Encyclopedia of Dubious Archaeology

Encyclopedia of Dubious Archaeology

From Atlantis to the Walam Olum

Kenneth L. Feder

GREENWOOD

AN IMPRINT OF ABC-CLIO, LLC
Santa Barbara, California • Denver, Colorado • Oxford, England

Library of Congress Cataloging-in-Publication Data

Feder, Kenneth L.
    Encyclopedia of dubious archaeology : from Atlantis to the Walam Olum / Kenneth L. Feder.
        p. cm.
    Includes bibliographical references and index.
    ISBN 978-0-313-37918-5 (hard copy : alk. paper) — ISBN 978-0-313-37919-2 (ebook) 1. Archaeology—Encyclopedias. 2. Antiquities—Encyclopedias. 3. Civilization, Ancient—Encyclopedias. 4. Archaeology—Philosophy—Encyclopedias. 5. History—Errors, inventions, etc.—Encyclopedias. 6. Pseudoscience—Encyclopedias. 7. Curiosities and wonders—Encyclopedias. I. Title.
    CC70.F43   2011
    930.103—dc22   2010025313

ISBN: 978-0-313-37918-5
EISBN: 978-0-313-37919-2

14   13   12   11   10   1   2   3   4   5

This book is also available on the World Wide Web as an eBook.
Visit www.abc-clio.com for details.

Greenwood
An Imprint of ABC-CLIO, LLC

ABC-CLIO, LLC
130 Cremona Drive, P.O. Box 1911
Santa Barbara, California 93116-1911

This book is printed on acid-free paper ∞

Manufactured in the United States of America

Some text reprinted from *Invisible Visitors: Explaining Archaeological Skepticism* and *The Lost Civilization in Historical Perspective: Déjà Vu All Over Again*, with appreciation to the Hall of Ma'at (www.thehallofmaat.com).

Text in "The Mars Face" entry reprinted from *The Skeptic Encyclopedia of Pseudoscience* by Michael Shermer, pp. 136–40. Copyright © 2002 by Michael Shermer. Reprinted with permission from ABC-CLIO, LLC.

CONTENTS

LIST OF ENTRIES

INTRODUCTION

Archaeology is one of a handful of sciences—astronomy is another example that comes to mind—that generates a tremendous amount of general interest outside of its small coterie of practitioners. In turn, that interest has led to a spate of sources of information about the human past directed to a general audience. There are, for example, a number of archaeology magazines aimed at public readership. Some, like *Archaeology* and *American Archaeology*, are pretty mainstream, with articles written by professional archaeologists or trained science writers. Others, like *Ancient American*, are less conventional and present a specific, unorthodox perspective about some element or elements of the human past.

Archaeological topics also are a staple of cable television documentaries. There are weeks when it seems that, if it weren't for archaeology, there would be an awful lot of dead air on cable or, at least, an overabundance of programs about Hitler or psychic pets (or maybe Hitler's psychic pets) on the History Channel, National Geographic, Discovery, and so on. I have appeared as an archaeological talking head on all of these cable channels and also on the SciFi Channel (now SyFy), the BBC, PBS's *Nova*, and even, improbably, the Weather Channel. Bookstore shelves—both real (take a walk through the bookshop at your local mall) and virtual—are replete with works about human evolution, lost continents and lost civilizations, ancient astronauts, the true meaning of Stonehenge or the Egyptian pyramids, and ancient Maya predictions about the end of everything.

Everybody finds fascinating and wants to know about human antiquity, and most people, justifiably or not, think they do know something about it. Often, however, what they think they know is, at best, questionable and, at worst, utter nonsense. While it may be difficult for most of us to propose or even contemplate hypotheses about string theory, quantum mechanics, or the time-space continuum, it's relatively easy for many of us to come up with or at least comprehend other people's speculations about who built the pyramids, the origins of the Maya civilization, or the purpose of Stonehenge. Plenty of people have speculated about such things and have even, in some cases, perpetrated outright fraud in attempting to convince others of the righteousness of their speculations—or just to make a bucket of money. Unfortunately, the cumulative weight of such speculations has led to an entire genre of archaeology based on dubious assumptions about the abilities of ancient people, dubious interpretations of artifacts and sites, dubious claims about the trajectory of the human past, and altogether dubious "proof" whipped out in someone's garage or basement and then planted in the soil in an attempt to fool people into accepting a particular scenario about the human past. This pervasive phenomenon provides a rationale for this encyclopedia as well as its title: *The Encyclopedia of Dubious Archaeology: From Atlantis to the Walam Olum.*

Archaeology is all about asking the question "Where do we come from?" in the broadest sense possible, and who's not interested in that? When did human beings first walk the Earth? How did civilization develop? What inspired human beings (or, phrased in a manner less accepting of human abilities, who taught primitive people) to build things like the pyramids, Stonehenge, the Great Sphinx, or Monk's Mound? Was there a single genius culture responsible for human intellectual development (and are they long lost, the victims of an ancient cataclysm of unimaginable proportion)? What connection, if any, is there between pyramidal monuments built in antiquity on either side of the Atlantic? Was there regular contact between the native people of the New World and ancient Egypt, China, or the Middle East? Did extraterrestrial aliens long ago visit the Earth and, serving in the role of a sort of intergalactic Peace Corps, teach our human ancestors agriculture, metallurgy, writing, and monumental construction? Further, did these extraterrestrials, through genetic manipulation or even just plain old interbreeding, contribute to the biological evolution of the human species?

If you were hoping for some earthshaking revelations about such things here, I'm afraid you're going to be disappointed. The archaeological evidence—the physical, empirical record of ancient artifacts, sites, and monuments—shows something far more stunning, actually, far more elegant and beautiful, and far more meaningful than all these dubious claims of ancient astronauts or peripatetic Atlanteans. That archaeological record shows the remarkable ability of human beings working collectively to produce spectacular works of art, mathematics, science, and architecture.

Science isn't about discovering great truths, but about achieving ever more accurate and precise explanations about the world around us, including the world of our ancient human ancestors. During the process of knowledge acquisition, we make mistakes, follow leads up blind alleys, and, yes, sometimes initially reject new ideas that ultimately turn out to be worthy of consideration. Nothing is ever written in stone in the scientific pursuit of knowledge—which, you will admit, is an interesting phrasing for a discussion about archaeology, where so much of our evidence *is* literally written in stone.

I cannot claim that—and would be greatly surprised if—all of my interpretations of each of the phenomena discussed in the entries in this encyclopedia are correct and complete in every case. Perhaps new data will be forthcoming to show that my skepticism about some of the unorthodox claims made in some of the entries here was unwarranted and that I am wrong. Maybe some of the claims or interpretations I include here under the rubric of "dubious archaeology" will turn out to be not dubious at all, but quite valid. So be it. This is the way science has always worked. This is the way science *must* work.

And if, as we approach December 21, 2012, whoops, I turn out to be wrong and the world, at least as we know it, really *is* about to come to a catastrophic end—I'll be the first to recognize my mistake and admit that maybe there was something to the whole Maya end-of-time thing after all. I hope my admission will make you feel better. But I won't count on it.

A

African Inspiration of the Olmec

The erroneous notion that the great civilizations of Mesoamerica were, at least in part, inspired by Africans has become part of **Afrocentrist** dogma, along with the extraordinary claim that skin pigment itself imparts supernatural powers (the more pigment, the darker the skin and the greater the paranormal abilities; see Ortiz de Montellano 1991 and 1992 for an exposé on these claims). Sadly, some of these discredited claims have even been incorporated into public school curricula.

The claim of an intimate connection between the ancient cultures of, especially, West Africa and the Olmec civilization of Mesoamerica has, as its chief proponent, historian **Ivan van Sertima** (1976). Van Sertima asserts, among other things:

- that there are references to "black Indians" in the writings of Christopher Columbus,
- that there also are in Columbus's reports references to a metal (*gua-nin*) being used by people in the New World that is claimed to be African in origin,
- that there are African features in the ancient skeletons found in the New World, and
- that there are artistic representations of people with decidedly African physical features in the paintings and, especially, the enormous, monolithic sculptures made by the Olmec people of Tabasco and Veracruz, in lowland Mexico.

The kinds of evidence van Sertima cites are inherently weak. Citing the writings of Columbus and his references to black Indians is unconvincing in the extreme. Columbus is merely passing along stories he was told by Indians with whom he was in contact; he never actually saw any himself. It should be pointed out that Columbus also reported that he was told that there also were Indians with tails. We cannot take his secondhand references to black Indians any more seriously than we can accept his secondhand accounts of a tailed race of New World native people.

Van Sertima's assertion that tools made of a non-American, African metal were present in the New World and reported on by Columbus is interesting and exactly the kind of evidence needed to assess claims of a pre-Columbian African presence in the New World. A nonnative raw material found in firm archaeological context anywhere in the New World in an undisturbed stratigraphic layer dated to before Columbus's voyages would represent convincing archaeological evidence of contact between native New World people and explorers or settlers from the Old World. But van Sertima's *gua-nin* is just a fantasy; no artifacts of *gua-nin*—whatever *gua-nin* is—or any other raw material traceable to Africa have been found in a pre-Columbian stratigraphic layer in the New World (Diehl 2004).

The claim that human skeletons with an African morphology have been found in pre-Columbian archaeological and stratigraphic context in the New World is similarly hollow. No trained forensic or biological anthropologist supports that claim. Simply stated, no demonstrably pre-Columbian skeletons have been found in the New World whose anatomical characteristics would suggest an African source.

Since van Sertima authored his major work on the topic in 1976, molecular archaeology has progressed remarkably quickly in ways no one could have imagined. DNA (both nuclear DNA, the genetic instructions in nuclei of each of our cells, and mitochondrial DNA [mtDNA], the much shorter DNA strands housed in the mitochondria of our cells and passed down in the female line) has been recovered from the skeletal remains of Native Americans. Beyond this, modern Native Americans have had their nuclear and mtDNA examined, as have modern people living across the globe.

In the case of mitochondrial DNA, a number of variants have been identified by their slightly differing patterns. These different variants are called *haplogroups*. Numerous haplogroups have been identified and defined in the human species, and these can be used to trace population movements across the face of the Earth.

Five distinct haplogroups have been identified among people who can trace their ancestry back to the early migrants into the New World: A, B, C, D, and X. The only other human group who express these same five mitochondrial variants are the Altatian, a group of people who live in central Siberia in proximity to Lake Baikal. The haplogroup data, unavailable when van Sertima wrote his major book, clearly show an Asian source for New World natives. There is no genetic evidence for any influx of African DNA before the arrival of Columbus in 1492.

Finally, interpreting artistic representations of human beings in terms of stereotypical racial or geographically clustered anatomical traits is always problematic. First, it depends on the assumption that ancient artwork is always anatomically accurate and, second, it depends on the accuracy of the viewer's interpretation of what ancient artists were attempting to convey. Finally, even if we could be certain that an ancient painting or sculpture is an accurate depiction of the anatomical features of the people in a region *and* that our interpretation isn't in some way biased, we need to remember that so-called racial traits are far from definitively associated with specific places. In fact, the racial stereotypes many of us harbor are very poor predictors of an individual's geographic origin. Dark skin is found in native people who trace their origin to Africa, south of the Sahara, to be sure, but it is also found in Australia and in southern Asia. Lightly colored hair of fine texture is found among the native people of northern Europe, but it is also found among the aboriginal people of Australia, many of whom have extremely dark skin.

The point here should be clear: the fact that an ancient artist's depiction of a human face appears to you to reflect the features of a person from another part of the world may reflect more the stereotypes you harbor and nothing at all about ancient patterns of contact or migration; it is weak evidence indeed to marshal in support of a hypothesis of such movement or contact.

What does this have to do with an African presence in Mesoamerica? Specifically, this: Van Sertima, among others, looks at one particular artifact category, the massive monolithic **Olmec Colossal Heads**, and sees what he believes to be anatomically accurate depictions of African rulers who, he surmises, brought civilization with them to the shores of the New World and to the Olmec people of lowland Mexico.

Altogether, 17 Olmec Colossal Heads have been found. They are quite impressive sculptures, all made from basalt, a dense, very hard volcanic rock. Even the smallest is huge, about 4.8 feet (1.5 meters) high (from chin to top of the head). The largest is a stupendous 11 feet (3.4 meters) high. Each one of them weighs many tons (the largest one just mentioned weighs a stunning 50 tons), and even the process of transporting the raw materials from their source was a monumental undertaking.

The sculpted heads date to the apex of Olmec civilization, between 3,200 and 2,900 years ago, and are interpreted as being the renderings of actual, historical rulers of the large Olmec ceremonial centers (Pool 2007). Here's where van Sertima jumps in. He maintains—and he's not the only one to do so—that the heads depict African faces. In fact, the faces depicted in the massive Olmec head sculptures do have broad, flat noses and broad lips. On the basis of those two facial traits and little else, therefore, van Sertima proposes that the heads depict ancient African rulers of the Olmec.

This proposition is fundamentally flawed and, to be blunt, just silly. One could just as readily argue that the Olmec heads present stereotypically Native American features, with very flat faces (in distinction to the forward-thrusting profile—technically, "prognathous"—of the mid- and lower face of many African people south of the Sahara). At the same time, the eyelids depicted in the Olmec heads show what appears to be the typical eye fold (the "epicanthic fold") seen in Asians and Native Americans that gives those peoples their distinctive eye shape (their actual eyes are the same shape as Europeans, Australians, and Africans; it's the skin in the surrounding eyelids that makes the shape appear distinctive and different). Finally, if you examine the full range of physical variation among the Native Americans of even just Central America, you'll find people with broad, thick lips and flat, broad noses, just like the Olmec heads. The facial features of the Olmec heads represent the weakest evidence possible to support the hypothesis that the Olmec rulers were actually transplanted Africans. As Olmec researcher Richard Diehl (2004, 112) puts it, "There can be no doubt that the heads depict the American Indian physical type still commonly seen on the streets of Soteapan, Acayucan, and other towns in the region."

Finally, it should be pointed out that monumental works like the Olmec Colossal Heads cannot be viewed in a vacuum. Monumental works don't make themselves. The ability to build a pyramid, conscript an army, build a palace, or produce a series of massive stone sculptures can develop only where other social, economic, political, and technological developments evolve in tandem. A physical infrastructure with quarries and roads for transporting the stones is needed. A social structure that provides for the conscription of laborers must be in place. The political wherewithal to organize and coordinate the labor of many hundreds, even thousands, of people is necessary. The economic basis for supporting these hundreds or thousands of workers—providing them with food and housing while they are engaged in monument-building and not in subsistence work and so can't feed themselves—is absolutely necessary, as is a system that can sustain a class of specialists, for example, the accomplished sculptors of the heads themselves. The point is, the ability to produce the Olmec heads is the result of a complex constellation of developments. It is unlikely that the appearance in ancient Mesoamerica of a boatload of people from anywhere in the world would suddenly inspire all of the necessary concomitants of civilization. In fact, the archaeological record shows the slow evolution in Mesoamerica of all of these social, economic, and political structures, along with the requisite technology. It did not arrive wholesale from Africa or anywhere else.

Further Reading

For more about the reality of the origins of the Olmec, see R. A. Diehl's *The Olmecs: America's First Civilization* (2004) and Christopher Pool's *Olmec Archaeology and Early Mesoamerica* (2007).

Afrocentrism

Afrocentrism has a laudable goal: to disclose the enormous, but often ignored, contributions made by African people to the sciences, medicine, philosophy, literature, and art. Unfortunately, in this effort some Afrocentrists ignore established historical and scientific fact and make claims of an African source for things that can clearly be shown to be non-African. The assertion is made by some Afrocentrists that much of European science and philosophy was literally "stolen" from African sources (James 1954).

For example, it has been asserted that the Greek philosopher Aristotle secretly visited the Egyptian city of Alexandria and pillaged the great library there, taking the best ideas of African thinkers and then presenting them to the world as his own. But this is an impossibility. Aristotle died in 322 BCE, but the library at Alexandria was not established until 297 BCE, 25 years after his death (Lefkowitz 1996). In fact, we know that the library was assembled by one of Aristotle's students and that most of the works there were written in Greek, not Egyptian.

Afrocentrism is as wrongheaded as Eurocentrism or any other "centrism" you might come up with (Feder 1998/1999). Every area in the world developed cultures that were, in their own way, sophisticated and elaborate. Fundamental technological achievements—including the domestication of plants and animals, mathematics, calendrical systems, a system of record keeping (generally writing, but not exclusively), monumental architecture, and long-distance trade—were independently developed in many places and many time periods. There was so single "genius" people or culture, nor a single source or cultural font where all of the great and significant advancements were made in the ancient world—spreading outward and raising all other peoples up from a natural state of barbarism. Africa wasn't the source, nor was Mesopotamia, Greece, Rome, Europe, or America. To state otherwise is to contradict the facts as seen in the archaeological and historical records, no matter how well intentioned the assertion might be (Ortiz de Montellano 1991, 1992).

Further Reading

To read more about the problems inherent in an extreme Afrocentric interpretation of history, see *Not Out of Africa* by Mary Lefkowitz (1996).

Alexandria Project

The Alexandria Project was an attempt to assess the efficacy of **psychic archaeology** in locating and identifying underwater archaeological sites, specifically in the harbor of the Egyptian city of Alexandria. Stephan Schwartz (1983), an ESP researcher and believer in psychic power, led a team of 10 psychics who used their purported abilities to remotely search for artifacts in the harbor. Using a procedure called "remote viewing," the psychics examined maps of the harbor and, through their ostensible paranormal abilities, then pinpointed places in the harbor where they believed archaeological material would be found.

The remote viewers were actually quite successful in accurately predicting the location of numerous objects buried in the mud in the harbor, leading to the discovery of Cleopatra's Palace and the Lighthouse of Pharos.

From this, it might seem that the Alexandria Project provides robust proof for the utility of remote viewing, at least for the location and identification of archaeological sites. A major problem with that interpretation is the same as that reflected in testing the efficacy of **dowsers** in finding water sources. When dowsers have been tested, they, too, have been very successful at predicting the location of water. However, this turned out not to be the result of some special, paranormal skill or of having tapped into some heretofore unrecognized energy field produced by flowing water or the Earth's magnetic field. Instead, the dowsers were right much of the time because even a *random* selection of places to look for water in the test region would have resulted in its discovery; just about anywhere researchers dug a well, water would have been found.

Alexandria is an ancient city that has seen an enormous ebb and flow of construction over the long history of its occupation. Alexandria's harbor is equally ancient and has been extremely active as a major center of Egyptian shipping and trade. Harbor cities suffer particularly from sea-level rise, and it is fairly common for the buildings in parts of ancient harbor towns to become inundated and, largely, lost. At the same time, active harbors are hubs for seagoing transportation and shipping, and with those activities come shipwrecks. In fact, the mud in Alexandria's harbor is littered with archaeological remains as a result. It would have been difficult for psychics *not* to find stuff in the harbor.

This does not prove that psychic power was *not* used in the Alexandria Project, but neither does the evidence presented prove that it *was*. Alexandria harbor is simply not a viable location for a test of remote viewing or the application of psychic power in finding sites because it is impossible to control all of the other, perfectly mundane reasons or ways in which anybody, psychic or not, could randomly put a pin in a map and, by sheer statistical chance, be highly likely to locate archaeological material.

Further Reading

To read about real-deal Egyptology, see *Building in Egypt* by D. Arnold (1991), P. A. Clayton's *Chronicle of the Pharaohs* (1994), and any of the articles in B. Manley's *The Seventy Great Mysteries of Ancient Egypt* (2003).

America B.C.

America B.C. (1976) was the first of three books written by Harvard University professor of invertebrate zoology **Barry Fell** (along with *Bronze Age America* [1982] and *Saga America* [1980]) in which he presented the case that the New World had been visited, explored, and settled by travelers from the Old World numerous times in antiquity. Fell's technical expertise was in fossil sea urchins, but he attained his greatest fame and notoriety when he ventured into the fields of epigraphy, archaeology, and history.

In *America B.C.* and in his other, subsequently published books, Fell argues that there is ample evidence, almost all of it in the form of written inscriptions, of the presence in the Americas of explorers and settlers he traces to Iberia (i.e., Spain and Portugal, dating to 3,000 years ago), Great Britain (the **Celts**, 2,800 years ago), Greece (2,500 years ago), Israel (the Hebrews, 2,000 years ago), northern Africa (the Phoenicians, about 2,000 years ago), and finally Egypt (about 1,500 years ago).

Fell not only claims in *America B.C.* that these groups accidentally made landfall in the New World, or even that they casually explored it; he argues for an active and elaborate process of substantial colonization of the Americas by these ancient Europeans and Africans. The primary evidence Fell offers in support of this hypothesis falls into three categories:

1. Word identities in Native American languages and the languages of Europe or Africa
2. Inscriptions found in the New World that Fell identifies and often translates, asserting that they are written in any one of a number of ancient Old World languages or writing systems
3. Dry-laid stone masonry seen throughout New England that Fell asserts was derived from the architecture of western European travelers to the New World in antiquity

Fell made very little reference to standard archaeological data—the lost, abandoned, or discarded refuse that archaeologists most commonly find and that constitutes the vast majority of the archaeological record. He scarcely cites any diagnostically Egyptian or Punic or Phoenician or Hebrew artifacts found in indisputable archaeological context in the New World. In the first place, I'm not sure he recognized that such items *must* be found here if those peoples explored and lived in the New World in antiquity. There is, perhaps, a more important reason why Fell makes scant mention of such kinds of essential and fundamental categories of archaeological evidence supporting his epigraphic interpretations: there is no such evidence.

America B.C. was not a scholarly work or an academic publication, nor was it intended as such. It was meant for a general audience, and it sold rather well, sparking the imagination of a public fascinated by the possibility that, essentially, everything that's claimed about American antiquity by orthodox archaeologists and in their standard pronouncements is wrong. Not surprisingly, those orthodox archaeologists almost universally derided Fell and all of his books, including *America B.C.* When Glyn Daniel, Disney Professor of Archaeology at Cambridge, editor of the venerable journal of European archaeology *Antiquity*, reviewed *America B.C.* in the *New York Times* in 1977, he didn't pull any punches, characterizing Fell (along with **Ivan van Sertima**, who wrote a book claiming an **African inspiration of the Olmec**) as a "deluded scholar" and *America B.C.* (and van Sertima's *They Came before Columbus*) as "ignorant rubbish" fraught with "badly argued theories based on fantasies." Though the wording is impolite, very few professional archaeologists would find reason to dispute those characterizations.

Further Reading

For more about a professional archaeologist's response to Fell's work, read Glyn Daniel's *New York Times* review (March 13, 1977).

American Genesis

Anthropologist Jeffrey Goodman asserted in his book *American Genesis*, published in 1981, that—contrary to the standard scenario laid out by anthropologists, archaeologists, and historians—American Indians had not arrived in the New World from Asia at the end of the Pleistocene Epoch (the Ice Age) when the sea level was lowered and a wide swath of land, the Bering Land Bridge, connected northeast Asia and northwest North America. Instead, Goodman maintained in his book that the standard scenario had things exactly reversed and that Asians and, ultimately, everyone else in the world had originated in North America—in California, to be precise, which Goodman (1981, 4) suggests was the location of the biblical Garden of Eden. Goodman asserts that modern human beings first appeared in California as much as 500,000 years ago, predating the earliest known modern-looking skeletal remains in the Old World by a few hundred thousand years. According to him, these first people spread out from California, populating the rest of the world.

Goodman continues in *American Genesis* to make claims concerning the great precocity of these first true human beings. Apparently we can credit the ancient Americans with everything from the invention of pottery and the discovery of insulin to the development of birth control pills and, rather incoherently, to me at least, "the applied understanding of the physics behind Einstein's gravity waves" (178).

There is, of course, not a scintilla of evidence for any of these claims. Skeletal evidence clearly supports the standard perspective that human beings evolved in Africa and spread from that incubator of human evolution. Archaeological, skeletal, and DNA evidence (to be fair, the last of these was not available when Goodman wrote *American Genesis*) all point to an Asian origin for American Indians. The oldest pottery found in the world dates to 11,000 years ago in Japan, at least 5,000 years before pottery is found in the Americas.

Though Goodman apparently believes all people are derived from American Indians, he never provides his opinion about where the Indians came from. After all, the vast majority of anthropologists point to the evidence of previous forms of humanity and evolutionary processes in their discussion of human origins. Since the earliest and most primitive of our prehistoric forebears are found in Africa, they propose that continent as the source of our species.

It is no wonder Goodman did not address this issue in *American Genesis*, though he does pose the question: "Was modern man's world debut the result of slow development or the result of a quantum leap inspired from some outside source?" (91). He does not answer that question in *American Genesis*. However, he does in a previous book, *Psychic Archaeology: Time Machine to the Past* (Goodman 1977). There, in discussing the inhabitants of a site in Arizona that Goodman cites in *American Genesis* as key evidence that modern humanity originated in the New World some 500,000 years ago (and that, apparently, was discovered entirely through **psychic archaeology**), Goodman passes on the information that the people there came from the Lost Continent of **Atlantis** and its Pacific counterpart, Mu (1977, 88).

When *American Genesis* was published, a journalist for the *Chicago Tribune* wrote an article about the implications of Goodman's thesis, topped with a headline that read: "Anthropologist Stuns Anthropological World." In fact, Goodman's work certainly didn't stun the anthropological world. Anthropologists, rather, were either amused by the book or ignored it entirely. *American Genesis* was a poorly written fantasy, and Goodman's claims were not backed up with even a shred of evidence. It was nonsense and seen for that by the scientific community.

Further Reading

For real archaeology assessing the story of the first Americans, see David J. Meltzer's *First Peoples in a New World* (2009) and Thomas Dillehay's *The Settlement of the Americas: A New Prehistory* (2000).

This feature (left) is called the "Sacrificial Table" by the owners of America's Stonehenge. Though the name lends an air of ancient mystery to the feature, such stones were fairly common throughout New England in the nineteenth century and were used for rather mundane purposes including the production of lye soap and the pressing of apple cider. The two photographs on the right show "cider press bedstones" that are quite similar to the misnamed "sacrificial table" at America's Stonehenge: (a) is on display at the Hadley Farm Museum in Hadley, Massachusetts; (b) is in the collection at Old Sturbridge Village, in Sturbridge, Massachusetts (K. Feder).

America's Stonehenge

Formerly known as Pattee's Caves and then **Mystery Hill**, America's Stonehenge is a site characterized by a fascinating amalgam of historical stonework, including dry-laid stone walls, stone chambers, menhirs (upright stones ostensibly reflecting **astronomical alignments**), passageways, and a feature called the "sacrificial table."

A number of different origins have been proposed for the North Salem, New Hampshire, site and its stonework. Some have proposed that the admittedly peculiar site was the handiwork of one or more of the admittedly peculiar Pattee brothers, members of a family that lived in the region in the nineteenth century. Others have suggested that the site was built by various pre-Columbian visitors to the New World, including, but not restricted to, sixth-century Irish Monks (the **anchorites**) or 4,000-year-old **Celts** (people like those who built Stonehenge), or by Native Americans.

The site is, indeed, fascinating and odd, certainly worthy of study, preservation, and a visit (it is open to the public and there is an on-site museum). It isn't clear exactly who built it or what its precise purpose was. However, the assertion that America's Stonehenge was built by pre-Columbian visitors to the New World has not been supported with any archaeological evidence of the kind discussed in the entry **Discovery of America**.

An extensive archaeological excavation was conducted at the site in the 1950s. Led by Yale University archaeology graduate student Gary Vescelius, the team recovered 7,000 artifacts, but none could be traced to ancient Celts. The artifact assemblage consisted of Native American stone tools and ceramics that are common throughout central and southern New England and likely date to occupation of the region before the stone features were constructed. The rest of the artifacts were typical eighteenth- and nineteenth-century ceramics, glass, and metal that reflect the known settlement of New England by Europeans in that time period.

When I visited the site while in graduate school, it was advertised as a Bronze Age European settlement of America. I noted, however, that the only artifacts on display were those that reflected a Native American presence on the hillside or a post-eighteenth-century European colonial presence. Where were the bronze objects that would support the assertion that the site was, in fact, a Bronze Age occupation? The person working at the museum responded by asking me a question: "You don't think those ancient people would have left all those valuable bronze tools just lying around, do you?" Actually, I *do* think exactly that would have happened, had the site dated to this period. In Europe, the ancient people did, indeed, leave "those valuable bronze tools just lying around." Archaeologists commonly find those bronze tools in Europe, as well as in Africa and Asia. That's how we know it was the Bronze Age. Without objects like bronze artifacts traceable to ancient Europe, the archaeological record at America's Stonehenge lends no support to the claim that the site was built by ancient European settlers of the New World.

One of the most interesting features at America's Stonehenge is the so-called sacrificial table. It is a flat slab of rock with a channel carved along its rectangular sides and an additional groove that appears to provide an outlet for whatever liquid accumulated in the channel. Of course, calling it a sacrificial table calls up images of young maidens being lovingly placed down on the table, their throats being cut, and then, as they bleed out, their virgin blood pooling up in the channel, flowing off of the stone through the exit channel, where it was collected in a ceramic vessel for some additional ceremony. A grisly scene, to be sure, but also a very far-fetched one. The purported sacrificial table at America's Stonehenge is something quite a bit more mundane than this scenario would imply.

The sacrificial table at America's Stonehenge is an impressive, though not entirely uncommon, artifact of eighteenth- and nineteenth-century New England, where similar stones were used in the production of lye soap and apple cider.

In the case of "lye stones" for soapmaking, wood ash from the hearth was placed in a bucket that had holes drilled in its base. The bucket was then placed in the center of the stone. Rainfall leached out the lye from the ash, and the liquid lye accumulated in the carved channel and flowed out the exit channel where not maiden blood but effectively liquid soap was collected in a bucket. Lye stones are common artifacts, usually found in rural areas of New England. They are common enough, in fact, that if you Google "lye stone," you will find antique dealers selling them as garden furniture. I have seen some that are so small that, if they *were* sacrificial stones, well, you could have sacrificed someone there, I suppose, but only if they were standing up. That seems a rather awkward way to sacrifice someone.

Very similar artifacts were used in the production of apple cider. The cider press was placed on top of a cider press bedstone, where the liquid squeezed from the apple pulp would collect in the channels carved along the margins and flow into a collecting bucket through an outlet groove. A stone very close in size and shape to the "sacrificial table" at America's Stonehenge can be seen today on the grounds of the Hadley Farm Museum in Hadley, Massachusetts. Another quite similar artifact is housed at the re-created nineteenth-century Old Sturbridge Village in Massachusetts. Documents clearly label both of these artifacts as cider press bedstones. The child in the photograph is my then four-year-old son Josh, and he provides my scale in the image. I actually asked him to lie down on top of the stone for the photograph, but when I told him the story of the sacrificial table hypothesis, he declined my request.

Anchorites

The anchorites were a group of Irish monks who, seeking isolation from the travails of "modern" life, journeyed to distant, out-of-the-way locales like desert caves or uninhabited islands to commune with God. During the sixth through eighth centuries CE, anchorites in ox-hide boats called *curragh* plied the waters of the northern Atlantic looking for islands on which to isolate themselves and pray. Archaeological evidence indicates that they actually made landfall and built monasteries on the Orkney Islands, north of the Scottish mainland, by 579, on the Shetland Islands by 620, on the Faeroe Islands by 670, and on Iceland by no later than 795. **Saint Brendan**—whose travels were recorded in the *Navigatio sancti Brendani abbatis*, or, in English, *The Voyage of St. Brendan, the Abbot*—was the best known of the anchorites.

The **Navigatio** tells of Saint Brendan's voyage to a land located far west of Ireland, at the edge of the Atlantic Ocean. It has been speculated that this land was located somewhere in the New World, making Saint Brendan the first European to make landfall in the Americas, beating Columbus by nearly a

Further Reading

Check out *Ancient American* for yourself at its Web site, www.ancientamerican.com, where you can read a sampling of articles.

Ancient Astronaut Hypothesis

Proponents of the ancient astronaut hypothesis assert that extraterrestrial aliens bearing an incredibly sophisticated technology have visited the Earth on multiple occasions in the ancient past, leaving behind archaeological evidence that attests to those visits. Proponents further believe that human history, as reflected in both the archaeological and historical records, reveals the active participation of these aliens in the affairs of our species, shepherding us along the pathway of biological evolution while serving as a sort of extraterrestrial Peace Corps and aiding in our species' cultural development. Adherents to the hypothesis claim, in fact, that human history and cultural evolution can be understood *only* by reference to the role played by these visitors from another star system.

Origin of the Ancient Astronaut Hypothesis

The ancient astronaut hypothesis has been roundly derided by scientists and historians alike for its stunning lack of evidence, absurd assumptions, and low regard for human intelligence. It is ironic, therefore, to report that the origin of the hypothesis may be traced to one of the most famous scientists—and certainly one of the most highly regarded scientific skeptics—of the twentieth century: astronomer **Carl Sagan**.

Sagan was fascinated by what he believed was the high probability that "we are not alone," that there are multiple intelligent civilizations scattered across the universe. Sagan was hopeful, though not overly optimistic, that even in his lifetime there might be proof, perhaps in the form of a radio signal picked up by a receiver on Earth, of the existence of an extraterrestrial civilization reaching out to us, at least electromagnetically. In fact, Sagan based his very popular novel *Contact* on this idea, and the story was made into a high-budget Hollywood movie of the same name. Unfortunately, by the time Sagan died in 1996, no such contact had occurred, nor has any occurred since.

Along with contact via radio waves, Sagan also considered the even more fascinating possibility that, at some time in the future, contact between Earthlings and extraterrestrials might take place on a face-to-face basis—the equivalent of *Star Trek*'s Captain Kirk or Jean-Luc Picard beaming down to Earth from the orbiting *Enterprise* and assuring us, "We come in peace."

Sagan also examined the possibility that such contact might already have occurred, that extraterrestrials had visited Earth in the distant past and that they had left evidence, perhaps inadvertently, of their arrival. Sagan focused on that prospect in 1963, in an article he wrote for a scientific journal, *Planetary Space Science*. In the article, Sagan asserted his belief that the probability of the existence of life beyond Earth was high.

In that same paper, Sagan also pondered the likelihood that an extraterrestrial civilization with a technology far more advanced than our own had mastered interstellar travel and might send a spacecraft to our planet. In assessing the viability of that scenario, Sagan reasoned that, in any given year, the probability that such a craft would arrive on Earth was extremely small, but, however small, that probability was not zero. Sagan held out hope that, because Earth's history is long, consisting of approximately 4.5 billion years, the infinitesimal probability of the arrival of extraterrestrial visitors in any given year mounted up to a much higher cumulative probability of such a visit having happened at some point during the entire course of our planet's history. Sagan concluded, therefore, that the most promising place to look for physical evidence of the hypothetical visits of extraterrestrials would be the billions of years represented in the ancient geological and archaeological records.

Sagan ended the article by alerting geologists and archaeologists to this possibility and went so far as to recommend that they be on the alert for evidence of otherwise inexplicable technologies in ancient layers of soil: a laser blaster in the same soil stratum as an ancient stone spear point, for example. It was a bold and fascinating suggestion by one of the boldest and most fascinating scientists of our generation.

Erich von Däniken

It is unclear whether or not the Swiss author **Erich von Däniken** was aware of Sagan's striking proposal. What *is* clear is that it was von Däniken who, beginning in 1968 with the publication of his book *Erinnerungen an die Zukunft* (Recollections of the Future), later widely known in the English-speaking world as ***Chariots of the Gods***, popularized the notion that humanity had been visited in antiquity by extraterrestrial beings. This speculation became known as the "ancient astronaut hypothesis."

Chariots of the Gods ultimately appeared in more than two dozen different languages and continues to reside high on the list of best-selling paperback books of all time. Von Däniken followed this first work with more than two dozen additional books, which have sold more than 60 million copies combined. In all of them, he made similar claims concerning archaeological evidence for the visits of extraterrestrial aliens to Earth in antiquity. Three underlying assertions can be gleaned from all of von Däniken's books:

1. Physical evolution of the human species was directly, even personally, managed by extraterrestrial aliens.
2. The archaeological and historical records are filled with examples of artistic depictions or written descriptions of extraterrestrial aliens, their spacecraft, and other elements of their technology.
3. The cultural development of humanity, especially as revealed by technological progress through time, was made possible by the active assistance of extraterrestrials.

Let's assess each of these in more detail.

Von Däniken is, essentially, an anti-evolutionist, at least as it relates to *Homo sapiens*. He apparently does not accept evolutionary scenarios in which the human species developed over great periods of time through the agency of natural processes. In his early works, he ignored the fossil evidence for human evolution almost entirely, and in his more recent publications, he has ignored or downplayed the genetic evidence for human evolution. Instead, von Däniken maintains that the modern human species is the result not of natural, evolutionary processes, but of a grand experiment in genetic engineering in which females in a species ancestral to our own—*Australopithecus*, perhaps, or maybe the Neanderthals—were selected by extraterrestrial visitors to be "fertilized," the term used by von Däniken. As a result, in von Däniken's words, "a new race would arise that skipped a stage in natural evolution" (1970, 11). In other words, humanity is the result of cross-breeding between ape-men (actually, ape-women) and ET.

It is unclear exactly how von Däniken thought these females were inseminated, but scientists have had great fun with this claim. Carl Sagan (1978) pointed out that a human ancestor would more likely be successful mating with a petunia than with an extraterrestrial. The petunia and the ancestral human at least evolved on the same planet and, therefore share, in the broadest sense and however tenuously, a genetic history. In a number of publications, I have called this scenario alternately the "Horny Astronaut Hypothesis" and the "Amorous Astronaut Hypothesis," imagining lovesick ETs arriving on Earth, whereupon they begin prowling the savannas of East Africa or the caves of Ice Age Europe, looking for love with primitive bipeds. You will admit that there is a certain "ick factor" in this scenario, but it is one of von Däniken's fundamental claims.

In any event, the likelihood of the DNA of two different *Earth species* being sufficiently similar as to allow for cross-fertilization and the production of offspring is already extremely low. The likelihood of creatures from *different planets* having DNA similar enough for cross-fertilization and the production of offspring is, effectively, zero. This claim is science fiction—and bad science fiction, at that—masquerading as alternative science.

Though it might seem paradoxical, while the ancient astronaut hypothesis sounds highly imaginative, its chief proponent reveals himself to be a man with a very limited imagination, or at least an imagination with a very narrow focus. When examining cave paintings, designs on pottery, or images etched onto the walls of temples, and when reading ancient religious texts like the Bible or the Mesopotamian Gilgamesh epic, he invariably sees the imprint of extraterrestrials and evidence of their sophisticated technologies, but his argument is all hand waving and speculation. Unaware of the cultural contexts of the artifacts he examines—after all, he is not an anthropologist, archaeologist, historian, or ethnographer (his training was in hotel management)—von Däniken habitually surrenders to speculations for which there isn't even a shred of evidence. Images of shamans or priests clearly wearing masks or headdresses are seen by von Däniken as aliens in space helmets. Enormous geoglyphs of spiders, condors, fishes, and monkeys produced in the highland desert of Peru by the ancient **Nazca** people are presumed by von Däniken to have been made possible only by extraterrestrials floating above the desert in antigravity aircraft. (Von Däniken does not explain *why* such extraterrestrials spent all that time essentially rearranging pebbles to produce the images of local creatures on a grand scale in a highland desert.) In von Däniken's one-track approach, stylized images of birds must actually be winged spacecraft and depictions of skeletalized human beings must mean that the extraterrestrial aliens were x-raying the locals—bringing modern medical care to the primitive folk, I presume.

Perhaps the most egregious example in *Chariots of the Gods* is von Däniken's interpretation of the sarcophagus lid of Pacal, ruler of the ancient **Maya** kingdom of **Palenque** in eastern Mexico. Pacal is a well-known historical figure who ruled his city-state between his ascension to the throne in 615 CE until his death in 683. He is buried beneath a pyramid in his city, entombed in a stone sarcophagus capped with a lid that bears a bas-relief of the great ruler. In the carving, Pacal appears to be suspended, perched between the underworld below that the Maya believed was populated by earth monsters and an eternal heaven above. Rather remarkably, von Däniken interprets this intricate carving, instead, as Pacal flying a spaceship. What even to an observer unfamiliar with Maya iconography looks like the beard of a strange beast located beneath Pacal becomes, for von Däniken, the smoky trail of a spaceship. An object dangling from Pacal's ear, looking for all the world like an earring, becomes, instead, an audio receiver, a sort of ancient astronaut iPod earbud. The widely agape jaws of a stylized snake poised to devour Pacal are interpreted as the walls of a spacecraft. It's all quite ridiculous, and archaeologists who have studied Pacal's tomb alternate between being appalled and amused by such nonsense. Finally, von Däniken does not explain how, if Pacal was, in actuality, the pilot of an extraterrestrial spacecraft, the mortal remains of the great ruler of Palenque—his bones were found within the sarcophagus when it was opened in the 1950s—are, in fact, undeniably those of a human being and, in all certainty, not those of an extraterrestrial.

Perhaps the most troubling of von Däniken's essential premises is the notion that the evidence of cultural change and development revealed in the archaeological record in most world regions cannot be explained as having been the result of human intelligence, ingenuity, and hard work. Instead, von Däniken denies credit to the human species, rejecting the cultural evolutionary timelines proposed by prehistorians and historians, ascribing the development of technology instead to the extraterrestrials. In von Däniken's world, calendars based on phases of the moon or the position of the sun at sunrise or sunset—both kinds are clearly evidenced in the archaeological record—could not have been developed by past peoples, but must have been introduced by ancient ETs. Von Däniken maintains this, though such calendars are based on fairly simple observations of the moon and the sun.

Von Däniken incorrectly asserts that **Egyptian pyramids** show up mysteriously all at once in antiquity and were far too sophisticated to have been developed by mere Egyptians. In this, von Däniken ignores much of Egyptology, which clearly shows evidence of a process of trial and error on the part of Egyptian architects, engineers, and builders in pyramid construction, lasting over a period lasting more than a century. Structures like the **Collapsed Pyramid** at Meidum, constructed at a too ambitiously steep slope and abandoned in mid-build, along with the **Bent Pyramid**, where the slope of the pyramid's surface was changed during construction because the façade began to crack (giving the building a very odd profile as well as an intriguing name), were the clear result of large-scale mistakes that, ultimately, were useful in teaching Egypt's builders the limits of their materials and skills. If collapsed and bent pyramids were the best the extraterrestrial aliens could do when engineering a simple structure, I, for one, would not be all that comfortable boarding one of their spaceships for a tour of the universe.

One always makes a mistake when one underestimates the abilities of ancient people to band together, labor communally, and rise to the challenges of digging a canal, developing a road system, perfecting a calendar, or constructing monuments or temples to their deceased rulers or gods. The archaeological record is clear on this point; the advanced technologies seen in antiquity invariably were prefaced by long periods of development, mistakes, trial and error, and plenty of examples of just, as the cliché puts it, "going back to the drawing board." That pattern of development is decidedly human, and our history is replete with examples. There is no support whatsoever for ancient astronauts anywhere in the entire process.

Mystery Park: The Ancient Astronaut Theme Park

Though the popularity of the ancient astronaut hypothesis waned in the late 1980s and through the 1990s, von Däniken remained busy writing books, making personal appearances, and in 1997, serving as a keynote speaker at the fiftieth anniversary of the alleged crash of a flying saucer in Roswell, New Mexico. He also, apparently, spent his time raising capital for an ancient astronaut theme park. You read that right. Having convinced a number of very well-known and ordinarily conservative companies, including Sony, Coca-Cola, and Fujitsu to foot the bill (something in the neighborhood of $60 million; it has further been revealed that the Swiss government also heavily invested in the park), **Mystery Park** opened in Interlaken, Switzerland, in 2003, closed in 2006 as a result of declining attendance and has been re-branded and re-opened under new management in 2010.

On a final note regarding von Däniken's notion that ancient human beings needed the assistance of extraterrestrial aliens to develop technologically, it is interesting to observe that, at least in *Chariots of the Gods*, his skepticism about the unaided abilities of ancient people is not exactly universal. Most of his examples—Polynesians spreading their populations across the islands of the Pacific, Native Americans developing calendars, Egyptians building pyramids—originate in Asia, the Americas, and Africa. Proportionally, very few examples of technology so advanced that von Däniken didn't believe local people were up to the task of developing it on their own are gleaned from the archaeological record of Europe. It may be a coincidence that in *Chariots of the Gods*, von Däniken ignores sites like the Colosseum in Rome or the Parthenon in Greece. Then again, it may not be coincidental. Von Däniken seems to believe that the European builders of these great monuments did not require the assistance of extraterrestrial engineers or architects, while the Egyptians, Maya, and Inca did.

This does raise the possibility that von Däniken's skepticism about the technological abilities of ancient people is confined to people other than Europeans. Von Däniken is, of course, a European. That would be a shame, for, if there's one thing the archaeological record shows, it is that ancient people all over the world, people who are the ancestors of every racial or ethnic category we currently conceive, were intelligent and capable and accomplished spectacular things, all without the assistance of a coterie of mentors, extraterrestrial or otherwise. The ancient astronaut hypothesis is entirely without merit. It is a notion as bankrupt as the theme park that it spawned.

Further Reading

It you are interested in Pacal and the ancient Maya, one of the best books around is Linda Schele and David Freidel's *A Forest of Kings* (1990). You can find quite a bit of information about Egyptian pyramid-building in Dieter Arnold's *Building in Egypt* (1991). To read more detailed criticisms of the ancient astronaut hypothesis, check out William Stiebing's *Ancient Astronauts, Cosmic Collisions, and Other Popular Theories about Man's Past* (1984) as well as my own *Frauds, Myths, and Mysteries: Science and Pseudoscience in Archaeology* (2010); I devote an entire chapter to the subject. Finally, though I do not recommend it, if you need to satisfy your morbid curiosity and go to the source, you can find equivalent nonsense in any of Erich von Däniken's books. *Chariots of the Gods* (1970) is as good—as bad, actually—as any.

Archaeoastronomy

Archaeoastronomy (sometimes called "astro-archaeology," but usually only by astronomers who don't get it that archaeology deserves top billing) is the study of the astronomical knowledge of ancient people through the study of their artifacts, monuments, architectural features, ritual structures, or even entire sites.

Remember that the calendars of most people, both ancient and modern, are astronomically based. The sun and the moon are, in fact, everywhere the most obvious and consistently visible astronomical objects in the daytime and nighttime skies. Our modern calendar and those of the ancients ultimately are based on the patterned sequences of movement and appearance changes in the sun and the moon in those skies and are, thus, based on the observation, tracking, measuring, and examination of astronomical bodies.

For example, an artifact interpreted as one of the oldest examples of a calendar is the Abri Blanchard bone plaque found in southern France. The artifact, a flat fragment of bone, dates to about 30,000 years ago and was produced by a people usually called Cro Magnon, among the earliest anatomically modern human beings in Europe. The plaque has about 70 distinct incisions etched onto its surface. The shapes of the markings change from one to the next in a consistent way: from a complete circle, each subsequent marking loses a bit from the same side until only half a circle remains. After the half-circle marking, each subsequent image depicts a little less of a circle, looking like an ever-diminishing crescent until only a tiny arc of a thin line remains. After that, an asterisk appears, looking for all the world like a placeholder signifying that the original disc shape has disappeared entirely. Following this placeholder, a thin arc-shaped line appears, but a mirror image of the mark appearing before the placeholder, a tiny crescent facing the opposite direction. Each mark that follows is a more substantial crescent until the makers incised a half-circle. Each subsequent mark the half-circle swells until, the makers repeated the full circle we began the pattern with.

The shapes of the markings, the sequence of changes seen in their morphology, and even the precise timing of the sequence—the number of individual markings between and including the first appearance of the crescent until the half circle (7) and then from that half circle up to and including the full circle (7), from that point back to half (7) and then through the diminishing crescents until the image is replaced by the asterisk we are here interpreting as a placeholder (7 more)— together are a perfect match for the sequence of phases of the moon in one lunar month. The Abri Blanchard artifact even repeats the sequence, as if to assure us that this is no coincidence, but that the makers were fully aware of the pattern and repeated it (and then repeated exactly half of the sequence again).

The Abri Blanchard bone plaque is an archaeoastronomical artifact, a lunar calendar, dating to 30,000 years ago. This is remarkable, but certainly not beyond the capability of ancient human beings. Speculations about the role of extraterrestrial aliens in the production of artifacts like the Abri Blanchard plaque include those of **Erich von Däniken**, who asks:

> Why did Stone Age men bother about astronomical representations? It is usually claimed that they had their hands full just to procure sufficient nourishment on endless hunts. Who instructed them in this work? Did someone advise them how to make these observations which were far above their "level"? (1973, 203)

The implications here—that our ancient ancestors were so busy in subsistence pursuits that they had neither the time nor the capacity, apparently, for a rich intellectual life—are wholly unwarranted, based on a woeful ignorance of the capacities of human beings of any era, and, put bluntly, simply absurd.

It should not be surprising that ancient human beings with brains precisely the same size and configuration of our own and who possessed, therefore, an intelligence and capacity for learning the equal to our own were capable of observing, interpreting, and recognizing the pattern of lunar phases and then memorializing it on a piece of bone.

And remember, the implication inherent in von Däniken's questioning above—that artifacts like the Abri Blanchard plaque were purely nonutilitarian, nonpractical works that would have taken away from the time needed to conduct subsistence pursuits—is yet another misapprehension of the role of science and art in ancient societies, where these human pursuits are inextricably linked to the practical necessities of life.

Our ancestors, in fact, were far more in tune with their natural surroundings than we are, because their survival depended on a knowledge of and sensitivity for things like animal migrations, seasonal availability of various food sources, and weather patterns, all of which are, essentially, time-of-year dependent. Just as we all rely on our personal planners, desktop calendars, iCal on our Macs, or schedulers on our smart phones to keep track of all of our deadlines, due dates, birthdays, holidays, and so on, ancient people needed to keep track of the days to schedule their movement and activities in rhythm with the course of year. With that in mind, a two-and-a-half-month, 30,000-year-old lunar calendar isn't so surprising after all. It's not just doodling, a form of artistic or impractical musing about the sky, that our ancient ancestors could ill-afford. In this case, the science and art behind the bone plaque provided a practical benefit to these people, who had to be able to keep track of time as part of their direct need to schedule subsistence activities, as well as their social gatherings, which had the practical consequence of organizing people's lives around food gathering, marriages, and births.

Another even more common element of archaeoastronomy focuses on the **astronomical alignment** or configuration of ancient roadways, monuments (including pyramids, palaces, or other buildings), or other features of the cultural landscape (earthen mounds, for example) in relation to points on the visible horizon that may have had astronomical significance to a past people, including especially solar or lunar rising or setting points, but also the rising and setting points of particular stars, groups of stars, or planets.

As the study of the capacity of ancient people to observe their world, to recognize patterns, to record those patterns in symbolic ways, and to exploit naturally sequenced patterns to produce calendars by which they might more efficiently, predictably, consistently, and safely schedule their own activities, archaeoastronomy shows us in the modern world that our ancient human ancestors were intelligent and capable. It affords no support whatsoever for hypotheses dependant on **lost civilizations** or ancient extraterrestrial visitors to Earth.

Further Reading

For more about archaeoastronomy, read any book written or edited by Anthony Aveni or Ed Krupp. Any of the chapters in Krupp's *In Search of Ancient Astronomies* (1978) is a great place to start.

Astronomical Alignments

One element in **archaeoastronomy** involves the construction by ancient people of monuments, roadways, structural elements, or even entire sites that align to points on the horizon that are of astronomical significance.

Ancient humans recognized the sequential patterning exhibited in the cycles of astronomical bodies, specifically lunar phases, and used those consistent, astronomical cycles as ways of marking time, as demonstrated by the Abri Blanchard bone plaque (see **Archaeoastronomy**).

Beyond lunar phases, there is the most obvious celestial cycle—the daily pattern of sunrise, sunset, and then sunrise again. The apparent movement of the

Ancient people recognized patterned sequences in astronomical objects—for example, the phases of the moon during the course of each month and the location of the sun and moon at sunrise and sunset during the course of the year—and used those patterns in producing calendars. The photograph is of the El Caracol observatory at the Maya site of Chichen Itza, the windows of which were aligned to the position of the planet Venus at its farthest north rise. (K. Feder)

sun, an astronomical body, has been used by all people to mark the progress of days and reflects the simplest kind of applied astronomy. The sun exhibits other cyclical patterns useful in the production of a calendar. One of those cycles involves the sun's location at sunrise.

If you ask most people where the sun rises, they will respond, "In the east," but this is imprecise. In fact, the location of the rising sun along the visible horizon shifts a bit from day to day from the standpoint of an observer on the Earth's surface. The change in the location of the rising—and setting—sun is a result of the tilt in the Earth's axis relative to the plane of the *ecliptic*, the imaginary plane on which the Earth's orbit around the sun resides. In summer, the Earth is tilted on its axis toward the sun, which causes the sun's rays to strike more directly and heat the atmosphere, and thus temperature is higher. Being tilted toward the sun in the summer in the Northern Hemisphere makes the apparent position of the sun upon sunrise farther to the north. The sun rises farthest to the north on June 21, the day of the *summer solstice*. By convention, we now call that the first day of summer, but historically the summer solstice was called "midsummer" and the sunrise on that day was called the "midsummer sunrise."

Conversely, in winter, the Earth's axis is tilted away from the sun in the Northern Hemisphere. Being tilted away, the sun's rays fall on the Earth less

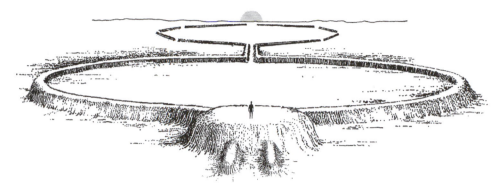

An artist's depiction of moonrise, aligned along the axis of the Octagon Earthworks in Newark, Ohio. (Courtesy of Timeline, Ohio Historical Society)

directly, heating up the atmosphere to a lesser degree than when they strike directly in the summer, and the temperature is colder. As winter approaches, the apparent position of the sun upon sunrise moves farther to the south in the Northern Hemisphere, reaching its most southerly point on December 21, the *winter solstice*. Again, we now call that the first day of winter, but historically the sunrise on that day was the "midwinter sunrise."

Stonehenge, in England, of course, is in the Northern Hemisphere. Standing anywhere in the region, especially on the flat Salisbury Plain where the ancient monument is located, in an area devoid of trees and without any large mountains on the horizon, an observer can see the rising of the sun and notice that, after December 21, each day its location is a little farther to the north of where it rose on the previous day. In fact, at the latitude of Stonehenge, if one were to mark the location of sunrise with a compass on December 21, the azimuth of the sun's disc just as it becomes visible on the horizon, is 129° (that is, a location 39° south of east, which is located at 90°).

An observant observer would see that each day thereafter, sunrise occurs farther north by a little and, obsessively following the movement, in three months, on March 21, the location of the rising sun would be seen to be due east (the aforementioned 90°). That day is designated as the *vernal equinox* and is the day when there is an equal amount of daylight and nighttime (12 hours and 12 hours, respectively). That same observer in the Salisbury Plain, even before Stonehenge was constructed, would have seen the location of sunrise continue its northward march until, three months following the vernal equinox, on June 21, the azimuth of the disc of the rising sun was at 51° (that's 39° north of due east on the compass).

The observer might have been surprised when, on the next day, June 22, instead of the sun being a little farther north at sunrise as had become routine, it was almost at exactly the same place it was on the previous day, or maybe even a bit back to the south. And then, by June 23, the position of sunrise would have shifted to the south and begun a steady march southward, that is, back toward the due-east position, where the sunrise arrives three months later, on September 21—the day called the *autumnal equinox*, like the vernal equinox six months earlier, a 24-hour period with an equal amount of daylight and nighttime.

The location of sunrise continues to the south as the daily temperature decreases and, eventually, three months later, a full year—365 days—after the beginning of the observations, the location of sunrise again reaches 129°. It is December 21 and the winter solstice has arrived, the day in the year with the greatest ratio of dark hours to daylight hours. But the observer, continuing the quest for understanding of the sequence of sunrise position, notes that on the next day, December 22, the sun has not continued in a southerly track, but has risen in about the same place it has on December 21, maybe a little to the north again, and in the subsequent days and weeks and months that follow, sunrise occurs a little farther to the north again.

Anyone following this pattern over the course of several years would note that is consistent and reliable. The dance of sunrise from the farthest south to the farthest north and back to the farthest south again always occurs, and it always takes the same amount of time, 365 days (plus a little). Anyone who comprehends this pattern has figured out the length of a year and can easily divide that year into four equal segments of three months each. Once you know that, you also know the march of the seasons during the span of a year, and you have a pretty good general handle, therefore, on what the weather ought to be like and when you should prepare the ground for planting, when you should plant your crops, and when you should harvest them.

In short, the location of the sun at sunrise is the result of our planet's tilt on its axis, whose direction changes relative to the Earth's orbit during the course of the year. So, if you keep track of where the sun rises, you know when every day fits into that yearly cycle. It's a natural calendar based on the location of an astronomical body: where the sun first appears in the sky each day.

We know that in a number of places at a number of times in antiquity, ancient people figured out the yearly cycle of sunrise locations on the horizon and marked those special days—the summer solstice, winter solstice, vernal equinox, autumnal equinox—sometimes with monumental, permanent structures. Stonehenge is a perfect example and seems to have been aligned primarily with the rising of the sun on the summer solstice (see the Stonehenge entry). The entire monument is generally aligned with the northernmost yearly rising of the sun (the opening of the horseshoe configuration of the trilithons points toward the rising sun on the summer solstice). More specifically, an observer in the dead center of the Stonehenge monument, looking out through the sarsens, would have seen the disc of the rising sun, directly over the heelstone, on June 21.

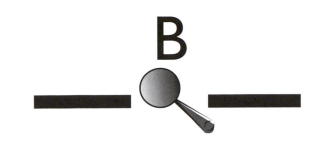

B

Bat Creek Stone

John Emmert was working as an archaeological field assistant to **Cyrus Thomas** of the Smithsonian Institution in 1889 when he excavated the Bat Creek Mounds located near the confluence of Bat Creek and the Little Tennessee River in Loudon County in eastern Tennessee (Mainfort and Kwas 2004).

Thomas had been given the job of director of the Division of Mound Exploration within the federal Bureau of American Ethnology in 1882. His primary task as director was to solve the mystery of the **moundbuilders**—to figure out who had built the mounds, when they had been built, and what connection, if any, there was between the spectacular earthworks encountered across the American Midwest, mid-South, and Southeast and the American Indians who inhabited those regions when Europeans first settled there. Over the course of about a dozen years, with a budget of $60,000 supplied by the U.S. government, Thomas directed or oversaw the investigation of some 2,000 mound sites scattered across 21 states, collecting more than 40,000 artifacts from those mounds. Those artifacts formed the basis of the Smithsonian's collection of Indian relics.

It was while excavating one of the mounds (Mound 3) at the Bat Creek site as part of the federal mound site survey that Emmert encountered the burials of nine individuals and recovered a number of artifacts from under one of the skulls, including two metal bracelets (he thought they were copper but they turned out, instead, to be brass), along with an inscribed stone. The stone object, Emmert said, immediately grabbed his attention because there appeared to be some sort of writing on its face. The artifact, which became known as the Bat Creek Stone, bore an inscribed message that Thomas believed represented the Cherokee writing system that was invented in 1819 by the Cherokee Indian Sequoyah to record his people's language. If that was the case, it proved that the Bat Creek Stone was very recent (no more than 80 years old at the time of its discovery) and, by extension, that at least some of the mounds were recent as well and had been constructed by the Cherokee—which was, apparently, Thomas's preferred hypothesis and his solution to the mystery of who had built the mounds.

The inscription on the Bat Creek Stone was unique. Unique artifacts are an enormous challenge to archaeologists. Difficult to assess and without other

The writing seen on the Bat Creek Stone has been shown to have been a nineteenth-century fake. (Cyrus Thomas)

stones bearing similar writing found in mounds to confirm its authenticity, the Bat Creek Stone was largely ignored. It was curious, inexplicable, and became increasingly isolated as subsequent solid archaeological data showed that the mounds were far older than the Cherokee syllabary. The Bat Creek Stone simply didn't make any sense within the growing consensus.

The Bat Creek Stone was an outlier, impossible to put into a genuine historical context, and, though few said it out loud, it was assumed by many that the artifact had been faked, perhaps by an overenthusiastic field assistant, probably Emmert, in an attempt to ingratiate himself with his boss. Emmert had a drinking problem and had been previously fired by Thomas. It was quite a coincidence that, newly rehired by Thomas to do archaeological fieldwork, Emmert had had the spectacular luck to find in a mound the first and only artifact with Cherokee writing on it, which just happened to support his boss's point of view.

As pointed out by Mainfort and Kwas (2004), the story stood there until Dr. **Cyrus Gordon**, professor of Mediterranean Studies at Brandeis University, closely examined the Bat Creek inscription in 1970 and asserted that it wasn't Cherokee at all but an ancient form of Hebrew on the Bat Creek Stone and that Cyrus Thomas had been looking at the object upside down! Gordon's declaration was largely supported by Ohio State University economics professor (and an abiding **diffusionist**) Hu McCulloch (1993). McCulloch also cited the presence of brass bracelets in association with the Bat Creek Stone (brass was a metal unknown to American Indians) and a very broad radiocarbon date range derived from charcoal recovered from the mound, which indicated an age of somewhere between 1,200 and 1,900 years, in dating the earthwork, and ostensibly the bracelets and the inscribed stone found therein.

Mainfort and Kwas (2004) have demolished this argument entirely. Metallurgical analysis of the bracelets (the proportion of copper to zinc) shows similarity to brass objects made anytime between the last few centuries BCE right up until the nineteenth century CE, so that proves nothing at all. Bracelets made in ancient Rome have proportions similar to those discovered in Mound 3 at Bat Creek (66.5–68.2 percent copper, 26.5–27.5 percent zinc), but brass bracelets made in England in the nineteenth century have exactly the same copper–zinc proportions (Mainfort and Kwas 1991). The style of the bracelet (made with a hollow core and exhibiting a seam) is common across a broad stretch of time as well, so that doesn't narrow down their age, either. The point is that the bracelets certainly could date to the nineteenth century and could have been inserted into the mound along with the fake tablet with writing. Again, as Mainfort and Kwas point out, there are no photographs of the artifacts in situ, no reliable field notes or records, no detailed mapping, and, in fact, no eyewitness corroboration of the discovery by any other fieldworker or Smithsonian employee, so no way of knowing whether Emmert actually found them or planted them.

How about the radiocarbon date? In all likelihood, that is genuine, but it has nothing to do with the bracelets or the Bat Creek Stone. Neither the bracelets nor the Bat Creek Stone can be dated directly. Radiocarbon dates can be derived only from organic remains, like preserved fragments of wood or bone, and that tells us, with some degree of certainty (barring any contamination, intentional or otherwise), only how old the wood or bone is. Applying the date derived from charcoal found in Bat Creek Mound 3 to the brass bracelets and the inscribed stone depends on the appropriateness of the temporal association between the artifacts and the charcoal. Without the requisite documentation and verification of Emmert's testimony, any claim of contemporaneity between the artifacts in question and the date cannot be supported. I could plant my iPod Nano into a site adjacent to charcoal radiocarbon-dated to 1,200 years ago, but that doesn't make the iPod that old.

Mainfort and Kwas (2004) seem to have identified the smoking gun in the Bat Creek Stone mystery. In a work published in 1870, the *General History, Cyclopedia, and Dictionary of Freemasonry*, there's a figure depicting a written message taken from a coin dating to the First Jewish Revolt against Rome in 66–73 CE. The writing on the coin as shown in that 1870 book is a dead ringer for the inscription on the Bat Creek Stone. The book was widely available in late nineteenth-century America and was, in all likelihood, the inspiration for the Bat Creek Stone **fraud**.

Further Reading

The definitive debunking of the Bat Creek Stone can be found in the article written by Mainfort and Kwas, "The Bat Creek Stone Revisited," in the journal *American Antiquity* (2004).

Beardmore Relics

At least ostensibly unearthed north of Lake Superior, near Beardmore in Ontario, Canada, in the 1930s, the famous—or more appropriately, infamous—Beardmore Relics consisted of four iron pieces making up three artifacts: two pieces of a sword, a spearhead, and a fragment of an artifact that cannot be definitively identified (perhaps part of the handle of a shield). If the artifacts were actually found where their owner, prospector James Edward Dodd, claimed to have found them, their style and degree of rusting implied great antiquity dating to, perhaps, the period when the Norse had reached Canada, which we now know predates Columbus by at least 500 years. Found long before the excavation of the demonstrably Norse site of L'Anse aux Meadows in Newfoundland, the Beardmore Relics were taken by many to be proof positive of an ancient Norse presence in Canada, though that presence, rather inexplicably, was not near the Atlantic Ocean across which the Norse actually did travel to the New World.

The relics were initially deemed genuine and important by the Royal Ontario Museum, which purchased them from Dodd and displayed them for 20 years. Many professional archaeologists and historians, however, were extremely skeptical right from the start. Investigation subsequent to the museum's purchase of the relics indicated that they, in fact, had been brought into Canada only in the 1920s. When Dodd's stepson, Walter, provided museum officials with a sworn statement that he had actually seen his father place the artifacts in the ground in order to perpetrate an archaeological hoax, the museum pulled the material from display.

The artifacts themselves appear to be genuine, that is, they are genuinely old Norse artifacts. Their appearance in Canada is not similarly genuine. According to Walter Dodd, his stepfather had found the objects in the basement of a house in Port Arthur, Ontario. The pieces, apparently, came from the collection of Andreas Bloch, a Norwegian illustrator, and ended up in Port Arthur when Bloch's son migrated to Canada. Once Dodd acquired the relics, for reasons known only to him (he made very little money on the objects, receiving only C$500 from the museum for them), he planted them near Beardmore just a short time before he claimed to have found them.

The artifacts were placed back on display at the Royal Ontario Museum in the early 1990s, not as evidence of an early Norse presence in Ontario, but as genuine Norse artifacts used in an infamous, if poorly carried out, archaeological hoax.

Benedictine Abbey of St. Mary at Glastonbury

The Benedictine Abbey of St. Mary at Glastonbury (near Bath), England, is reflected in the ruins of a church whose origins can be traced back to about 600 CE.

Along with presenting lovely and picturesque ruins, the Abbey of St. Mary is supposed to have, at one time, housed the remains of King Arthur and his queen, Guinevere. Legend, at least, has it that their tombs were discovered by the Benedictine monks on the grounds of the abbey in 1191. The legend maintains that Arthur and Guinevere's remains were reburied there, but then removed and forever lost sometime during the Reformation.

The abbey's connection to speculative archaeology rests in the strategy employed in its investigation by British architect **Frederick Bligh Bond** in 1909. Bond claimed that in his analysis he relied on guidance from the spirits of dead Benedictine monks, as well as that of one of the church's builders, especially in deciding where to conduct the archaeological search for two of the chapels—Edgar and Loretto—at the abbey. Though Bond was successful in locating the two chapels in question, there is every reason to believe he did so on the basis of prosaic sources of information he had access to, including early drawings of the abbey and his own working knowledge of the architectural layout of old English churches. There is nothing even approaching convincing evidence that Bond actually was in contact with dead monks.

Bent Pyramid

The Bent Pyramid represents the second—and still unsuccessful—attempt by **Egyptian pyramid** builders to construct a true pyramid burial chamber for the pharaoh Snefru. After abandoning the project at Meidum, now known as the **Collapsed Pyramid**, the builders moved north to Dashur, where they made their second effort to construct Snefru's final resting place. Unlike the Collapsed Pyramid, which began as a step pyramid and was changed in midbuild, in this instance the architects started from the very beginning with the intention of constructing a true pyramid. Having learned a valuable lesson in their construction of the Collapsed Pyramid and recognizing that its steep angle (more than 70°) contributed to construction problems, the builders used a gentler angle—54.5°—when building the Bent Pyramid's faces. But even at this gentler angle, cracks developed on the facing of the structure, in part because the builders made the mistake of positioning three corners of the pyramid on unmovable bedrock, while the fourth corner was built on a compressible gravel base (Brier and Houdin 2008). The great weight of the monument on the soft gravel resulted in inconsistent overall settling. As a result, the structure developed significant cracks on its exterior surface and a near collapse in the interior burial chamber.

The builders came up with an interesting solution to this problem. Rather than abandoning the project in its entirety after discovering cracks in the lower courses of the pyramid blocks, the builders changed the angle of the slope to an

The Bent Pyramid was the second failed construction attempt of a true pyramid form as the burial monument of an Egyptian pharaoh. The Collapsed Pyramid was the first failed attempt for the same ruler, Snefru. The slope at the lower end of the pyramid was too steep, and cracks developed at the base. Builders attempted to deal with this by lessening the angle at the top, giving the monument its rather odd "bent" appearance. (M.H. Feder)

even gentler 43.5°. Their hope, which proved successful, was that by lessening the angle, they would lessen the amount of stone needed to cap off the pyramid and, thus, reduce the weight of material resting on the lower portion of the pyramid. This change in slope gives the pyramid its name—the Bent Pyramid—because it does, indeed, appear to be bent.

Here, as in the case of the Collapsed Pyramid, we see an obvious example of the trial-and-error process reflected in the evolution of pyramid construction. This is precisely what we would expect if human beings in ancient Egypt developed the technologies necessary for building monumental pyramids. Those who claim that pyramids were built by an advanced, perhaps extraterrestrial, civilization have a difficult time explaining why a technology capable of interstellar spaceflight had such a difficult time piling up rocks in the form of a stable pyramid structure.

Further Reading

To read about the Bent Pyramid in context of the history and development of the Egyptian pyramids, there's no better source than Mark Lehner's *The Complete Pyramids* (1997).

To read about the Bent Pyramid in the context of pharaonic history, see Peter Clayton's *Chronicle of the Pharaohs* (1994). For a useful discussion of the problems that developed in mid-build of the Bent Pyramid, see Bob Brier and Jean-Pierre Houdin's *The Secret of the Great Pyramid* (2008).

Bhaktivedanta Institute

The Bhaktivedanta Institute is a branch of the International Society for Krishna Consciousness. The institute offers what it asserts on its Web site to be "the world's first (and so far the only) full-fledged graduate degree (M.S./Ph.D.) program in 'Consciousness Studies'" (www.bvinst.edu). You'll need to go to the institute's Web site for an explanation of what that is. I've read it and admit to having no clue what they're talking about.

In the past, the Bhaktivedanta Institute published a number of books about archaeology and paleoanthropology, which appear to have been based on a literal interpretation of Hinduism. The first and most significant of these was *Forbidden Archaeology: The Hidden History of the Human Race* by Michael A. Cremo and Richard L. Thompson. Neither author was an archaeologist or paleoanthropologist, though both were members of the International Society for Krishna Consciousness.

Bond, Frederick Bligh

Frederick Bligh Bond (1864–1945) was a British architect who, in 1909, was hired to investigate the ruins of the **Benedictine Abbey of St. Mary at Glastonbury** and, at the same time, to shore up the walls to make them safe for visitors to remnants of the old church. Among Bond's duties was the production of a guidebook to the abbey's ruins, and among the techniques he used to illuminate the history, appearance, functioning, and architecture of the building was archaeology. Bond excavated among the church's ruins in an attempt to better tell the story of the building.

Along with using standard methods of historical investigation, though, Bond decided that it might prove fruitful to contact some of the monks who had actually lived and worked at the abbey. Obtaining oral histories is a well-accepted method used in history and historical archaeology, but in Bond's case, we're not talking about him commiserating with a cohort of aging Benedictines who were living out their golden years at the retirement home for aged monks. Rather, as Bond later claimed, he was in direct contact with the spirits or ghosts of decidedly dead monks and the similarly long-dead Abbot Beere, who is supposed to have built the Edgar Chapel at the abbey in the sixteenth century.

The deceased monks and especially Abbot Beere advised Bond, he said, as to where to locate his archaeological excavation units and, in this way, revealed to him the locations of two chapels (the Edgar and Loretto chapels) in the abbey.

In this particular case of the application of what amounts to spiritualist archaeology, there were no scientific controls whatsoever. Though Bond indeed was able to locate the two chapels mentioned, there is no way at all to ascertain whether he did so because of the information provided him from the great beyond or if, as an architect with a reasonable working knowledge of churches and access to early drawings of the abbey, his source of information was a bit more mundane than dead monks. The excavation of the Benedictine Abbey of St. Mary at Glastonbury provides no evidence for the successful use of anything more than common sense in its excavation.

Bosnian Pyramids

The construction of pyramids as monuments in the ancient world is not restricted to Egypt. Using a broad definition of the term, pyramids of various forms are found in Mesoamerica (the **Maya** and Aztec built lots of pyramids, as did the predecessors of the Aztec, the people of Teotihuacán); American Indians north of Mexico built pyramids of earth; there are enormous pyramid monuments in western China; and there are other examples. It makes perfect sense, of course, that ancient people all over the world came upon the same general form for constructing massive monuments. The pyramidal form, a structure broadest and widest at the base and becoming smaller as it rises up, is inherently stable. You don't need to build support structures like the flying buttresses of medieval churches to hold up the walls, and you don't need to keep each subsequent course perfectly aligned as you proceed upward. Certainly, there are problems with complex additions, like separate facing stones (as in many **Egyptian pyramids**), but the general pyramidal form is enormously stable. People all over the world figured that out and used the pyramidal form in their monumental construction projects.

Therefore, it would not be the least bit surprising if ancient people near the modern city of Sarajevo, Bosnia, did that same thing; the recently made claim that there are ancient pyramids in Bosnia is not, in and of itself, outlandish. What *is* outlandish, however, is the assertion that the Bosnian pyramids are upwards of two and a half times taller than **Khufu**'s pyramid, the largest in all of Egypt, and that the Bosnian pyramids predate the Egyptian monuments by 8,000 years.

The Bosnian pyramid claims have been made primarily by one man, Semir Osmanagic, a metalwork contractor of Bosnian extraction in Houston, Texas.

Though actually just a hill, the result of well-known and entirely natural geological processes, the author Semir Osmanagic calls this the "Pyramid of the Moon," and claims it reflects the work of an ancient Bosnian civilization twice the age of ancient Egypt. (AP Photo/Hidajet Delic)

Though not an archaeologist, geologist, historian, or scientist, Osmanagic certainly has been a terrific salesman for his claim.

Osmanagic has been able to get funding for archaeological work at the so-called pyramids, primarily by appealing to the ethnic and national pride of Bosnians, who have suffered greatly in the recent past as the result of the internecine strife that devastated their country. Whether his claims serve a valuable emotional purpose or not, however, cannot be considered when we examine Osmanagic's archaeological and geological evidence. Essentially, there is none.

The pyramids he assigns colorful names to—the Pyramid of the Sun, the Pyramid of the Dragon, the Pyramid of the Moon, the Pyramid of Love—are nothing more than natural features, hills that do share with pyramids the characteristic of being broader on the bottom than on the top, but that's not exactly a convincing argument. There isn't a shred of evidence that the mountains and hills Osmanagic is excavating are artificial in the least. Bosnian geologists have long studied these features and reject Osmanagic's assertions of a cultural origin to them; these scientists have identified the geological features that have produced the angular characteristics of some parts of the hills, features that Osmanagic identifies as edges of artificial pyramids.

In his most extreme musings, Osmanagic relates the Bosnian pyramids to those of Egypt and the Maya and manages to trace them all back to **Atlantis** and **Lemuria**. Suffice it to say, there is no geological evidence whatsoever to support his claims that the hills around Sarajevo are astonishing, enormous, 12,000-year-old, human-made monuments. Nor is there any evidence that supports the notion that an incredibly precocious ancient society lived in the vicinity of Sarajevo and built these remarkable structures.

Archaeologists describe the civilization of Bosnia 12,000 years ago as reflecting a hunting-and-gathering economy characterized by the use of stone tools and living a nomadic way of life. There is no 12,000-year-old city nearby; no archaeological evidence of a densely packed settlement or vast dormitories of peasant pyramid workers; no infrastructure characterized by a complex set of roads for bringing in raw materials; no enormous bakeries or kitchens to feed the builders; no evidence at the time the pyramids are purported to have been built of a rigidly stratified society of noblemen and women, specialist craftsmen and women, merchants, and soldiers; and no evidence of a system of writing to maintain the records necessary to coordinate the construction of so impressive a series of monuments. The evidence just enumerated *is* found in other parts of the world where such vast and impressive construction projects were carried out, for example, in ancient Egypt. The fact that such evidence is entirely lacking here is just another damning piece of evidence that the Bosnian pyramids are little more than Osmanagic's fantasy.

Further Reading

The best summary of the Bosnian pyramid hoax can be found in an article published in *Archaeology* magazine (Kampschror 2006).

Brendan, Saint

Born in 484 in County Kerry, in the southwest of Ireland, Saint Brendan was the most well-known Irish cleric among a group called the **anchorites**, who, in their ox-hide boats (*curragh*), plied the waters of the northern Atlantic in the sixth century, seeking out places of solitude where they could meditate and commune with God. Archaeological evidence indicates clearly that anchorites actually made landfall and established monasteries on the Orkney Islands, north of the Scottish mainland, by 579; in the Shetlands by 620; in the Faeroe Islands by 670; and on Iceland by no later than 795.

Brendan's seafaring exploits, which likely occurred soon after 510, were immortalized in a book titled *Navigatio sancti Brendani abbatis*, or, in English, *The Voyage of St. Brendan, the Abbot*. Along with describing places and features (like icebergs and volcanoes) present in the Northern Atlantic, the *Navigatio* tells the tale of Brendan's seven-year voyage, with as many as 60 followers, to a place far to the west of Ireland, at the far end of the Atlantic Ocean, a place called the "Land Promised to the Saints." If, as some have asserted, this land was located in North America, Saint Brendan would have been the first European to have arrived on the shores of the New World, beating both Columbus and the Norse here by centuries. However, there is no archaeological evidence whatsoever to support this claim; there are no artifacts found in pre-Columbian context in the New World traceable to sixth-century Irish monks.

That is a deal-breaker from an archaeological perspective.

Brendan died in 577. Soon thereafter, he was made a saint, and rather appropriately Brendan became the patron saint of sailors and travelers.

Burrows Cave

Burrows Cave is one in a long line of ostensible archaeological discoveries in the Americas (others include the **Michigan Relics**, the **Davenport Tablets**, and the **Newark Holy Stones**) that have been used by proponents to support a hypothesis of pre-Columbian contact between the Old and New Worlds and even the settlement of places in North and South America. The case of the Burrows Cave discoveries is significant if only because of the extraordinary number of objects claimed to have been found there; one accounting numbers the artifacts at over 4,000 (www.the-book-of-thoth.com/content-69.html).

In the usual telling of the story, Russell Burrows discovered the cave that now bears his name entirely by accident when he stopped for lunch while hiking across a bluff in southeastern Illinois sometime in 1982. Upon falling into a pit, Burrows states that he found the carving of a human face that didn't look anything like an Indian or like any Indian artifact that he had ever found in the state. Then, he reports, things got even stranger when he discovered in the cave a human skeleton laid out on a block of stone; all around the skeleton were marble axheads, bronze spears and swords, and, to top it off, hundreds of objects, including armbands and headbands, of solid gold.

After that initial investigation of the cave, Burrows apparently returned, finding altogether 13 astonishing crypts and thousands of artifacts inscribed with all manner of writing. According to the supporters of the authenticity of Burrows's story, the writing systems reflected in the artifacts are a mixture of Egyptian hieroglyphs, Mesopotamian, Hebrew, Etruscan, and ancient Greek, among other archaic languages. (For photos of some of the objects Burrows says he found in the cave, see www.the-book-of-thoth.com/content-69.html.)

If any of the story told by Burrows is true, well, the stereotypical reaction to a momentous new archaeological discovery where "we're going to have to rewrite the textbooks" would certainly apply. But before we go around rewriting those books (some of which were written by me), there are some reasonable expectations we would have of the researchers presenting the claims. How about, at a very minimum, a series of photographs of the artifacts and human remains in situ? How about documentation of how the objects were positioned when discovered and a detailed accounting of how they were recovered? How about organic remains and their analysis? Was any charcoal recovered suitable for radiocarbon dating? Any plant remains? And were there 13 human skeletons recovered in the 13 crypts? How many males? How many females? What were their ages as indicated by skeletal development? Were any pathologies presented in the bones that might suggest a particular geographic source? And how about a chemical analysis of the bones? This has been used to great effect to identify the place on our planet where an individual lived; the trace elements in the soil end up in the food and then end up in the bones. How about presenting the remains for a genetic analysis that might enable tracing the bones to a particular human group living in a particular geographic region? And finally, how about bringing a bunch of skeptical archaeologists down into the cave? That would show us! How great would it be to see the looks of shock, recognition, and then resignation on our faces when we realized that there was no way we could explain away the amazing implications of Burrows Cave?

Perhaps it is not so amazing that none of the above has yet occurred. Photographs of a handful of artifacts don't add up to a very convincing case. **Carl Sagan** is credited with codifying the following rule of scientific reasoning: Extreme claims require extreme levels of proof. But extreme levels of proof, even regular levels of proof, even *weak* levels of proof, have not been forthcoming by the Burrows Cave proponents. According to one source (Joltes 2003), no one but Burrows has actually been inside the cave; folks who would seem to be natural allies of a claim that a cave in Illinois houses ancient objects from all over the world (the Early Sites Research Society) were supposed to be given a tour of the cave, but even they were summarily disinvited when they sought to apply some very tepid scientific controls.

When individual objects *have* been made available for analysis by scientists, the verdict has not been very supportive. In a report provided by Richard Joltes (2003), it was noted that, in the case of the stone artifacts, the condition of the raw material from which the objects were made indicate a very recent date of manufacture.

As we see elsewhere (the **Michigan Relics** or the **Tucson Artifacts**, for example), a fundamental problem in sites like Burrows Cave rests in this simple fact: A single site—even one with lots and lots of artifacts—is fundamentally easy to fake. But the existence of a site like Burrows Cave, if genuine, brings along with it a host of implications about what the archaeological record must look like, not just in the cave but in a vast area around that cave. If a substantial population of people from the Old World were stashing copious quantities of cool stuff in a cave in Illinois, local people who had lived in the area for untold generations would have known about the cave, would have known how to get into it, and would have taken some of the objects, and archaeologists would have found these stolen artifacts when digging in local village, ceremonial, and, maybe especially, burial sites. And where did the people who used the cave live? Where are their villages, their habitations? Did they only bring in gold objects with a mash-up of writing styles? Where is their dishware, their cutlery, their woodworking tools, their distinctive house forms, burials, and trash heaps? We should have found the archaeological evidence of their ordinary, everyday lives—ordinary and everyday, but distinctly and uniquely their own. Without that kind of evidence being found by archaeologists, it's quite impossible to believe that they were there at all.

Ultimately, it is unclear whether any of the claims of Russell Burrows are in any way accurate. It should give strong supporters pause when reading that many of the gold objects found by Burrows may have been melted down or sold on the antiquities market. And, indeed, even some strong advocates are perplexed by the apparent amalgam of ancient languages supposedly present in the cave. Why would there be so many different ancient Old World languages—by the way, from differing time periods—in one cave in Illinois (and nowhere else)? One of the supporters suggested that the cave houses a vast and varied array of booty stashed there by pirates who, in antiquity, stole the stuff from all over the world, and then cached it in . . . southeastern Illinois. Remarkable. And wildly unlikely.

Further Reading

For the best job of breaking down the elements of the Burrows Cave folly, check out the online article titled "Burrows Cave: A Modern Hoax" by Richard Joltes (2003).

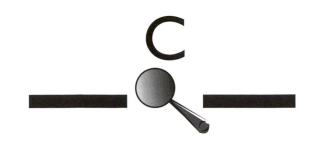

Calaveras Skull

The Calaveras Skull was a somewhat fragmented human cranium found in February 1866, at a depth of 130 feet below the surface, deep in a mine in Calaveras County in central California, southeast of the capital, Sacramento. The depth at which the human remains had been found and the fact that it appeared to originate below a layer of lava seemed to provide evidence for the great antiquity of a human presence in the New World, specifically, California, precisely at a time when there was a considerable amount of controversy concerning the timing of the first human entrance into the New World.

Many archaeologists in the New World were convinced that—especially in comparison to the archaeological record of Africa, Asia, and Europe—the Americas were occupied comparatively only relatively recently, and there was not just a little envy among American scientists over this state of affairs. The archaeological record of the Americas was viewed as rather thin, with humans arriving on these shores only relatively recently—rendering, in the minds of some, the New World rather less significant than the Old.

The skull found in the mine in Calaveras County seemed to provide evidence that this pessimistic view of American prehistory was unwarranted, that, indeed, the time depth of a human presence here rivaled that of the Old World. If the cranium was really found where it had been reported, it was possible that human beings had been in the New World deep into the Pliocene Epoch, as much as 5 million years ago.

The cranium was not recovered in excavation by archaeologists, but was ostensibly unearthed by miners working in the mine. It ended up in the possession of J. D. Whitney, the state geologist of California and a geologist at Harvard University. An individual with a rather reserved and patrician air, Whitney had engendered more than just a little resentment among the locals, being an Easterner and an intellectual; he was uncomfortable in his dealings with the miners and, as a result, unpopular among them.

Whitney became the chief champion of the authenticity of the cranium, and, in a sense, he was correct. The remains, rather obviously, were genuine. It really was an almost entirely intact human cranium (the skull without the mandible, or lower jaw). However, Whitney had not been in the mine when the cranium was found and therefore had to rely implicitly on the testimony of the miners concerning the stratigraphic provenience of the cranial remains. But remember, these were the same miners who disliked Whitney for his intellectual airs.

Almost immediately, stories were told of the **fraudulent** nature of the cranium's find-spot. As early as 1869, only about three years after its discovery and official announcement of its significance by Whitney, a San Francisco newspaper noted that workers in the Calaveras County mine where the remains had been found were more than willing to talk about the hoax they had perpetrated on Whitney. Then, in 1901, Frederick Ward Putnam, also an archaeologist at Harvard's Peabody Museum, investigated details surrounding the discovery of the cranium and was told that Indian skulls had been excavated near the mine in 1865, just about a year before the miners reported their discovery of the Calaveras Skull, and that one of those skulls had been planted in the mine, knowing that, as the state geologist, it would end up on Whitney's desk. To add another layer of confusion to the story, a detailed description of the skull the miners originally found doesn't match the appearance of the skull that was provided to Whitney, so for some reason and somehow, the skull was switched somewhere along the way.

The entire thing, rather obviously, is a silly mess filled with confessions of a hoax, an unpopular target of the hoax, and mixed-up skulls. Quite simply, the Calaveras Skull does not prove that human beings were in California 5 million years ago. As archaeologist Ralph Dexter characterized the affair in 1986, the entire thing had been a practical joke from the beginning.

Further Reading

For an archaeological debunking of the Calaveras Skull story, see Ralph Dexter's article "Historical Aspects of the Calaveras Skull Controversy," in the journal *American Antiquity* (1986).

Cardiff Giant

The more than a little ridiculous tale of the Cardiff Giant—at least, the public part of the story—begins on Saturday, October 16, 1869, when workers digging a well on Stub Newell's farm in Cardiff, New York, encountered a hard object at a depth of approximately three feet. After a little cleaning up, the discovery appeared to be made of stone and in the perfect form of an enormous human foot. Perplexed about the presence of such a thing in the clean, rich, agricultural soil along Onondaga Creek, the workers expanded their excavations until, after a relatively brief time, they had revealed the rest of what clearly appeared to be a huge human body attached to the foot. It seemed as if a giant human being, more than 10 feet in height, at some time in the distant past had traveled through this region of New York State and had died there, after which his body was covered by the alluvium deposited by the creek and then, despite what in the nineteenth century was already well known about the geological process of petrification, had turned to stone, just like a petrified tree.

Thus began the short, sad career of the Cardiff Giant as an archaeological humbug. It was called by some the "Goliath of Cardiff" in a deliberate reference to the character in the Old Testament, a giant Philistine warrior who was slain by David, a diminutive representative of the Israelites. That story has ever been the symbol of good overcoming evil, of the small and meek defeating a far more powerful force, of right prevailing over might, no matter the odds or material unlikelihood.

Now in silent repose at the Farmers Museum in Cooperstown, New York, the Cardiff Giant was a transparent archaeological fraud, done for the money. (K. Feder)

Ostensibly just a simple farmer, Newell had a circus tent erected over the giant and shortly began charging the public first 25 and then 50 cents to view the remains of a biblical giant from before Noah's flood. It was a good bet that the giant would interest people enough to make a trip to examine him. After all, Goliath was only the most famous of the giant men and women noted in the Old Testament, and the Cardiff representative of this ancient species now served as proof of these biblical references.

Whether to verify a biblical claim or out of simple curiosity, the paying public came in droves. It is estimated that between 300 and 500 people visited the Newell farm on a daily basis in the weeks after its discovery. Newell was making more money than farming ever could have provided, and he wasn't the only one reaping an economic bonanza from the petrified man. Hotels and restaurants in the surrounding area saw an enormous influx of tourist dollars. Syracuse, New York, especially, as the largest nearby town, experienced a miniboom in hotel registrations.

A consortium of local businessmen, enthusiastic about the presence of a new attraction nearby, grew concerned that the yokel in charge, tiring of the work involved, feeling he had made enough money, or simply getting bored, might do something precipitous like bury the thing or, even worse, sell it to the highest out-of-town bidder. The businessmen had reason to be concerned, knowing that circus impresario P. T. Barnum had offered a large sum of money to Newell to purchase the giant. The Syracuse consortium ended up paying Newell $30,000 for a three-quarters interest in the giant. After continuing to exhibit the giant on the Newell farm for nearly two weeks (and already having made back $12,000 of their investment), they decided to raise the giant up out of his place of discovery and transport him to Syracuse, where they felt they could make even more money more quickly.

Though the owners seemed to have come up with a pretty good business model, they could not foresee a significant problem: Stub Newell had a big mouth and began spouting off about the great joke he had pulled off with a decidedly fake archaeological specimen. Apparently it was Stub's inability to keep a secret that led to a full confession by his co-conspirator, the real brains behind the hoax, Newell's cousin George Hull.

Hull revealed in a newspaper interview that he had purchased a block of gypsum more than a year previously in Fort Dodge, Iowa, with the intention of producing an archaeological fake after an animated discussion with a preacher. Hull was an atheist, a scoundrel with a number of run-ins with the law, but also a successful entrepreneur of sorts. He was inspired by the conversation with the minister to produce a fraudulent artifact that would seem to supply proof for a biblical tale, feeling that with such a specimen, he could take advantage of gullible believers.

Hull's hoax would involve proof of biblical stories of giants (it could just as well have been evidence of the existence of **Noah's ark** or Christ's cross). He shipped the large block of gypsum to Chicago, where he hired two sculptors to produce a work of a giant naked man in repose. Upon its completion, Hull shipped the giant to New York and, then to the Newell farm where, with the knowledge and assistance of his cousin, the giant was buried and allowed to "season" for about a year before the sign was given to Newell to hire men to dig a well in the exact location where the giant was interred.

With the confession, the Cardiff Giant's economic value plummeted; few wished to pay much of anything to see a transparent fake of a petrified man. The Giant was placed in storage and trotted out occasionally for fairs and such. Then the Giant made a brief sojourn to Iowa, the source of the gypsum from which it was made. Gardner Cowles, an Iowa newspaper owner, bought the Giant, had him shipped west, and then displayed him in the basement of his house. The Giant can be seen there in a photograph published in the August 1939 issue of *National Geographic* in the context of an article about Iowa. Then, in 1947, the new director of the New York State Historical Association purchased the Giant from Cowles and returned it to the scene of the crime, installing it as an exhibit at the Farmers Museum in Cooperstown, New York, reasonably nearby to what had been the

Newell farm. The erstwhile biblical giant, in all his glory, resides at this outdoor museum, where he continues to amaze the paying public—though not as proof of biblical tales. Rather, tourists now gaze in amazement at a fake so obvious it is truly remarkable that it fooled anybody at all.

It is important to point out that, in fact, the Cardiff Giant fooled no scientists or, for that matter, artists. Geologists such as J. F. Boynton at the University of Pennsylvania recognized the stone from which the sculpture was carved and, knowing full well that gypsum is a sedimentary rock and decidedly not the product of petrification, declared it to be a **fraud** placed in the ground no more than a year previously. His conclusion was spot on, as was the determination of Eratus Dow, a well-known sculptor, that there were tool marks on the Giant, the obvious result of human artifice. O. C. Marsh, the most famous paleontologist of the day, also declared the Giant to be a clumsy fraud.

Despite the pronouncements of scholars and sculptors, the public believed in the Giant because they wanted to believe in giants. As absurd as the Giant was, and as unequivocal as the scientists and artists were about its fraudulent nature, the public continued to look on it in awe. It took the confession of the perpetrator to convince them otherwise.

Perhaps the most hilarious element of this already funny episode in human history is this: Newell's rejection of Barnum's offer to purchase the Giant did not deter the showman in the least. Barnum actually had a fake Cardiff Giant made—that's right, a fake of what was already a fake—and exhibited it in his sideshow. Adding insult to injury, the real Cardiff Giant (the real fake, that is) traveled to New York to be exhibited coincidentally, at the same time that Barnum's circus was in town. Barnum's fake (that is, the fake fake) actually outdrew the real fake. Mark Twain was so amused by this turn of events that he composed the short story , A Ghost Story, in which even the Cardiff Giant's own ghost was fooled by Barnum's copy, as he haunts the wrong body in an attempt to have the real one laid to its final rest.

Further Reading

The definitive work on the tale of the Cardiff Giant is Scott Tribble's *A Colossal Hoax* (2009). I also devote a chapter to the story in my book, *Frauds, Myths, and Mysteries* (Feder 2010).

Carter, Howard

Howard Carter (1847–1939) was an English Egyptologist. He began his career as an artist and illustrator of Egyptian antiquities and learned excavation from Sir Flinders Petrie, one of the best-known Egyptologists of the late nineteenth and early twentieth centuries.

Carter found financial backing for his own excavations from British nobleman George Herbert, Earl of Carnarvon. The Earl hoped that his investment would pay big dividends if Carter found the undisturbed tomb of a pharaoh. As was the practice in the late nineteenth and early twentieth centuries in Egypt, European benefactors signed contracts with their archaeologists that formalized the distribution or "ownership" of any artifacts discovered in their excavations. Such contracts were more like mining agreements than scientific arrangements; financial backers like Carnarvon commonly got first claim of material recovered and often kept the best pieces or distributed material to museums. (The contract was not enforceable once the Egyptian government declared that the treasures in the tomb were the patrimony of Egypt and property of the nation.)

Carnarvon and Carter's most important discovery was, of course, the unplundered tomb of the pharaoh Tutankhamun, reputedly protected by **King Tut's Curse**. The curse, however, didn't exist; there was no epidemic of deaths surrounding the opening of the tomb or the analysis of Tut's mummy or associated artifacts. The lack of a curse or, at the very least, its complete inefficacy is best exemplified by this: Howard Carter, the person most directly responsible for finding and opening the tomb and the individual most directly involved in handling and examining the mummy and associated materials, was 48 years old when he first entered the tomb and lived for an additional 16 years, spending much of that time analyzing the site. It would have been an odd curse indeed that afflicted as disparate and tangentially associated people as assorted taxi cab drivers, tourists, guards, and the like, but passed over Carter. Carter ultimately admitted that he encouraged the fiction that there had been a curse expressly to scare away any who might attempt to enter the tomb illegally in order to spirit away any of its valuable treasure. On his grave marker is inscribed the phrase: "May your spirit live / May you spend millions of years / You who love Thebes / Sitting with your face to the north wind / Your eyes beholding happiness."

Cayce, Edgar

Edgar Cayce (1877–1945), called by some the "sleeping prophet," was an American who claimed abilities that might be labeled "psychic." During the course of his life, Cayce provided psychic readings in a trance or trancelike state—hence the epithet "sleeping"—in which, among other pronouncements, he described life on the Lost Continent of **Atlantis** to clients or patients who consulted him and who, according to Cayce, had lived on Atlantis in a past life.

Cayce's description of Atlantis is mundane, a pastiche of science-fictiony musings about the future, firmly ensconced within early twentieth-century sensibilities (see Jordan 2001). For example, Cayce's Atlanteans had lasers, elevators (tubes powered by compressed air and steam), submarines, nuclear power, and telephones. His descriptions of Atlantis sound less an Atlantis where he had actually lived—Cayce was, apparently, the reincarnation of an Atlantean priest— and quite a bit more like a description of one of those lame 1960s World's Fair displays of the future where, by the turn of the twenty-first century, we were all to be driving our own "autogyros" (personal helicopters) instead of cars, an abundance of energy would be produced from nuclear fusion so cheaply that the utilities companies wouldn't even be able to measure the usage on a standard meter, and families would be taking summer vacations at a Club Med resort on the moon. The future never quite pans out the way futurists expect or predict, and the highly advanced technology of Atlantis as described by Cayce consists of little more than exaggerations of technologies already available or in the works when Cayce was alive. He never described Atlanteans with laptops, iPods, iPads, or cell phones— not because there was a real Atlantis that just hadn't developed such things, but because these bits of twenty-first technology were beyond the imagination of even someone with as vivid imagination as his.

Specific predictions made by Cayce, prognostications that can be assessed because either they happened or they didn't, have turned out not to be true. For example, Cayce predicted that Japan would disappear beneath the waters of the Pacific, that New York City and parts of Georgia and the Carolinas would be swallowed up by the Atlantic, and that new land would rise up out of the Atlantic. These are all inevitable, at least in geologic time, but Cayce (1968, 157–59) claimed that his psychic visions told him this all would occur, or at least begin to occur, in 1968 or 1969. Enough said.

Cayce maintained that some Atlanteans escaped death and journeyed to Egypt sometime before 10,000 BCE. They brought with them books or other records that contained at least some of the accumulated knowledge of their advanced civilization. They secreted these materials in an underground chamber Cayce called the **Hall of Records**.

None of Cayce's descriptions of Atlantis have, needless to say, any evidence to support them. This is not surprising, as Atlantis itself was not a real place, but a fiction concocted by Plato in order to make a point about the perfect society in the *Critias* dialogue. No artifacts from Atlantis have ever been found. A Hall of Records has yet to materialize in any archaeological excavations in Egypt or anywhere else. Cayce's pronouncements on Atlantis are nothing more than science fiction.

Celt Discovery of America

Some writers—though not many, if any, who are trained archaeologists or historians—suggest that North America was discovered, explored, and settled by Europeans, especially Celts from western Europe, long before the voyages of exploration of Christopher Columbus. These authors, prominent among them

Barry Fell, assert that the evidence of this early **discovery of America** is centered in, but not confined to, the northeast, especially New England. In most of the proposed scenarios, ancient Celts did not just briefly wander through North America. They arrived, as much as 4,000 years ago, explored, and then settled in great numbers. The proposed Celtic presence in North America, in fact, is usually claimed to be substantial; Fell, for example, describes "Celtic kingdoms" in pre-Columbian North America.

If this were true and if the presence were that extensive, archaeological evidence of an ancient Celtic presence should be abundant and obvious. That evidence should include elements of material culture. Diagnostically Celtic tools—unlike anything known to have been made and used by native people and made of raw materials unavailable in North America but traceable to Europe—should be found by archaeologists in pre-Columbian stratigraphic contexts, in sites that seem obviously to be intrusive, looking unlike the sites of native people, along with settlement, housing, trash disposal, toolmaking, and burial patterns that look unlike anything seen at archaeological sites before their "invasion." Those patterns should, instead, appear to match those seen in Celtic habitations in such places as England, Scotland, Ireland, and Wales. Where conditions have been conducive to the preservation of organic remains (those conditions are rare in the east), human skeletons should be found that anatomically share more in common with those of Europeans than Native Americans. Mitochondrial DNA analysis of these skeletons should reflect haplogroups found in Europe, as opposed to the mitochondrial varieties (A, B, C, D, and X) that are known among Native Americans and East Asians.

All of these expected varieties of archaeological and skeletal evidence that would support the hypothesis of the presence of Celtic people are, in fact, found in northeastern North America in a *post*-Columbian temporal context. That is to say, artifacts typical of western Europe, raw materials whose source is western Europe, settlement patterns, housing patterns, trash disposal practices, burial traditions, and even the skeletal remains of western Europeans are found in northeastern North America in sites and contexts that date to as early as, but not before, the early seventeenth century.

The primary data marshaled in favor of the claim that northeastern North America was populated by ancient Celts consists of epigraphic evidence and the argument that stone structures found here are of ancient Celtic origin.

Most of the epigraphic evidence consists of idiosyncratic interpretations of tally marks, glacial scratch marks, and modern inscriptions in **Ogham**, a written language known to have been used in Ireland, Scotland, and Wales between the third and sixth centuries. Experts in the Celts and Ogham are not sympathetic to Fell's interpretation, however, and do not agree that there is any evidence of Ogham in the New World.

The other significant source of data used to support the claim that ancient Celts were present in the New World is an interpretation of stone structures found all over New England, such as **America's Stonehenge** and **Gungywamp**. Various kinds of chambers and vaults, generally made of fieldstone with dry-laid masonry, are ubiquitous in New England and eastern New York State. They are almost always associated with historic farmsteads, in all likelihood served as storage buildings, often for cold storage, which is why they are historically called "root cellars." The architecture and historical context of these outbuildings have been researched (for example, in Vermont [Neudorfer 1980] and Massachusetts [Cole 1982]). The structures are in no way mysterious; they are part of a tradition of vernacular architecture—homebuilt facilities in farm country where stone is abundant—their construction is sometimes recorded in historical documents, and their archaeology shows no evidence of ancient Celtic artifacts. Excavation of the stone chambers has revealed only the material culture of seventeenth-, eighteenth-, nineteenth-, and twentieth-century New Englanders.

Supporters of the claim that the stone chambers were built in pre-Columbian times are therefore left only the argument that the architectural style of the chambers is reminiscent of that of ancient western Europe. In a sense, this is true. Historical archaeologist Robert Gradie (1981) points out that the architectural styles incorporated in the stone chambers of New England are ancient and long lived in Great Britain and Ireland. In other words, ancient Celts, thousands of years ago, made stone structures in much the same way that their descendants did in England, Scotland, Ireland, and Wales far more recently, in the seventeenth through early twentieth centuries. Many of the seventeenth-, eighteenth-, and nineteenth-century settlers of New England were Celtic people who established farmsteads and built outbuildings, including root cellars, in the traditional way.

The point is, those traditions go back to the ancient Celts. So, the fact that stone chambers in New England may resemble the architecture of ancient Great Britain in no way means those stone chambers date to antiquity. The only way to show that the stone chambers of New England were built by ancient Celtic visitors and settlers would be to find diagnostically ancient Celtic artifacts in firm stratigraphic context within or under (predating) the chambers. Such evidence has not been found, so the claim that ancient Celts discovered America has not been definitively supported by archaeological evidence.

Further Reading

The best antidote to the claim that ancient Celts settled New England in antiquity and built the ubiquitous stone chambers found here as religious temples, shrines, or whatever can be found in Giovanna Neudorfer's book *Vermont's Stone Chambers* (1980). For a general discussion of this issue, see the chapter "Who's Next" in my book *Frauds, Myths, and Mysteries* (Feder 2010) as well.

Chariots of the Gods

Chariots of the Gods is the English title of a book first published in Europe in 1968, in German, under the title *Erinnerungen an die Zukunft* (Recollections of the Future). The book's author is the Swiss writer **Erich von Däniken**. *Chariots of the Gods* is the first of 29 published books written by von Däniken, all with a common theme: that the Earth was visited in antiquity by extraterrestrial aliens who became directly involved in the physical evolution of our species—through genetic engineering, perhaps, or even the old-fashioned way, by actually mating with our ancestors—as well as the cultural evolution of humanity by helping us along in science, engineering, mathematics, and so forth. Von Däniken's fundamental claim is referred to as the "**ancient astronaut hypothesis.**"

In von Däniken's own account of the story behind *Chariots of the Gods*, he became certain of the role of extraterrestrial aliens in the development of human culture after a number of tourist visits to significant archaeological sites across the face of the globe. Convinced that mere humans, and ancient ones at that, were wholly incapable of having produced the spectacular technological achievements exhibited in the archaeological record of places like Egypt and South America, von Däniken decided to lay out his remarkable realization in a manuscript. That manuscript became *Erinnerungen an die Zukunft.*

When von Däniken shopped around the manuscript, most publishers responded decidedly negatively, concluding that his scientific credentials were nonexistent, his argument was weak at best, and acceptance of his "proof" required a complete ignorance and rejection of much of what archaeology has been able to tell us about the ancient civilizations that were the focus of the book. In fact, a series of publishers turned the manuscript down flat. Eventually, however, a small German publisher decided that the manuscript was worthy of publication, but was still unconvinced that the book would do especially well and ordered a small initial print run.

At least from a business perspective, the publishers who turned down *Erinnerungen an die Zukunft* were quite mistaken. The book became an immediate sensation, the small run sold out very quickly, and thousands more copies were hurriedly printed to fulfill demand. The book ultimately sold millions of copies, was translated into more than 20 languages, led to a series of 28 more books by von Däniken, and effectively spawned an entire ancient astronaut industry replete with television documentaries, movies, conferences, magazines, and a theme park (**Mystery Park**). The mistakes and misrepresentations of human antiquity found in the book are so egregious that some have questioned whether von Däniken actually believes any of it. This has also led some, the author of this encyclopedia included, to suggest that, far from being a writer of alternative human histories, von Däniken is instead a writer of fantasy and science fiction.

Chinese Discovery of America

Author Gavin Menzies in 2002 wrote a popular book titled *1421: The Year China Discovered America*—which spawned an accompanying cable documentary—that purported to prove that Chinese explorers had circumnavigated the globe, discovering and exploring the Americas in the process, 71 years before Columbus, in 1421.

Historians are well aware that a Chinese admiral, Zheng He, commanding a fleet of ships, did in fact set out on a journey of exploration in 1405 and indisputably traveled as far as the east coast of Africa and entered into the Persian Gulf. Though historians can trace Zheng He's return to China in 1421 after these sojourns and point to historical evidence that suggests his fleet of exploration was thereafter abandoned, Menzies, on very little evidence, suggests that at least a part of the fleet, led by four of Zheng He's rear admirals, did not return and continued exploring the world.

Most of Menzies' argument focuses on fifteenth- and sixteenth-century cartography—maps like the **Piri Reis map**—which he argues shows a preexisting knowledge of the world's oceans and coasts on the part of European navigators like Christopher Columbus. That knowledge, Menzies argues, came from the records and maps produced by Zheng He's underlings in their 1421–1423 circumnavigation of the globe.

If a Chinese fleet did circumnavigate the globe between 1421 and 1423 and if they "discovered" America, making landfall and exploring, we would expect there to be physical, archaeological evidence of their presence here. There would be encampments. Perhaps they would have traded Chinese goods with the natives, and perhaps one of their crew may have died and would have been buried here. Maybe anchors would have been lost along the American coast by ships in the Chinese fleet; but to date, the only Chinese anchors discovered in American waters, the **Palos Verdes Stones**, have been shown to have been made not of Chinese but of California stone and to date to a much later contingent of Chinese immigrants to the New World.

As reviewers of his book have pointed out (e.g., Barrett 2002), while we cannot rule out the possibility of a Chinese **discovery of America** before Columbus, no indisputably diagnostic fifteenth-century Chinese artifacts have been found in the New World that would support the Menzies scenario. This may mean:

1. their contact here was so brief, fleeting, and ephemeral that archaeological evidence is entirely lacking,
2. they were exceptionally neat, picked up all their trash, brought their dead back home with them, and essentially left nothing behind, or
3. they simply weren't here.

Applying **Occam's Razor**, possibility 2 is archaeologically highly unlikely and, though we cannot rule out explanation 1, it is most sensible to go with the third explanation for the lack of fifteenth-century Chinese artifacts in the New World—they weren't here—until convincing archaeological evidence is found in firm, pre-Columbian stratigraphic context proving their presence in North America.

Further Reading

Read the book by Gavin Menzies, *1421: The Year China Discovered America* (2002), to get a firsthand view of his hypothesis.

Collapsed Pyramid

Located at Meidum, along the Nile in Egypt, the Collapsed Pyramid was originally intended as the burial chamber for the pharaoh Snefru, the first pharaoh of the 4th dynasty. Snefru ruled from 2613 to 2589 BCE and likely was the father of **Khufu**, whose Great Pyramid at Giza is the largest burial structure built by the Egyptians and remains as one of the triad of **Egyptian pyramids** that together constitute the only still intact example of the Seven Wonders of the Ancient World.

The Collapsed Pyramid was originally conceived as a step pyramid, like the previous pharaoh **Djoser**'s, but in midconstruction its architects decided to fill in

The first attempt by ancient Egyptians to construct a true pyramid ended in failure. The result, the so-called Collapsed Pyramid, stands in mute testimony to the trial-and-error process that characterized the evolution of Egyptian burial architecture. (M.H. Feder)

the steps and produce a true, geometrical pyramid form with four triangular faces meeting at a common apex. Unfortunately for its builders, in this, their first attempt to construct a true pyramid, they did not realize that the slope (greater than 70°) was far too steep for their building materials to sustain. Significant problems developed, and the project was abandoned. Those builders then moved north to Dashur, where they made another attempt at the construction of a true pyramid, the **Bent Pyramid**.

The Collapsed Pyramid is best understood as an example of a predictably human process of trial and error by the architects, engineers, and builders that typifies the evolution of human technology both in the ancient and modern worlds. Writers, like **Erich von Däniken**, who argue that pyramid construction appeared instantaneously and perfectly in ancient Egypt—and therefore must have been introduced by some outside, technologically advanced civilization— have to explain why such an advanced civilization initially had so much trouble piling up rocks at an angle that didn't result in their collapse.

Further Reading

To read about the Collapsed Pyramid in context of the history and development of the Egyptian pyramids, there's no better source than Mark Lehner's *The Complete Pyramids* (1997). To read about the Collapsed Pyramid in the context of pharaonic history, see Peter Clayton's *Chronicle of the Pharaohs* (1994).

Critias

Critias is the name of an actual, historical figure in ancient Greece, and it is also, significantly in the context of this encyclopedia, the name **Plato** gave to a dialogue he wrote toward the end of his life in 347 BCE. The historical Critias is used by Plato as the central character in the dialogue; in Plato's dramatic presentation, Critias provides the story to an assembly that consists of another Greek philosopher, Socrates, and Socrates' students.

Critias (the Younger) was an Athenian poet and teacher. Born in 460 BCE, he may have been Plato's uncle or even his great-grandfather. The story he tells in the dialogue that bears his name was inspired by what amounts to an assignment given by Socrates to his students. Referring to a conversation Socrates and his students (including Critias) had, ostensibly on the previous day, about the workings of a perfect society, Socrates mentions having asked his students to come up with an example of such a perfect society in action:

> I should like to hear some one tell of our own city [his hypothetical perfect society] carrying on a struggle against her neighbors, and how she

went out to war in a becoming manner, and when at war showed by the greatness of her actions and the magnanimity of her words, in dealing with other cities a result worthy of her training and education.

Critias responds to Socrates' assignment by saying:

When you were speaking yesterday about your city and citizens, the tale which I have just been repeating to you came into my mind, and I remarked with astonishment how, by some mysterious coincidence, you agreed in almost every particular with the narrative of Solon.

Critias then relates the story of the ascendance and subsequent fall and destruction of the nation of **Atlantis**, including its military defeat at the hands of Athens and its annihilation as the result of a natural cataclysm initiated by the gods as punishment for their hubris.

It is important to point out a number of things regarding Critias's telling of the Atlantis story:

1. Though Critias prefaces his telling with the claim that it is a true tale, that was typical of Plato, having characters in his dialogues claim that what they were saying was true, even in instances when we know for certain that it was not. Claiming that a story about to be told is true is a common strategy in horror stories, late-night talk show monologues, and those annoying chain-letter e-mails. Claiming that something is true does not make it so. And furthermore, though you will sometimes hear people assert something to the effect of "Plato himself claimed that the story of Atlantis was true," that is incorrect. Plato has a character in a dialogue make that claim. Authors commonly put words into the mouths of their characters that they (the authors) do not believe. The conversation ostensibly that took place the day before Critias tells the Atlantis tale was about the nature of a perfect society. The details provided by Critias about an ancient Athenian society (members of the military live communally and possess no wealth; everyone engages in gymnastic exercise) sounds so much like Plato's discussion of a perfect society in his *Republic* dialogue that that is almost certainly what Critias is referring to. *The Republic*, however, was written several years previously. Plato apparently decided to revisit his discussion of a perfect society and did so through the fiction that Socrates needed to hear about that hypothetical society engaged in overcoming adversity or responding to a challenge so great that its response would provide an object lesson in its perfect qualities.

2. Critias is forthcoming in how indirectly the story was handed down to him; he heard it, he says, from his grandfather (Critias the Elder), who first told the story in a competition during the Apatournia festival. Critias the Elder

heard it from his own father, Dropides, who heard it from the Greek sage Solon, who, in turn, supposedly heard it from Egyptian priests when he visited there in 590 BCE.

3. Other than Plato's *Critias* dialogue, there are no other Greek accounts of the Atlantis story. There are a number of thorough Greek histories written around Plato's time, but none of them mention anything even vaguely like the Atlantis story. This would be incredibly odd for a true historical account of what can be interpreted as the most significant military victory and formative event in all of Greek history. It would be the equivalent in the United States of one individual, years after the fact, presenting for the first time the tale of the Revolutionary War, previously entirely unknown to the entire population.

4. No Greek historians commented—either positively or negatively—about the *Critias* story. That is, no Greek historians rose to either confirm or dispute it. They did not write about this glorious new page in Greek history revealed by Critias in any context. The *Critias* story elicited no reaction whatsoever from Greek historians, which is exceptionally odd if they interpreted Plato's telling of the tale as an attempt to reveal a veritable history.

5. Finally, the *Critias* dialogue is not a transcript of something that actually happened. One of Plato's strategies—perhaps intentionally to avoid the fate of Socrates, who was forced to commit suicide as a result of his unpopular beliefs—was to make it sound like he was merely reporting the statements of others. In all likelihood, those other people never actually had the conversations that Plato attributes to them, and many of them were dead when Plato presented them. In fact, in the case of the *Critias* dialogue, Plato asserts that it took place at a time that corresponds to 421 BCE in our calendar. Plato was smart and I'm sure precocious as a child, but in 421 BCE, he was only seven or eight years old. It is unlikely that he heard, understood, and made a stenographic transcript of Critias's telling of the Atlantis tale

Critias was a real person, but he did not reveal the true history of ancient Greece in the telling of the Atlantis story. As Aristotle later told it, "Plato alone made Atlantis emerge from the waves, and then he submerged it again."

Further Reading
You can find the *Critias* dialogue online at http://philosophy.eserver.org/plato/critias.txt.

Crop Circles

I saw my first crop circle in 1996 during a visit to the more than 4,000-year-old megalithic site in Avebury, in the south of England, an enormous circle of dozens of

Crop circles were a craze primarily of the 1990s. Though clearly the work of pranksters, and often beautiful and always intriguing works of performance art, they are wholly unrelated to the ancient stone circle megalithic sites of western Europe. (KEYSTONE/Sandro Campardo)

standing stones left by the area's ancient inhabitants. There was a clearly discernible pattern in the form of mashed-down rapeseed (a name so disturbing that in the United States it has been changed to canola) that had been planted just outside of the stone circle. It wasn't nearly as elaborate, impressive, large, or as artistically sophisticated as the more famous circles that had appeared in England during the previous few years—it was little more than a perfectly circular patch of vegetation that appeared to have been neatly pushed down—but it was fascinating nonetheless.

Playing dumb (which is always easy for me), I inquired of a local shopkeeper as to whether what I had seen nearby was a crop circle. I should point out that this particular shop was filled to overflowing with all manner of New Agey bric-a-brac, including crystals, pendulums, Ouija boards, tarot card decks, **dowsing** rods, and, perhaps not coincidently, plenty of literature about crop circles, including back issues of *Cerology*, a magazine devoted to their analysis.

The shopkeeper cheerfully shared with me the fact that, yes, indeed, that was a crop circle I had seen. He added that crop circles regularly appeared in the fields adjacent to the ancient Avebury stone circle and intimated that there was some sort of ineffable connection between the ancient stone monuments built at Avebury, at **Stonehenge** just down the road, and at the hundreds of other stone circles that dot the British Isles (Burl 1995).

Beginning close to 5,000 years ago, the ancient inhabitants of the British Isles, did, indeed, launch a building program that resulted in the construction of hundreds of stone circles, some consisting of just a very few, rather small stones encircling an area just a few feet in diameter, to the far more elaborate Stonehenge with its 30 enormous, upright sarsens, each standing more than 10 feet tall and weighing more than 22 tons, capped by lintel stones weighing in at 6 tons each, not to mention the 5 trilithon sets, whose largest component stones weighed upwards of 50 tons each. The nearby Avebury circle, though not as elaborate as Stonehenge, was nonetheless an impressive stone circle, enclosing an area more than 1,100 feet (335 meters) in diameter, nearly 22 acres (8.5 hectares).

It is the circular form of the ancient megalithic monuments constructed between close to 5,000 years ago and a little more than 3,000 years ago that has caused some people to assert a connection between these monuments and the modern crop circle phenomenon. Perhaps ancient people encountered circular patterns impressed into their crops—the builders of the ancient stone circles were, after all, farmers, bearers of the benefits of the agricultural revolution that had begun in the Middle East more than 10,000 years ago and had spread its influence to the British Isles around 5,000 years ago. Inspired by the mysterious crop circles, perhaps the ancients attempted to memorialize them by constructing replicas in the far more permanent medium of stone.

I asked the New Age shopkeeper if the crop circle we could see from his window was "genuine." He leaned over the counter toward me and in a hushed, nearly conspiratorial tone assured me, "No, sir, that circle is just a prank. It's not the real thing." At that point, I leaned in toward him and queried, "Well, how can you tell a real circle from a fake one?" He just smiled, shook his head a little, I assume at the naïveté of my question, and with a sparkle in his eyes, whispered, "It's all in the magnetics."

Of course it is. That sounds like a far more scientific explanation than those that involve "earth energy **vortexes**" (whatever those are), sex-crazed hedgehogs, or extraterrestrial aliens. One particularly clever crop circle included a monumental message in English: "WE ARE NOT ALONE," which some took to be a communication from the aliens. In fact, it was a message sent by the pranksters who produced the circle and referred not to extraterrestrials, but to other underground artists making other crop circles.

The truth, however, is far more mundane than mysterious magnetics, vortexes, crazy hedgehogs, or extraterrestrials. There is no evidence whatsoever of the crop circle phenomenon dating to much earlier than the 1980s. We can even trace their origin to two erstwhile artists, Dave Chorley and Doug Bower, who owned up to the whole thing in 1991. Inspired by their puckish senses of humor, the guys decided to use their artistic skills to prank their neighbors by making a grandly scaled pattern in a local farmer's field. They devised a simple tool for flattening crops with a steel bar and then, later, wooden planks. It was, in many ways, a perfect prank, getting the attention, first, of their neighbors, then their country, and ultimately the world. All this, and the crops themselves were fine, continuing to grow and in no way inconveniencing the farmer whose crops they flattened. No harm, no foul.

Dave and Doug's exploits inspired other would-be artists, who viewed crops as an interesting medium in which to produce art and, especially in the 1990s, the phenomenon exploded. Circles and triangles and far more mathematically complex forms appeared almost on a nightly basis both in England and, eventually, Canada and the United States. Crop circles became a form of underground artistic expression and, like modern graffiti artists, collectives of artists—relying on stealth, mathematical equations, computers, fractals, and an intense desire to inspire wonder—began outdoing Dave and Doug and one another with increasingly complex patterns.

To be sure, there have always been "cerologists" who claim a great antiquity and mystery for the phenomenon and view Dave and Doug as mere posers, perhaps intentionally set up by the authorities to deflect attention from the *real* circles. You know, the ones with the inexplicable "magnetics."

Some of those crop circle experts had their expertise called into serious question when they arrived at a circle and, in front of God and the BBC, declared it genuine, far beyond the capabilities of mere mortals. They even mentioned the magnetics of the thing. It was all quite interesting until the BBC crew revealed that they had filmed Dave and Doug the previous night as they had produced the circle just judged by the "experts" to be entirely genuine. Perhaps it's not in the magnetics after all. Paraphrasing Shakespeare, the fault lies, not in the magnetics, but in ourselves—in our desire to see mystical properties where this is little more than human creativity, imagination, and wit.

Further Reading

For a fantastic description of the entire crop circle phenomenon, read Jim Schnabel's book, *Round in Circles: Poltergeists, Pranksters, and the Secret History of Cropwatchers* (1994). (Though Schnabel is a bit unclear on this point, he actually was a crop circle prankster himself.) More recently, a couple of the more active circlemakers, Rob Irving and John Lundberg, have written and published their own history of the phenomenon: *The Field Guide: The Art, History, and Philosophy of Crop Circle Making* (2006). It's informative, and a hoot—a must for anyone interested in the fascinating study of the crop circle phenomenon. See also the Web site of one of those groups of merry pranksters for a somewhat veiled discussion of their role in the production of crop circles (http://circlemakers.org).

Crystal Skulls

The story of the crystal skulls, mystically charged artifacts ostensibly produced by an ancient Mesoamerican civilization—sometimes Aztec, sometimes **Maya,** or perhaps manufactured by ancient extraterrestrial visitors to Earth—has been traced back by researcher Jane MacLaren Walsh to no earlier than 1856 when one showed up at the British museum in London. The crystal skulls are just that; artistic representations of human skulls, carved into quartz crystals (though some recent knock-offs turn out to have been made of glass or even artificial resin). Some are quite crude and schematic, others have more detail, and one (the Mitchell-Hedges Skull) even has an associated lower jaw. They vary widely in size—the earliest specimen is only about an inch (2.5 centimeters) tall, a few are 3 or 4 inches (8–10 centimeters) high, a couple are life-size, and one or two are even bigger than life-size.

Though purported by some to have magical power, the crystal skulls are nineteenth-century fakes which, when looked at under a microscope, exhibit evidence of their manufacture with nineteenth-century lapidary equipment. (AP Photo/Gregory Bull)

Whatever their size or degree of artistic sophistication or level of detail, one thing is absolutely true about all of the crystal skulls: there is absolutely no archaeological context for any of them.

One of the most important measures by which archaeologists assess the significance of archaeological specimens, including their authenticity, is their *archaeological context*—the precise position in the soil in which they were discovered, the objects found in direct spatial association with them, and especially their *stratigraphic context*, meaning the layer or *stratum* in which an artifact was found. When artifacts are found firmly ensconced in specific soil layers, they can be dated, or at least put in chronological sequence. Obviously, objects found in more recently deposited soil layers, barring any soil disturbance or upheaval, are younger than those located in older layers. By the same token, objects found in the same layer ordinarily date to approximately the same time period. The *provenience* of an artifact—its precise, three-dimensional location of discovery—is vital in assessing an object's meaning and function within an ancient culture, as well as its chronological context. In fact, archaeologists understand that unless an object was located *in situ*, meaning just exactly where it was left—whether dropped, lost, discarded, or deposited—by an ancient person, the artifact has been removed from its context and its precise meaning is much more difficult to assess.

The point of this little diversion is this: none of the crystal skulls have any reliable archaeological context at all. Not one was recovered in a professionally directed excavation, not one has any record of its spatial context, not one has a map of its precise location of discovery, not one has a recorded provenience, not one is mapped in a stratigraphic profile, not one has any record of being recovered from an in-situ context. All of the crystal skulls appeared, usually on the antiquities market, essentially out of thin air. That does not highly recommend their authenticity to any serious archaeologist or historian.

Jane MacLaren Walsh is an archaeologist at the Smithsonian Institution and has conducted more research on the crystal skulls than virtually anybody else. In her enumeration of the known specimens, she mentions a larger-than-life skull that was unknown until 1992 when—are you ready?—it arrived at the Smithsonian in a package with no return address. Adding to the mystery, the source remained anonymous in the enclosed note, which merely gave possession to the Smithsonian (Walsh 2008).

Once the first of the skulls appeared in the nineteenth century, more followed, all of them carved from clear or milky quartz crystals, some small and some quite large. According to Walsh (2008), two specimens were shown at the Exposition Universelle in Paris in 1867 (an early version of a World's Fair). These two skulls were exhibited by a Frenchman, Eugène Boban, a man whose name shows up subsequently in conjunction with a number of the crystal skulls. Another name that is attached to another of the skulls is Frederick Arthur Mitchell-Hedges, who, as nearly as can be determined, purchased one in 1943. Mitchell-Hedges was, according to all who knew him, a teller of tall tales, so it is not terribly surprising that his skull has achieved a kind of fame the others haven't and is sometimes called the "Skull of Doom" because its mere presence supposedly leads to all manner of bad luck.

Whatever tales have been concocted about the source, age, or paranormal influences of the skulls—and despite the fact that they served as the focal point of the 2008 Indiana Jones movie, *Indiana Jones and the Kingdom of the Crystal Skull*, where they turn out to be extraterrestrial in origin—one thing is clear: The existing skulls analyzed by Walsh cannot be traced to ancient native cultures of Central America. None fit into any native artistic tradition. They simply don't bear the recognizable artistic or stylistic imprint of Aztec or Maya or Mixtec or Toltec or Teotihuacano or any of the other myriad cultures that have been identified in Mesoamerica. Perhaps more definitively, however, when examined using modern analytical equipment, including high-powered scanning electron microscopes, all of the skulls clearly show the use of modern lapidary equipment. In other words, all show the typical microscopic scratch marks left behind by a grinding wheel. Grinding wheels were unknown to the ancient people of Mesoamerica (so they didn't make the skulls) and would be quite unexpected on skulls produced by laser-wielding extraterrestrial aliens.

Modern movies, tabloid newspapers, and even modern museums aside (Mexico's national museum displays skulls it asserts are the work of Aztec and Mixtec carvers), the crystal skulls are nineteenth- and twentieth-century fakes.

Further Reading

The best place to find an accurate assessment of the crystal skulls of Mesoamerica is the article by the archaeologist who has most closely examined them, Jane MacLaren Walsh, in the May/June 2008 issue of *Archaeology*.

Cult Archaeology

Cult archaeology is a term used first by archaeologist John Cole to designate a certain variety of **pseudoarchaeology**. Cole did not intend to signify that adherents to certain pseudoarchaeological claims were members of a cult; Cole used the word "cult" in a very specific, anthropological sense.

The anthropological term *cargo cult* was first applied to isolated human groups who had limited contact with Western societies and only a rudimentary understanding of who those outsiders were. In some instances, these non-Western people thought they could induce the outsiders to come to their territories and share their goods, their "cargo," with them. Unsure how to initiate that contact, some of these people went through the motions of what they thought would be effective inducements, not fully understanding their context.

During World War II, for example, some isolated Pacific Islanders who were aware of the presence of Europeans and Americans on other islands had some knowledge of the alien technologies they brought with them (including airplanes). They learned that islands where the aliens visited, bringing all manner of wealth with them, which they then spread around, had certain features—airstrips and control towers, for example—which their own islands lacked. In an effort to address this, some of these islanders actually constructed simulated airstrips and control towers, thinking this would induce the planes to land on their islands to disperse their cargo, all that juicy Western technology that other islanders had access to.

Cole used the term *cult archaeology* in that way, viewing some pseudoarchaeology as the equivalent of cargo cults. For instance, though the adherents did not comprehend the need to conduct objective, scientific investigation of the human past, they knew that "real" archaeologists had meetings where colleagues presented papers, so the cult archaeologists had meetings and invited speakers to present their thoughts. Real archaeologists published journals, containing scholarly articles with footnotes and bibliographies, so the cult archaeologists published their own journals and their articles were replete with footnotes and bibliographies. In Cole's view, the cult archaeologists are only superficially mimicking the science of archaeology and never actually doing the objective analysis of data and hypothesis testing required in science.

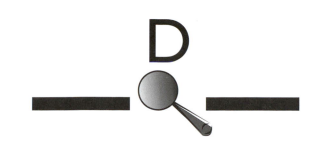

Davenport Tablets

In 1877, the Reverend Jacob Gass discovered two inscribed slate tablets in a mound on a farm in Davenport, Iowa. One of the tablets had a series of inscribed concentric circles with enigmatic signs believed by some to be zodiacal. The other had various animal figures, a tree, and a few other marks on one face; its reverse face had a series of apparently alphabetic characters from half a dozen different languages across the top, and the depiction of a presumed cremation scene on the bottom. Gass discovered or came into possession of a number of other enigmatic artifacts ostensibly associated with the **moundbuilder** culture, including two pipes whose bowls were carved into the shape of elephants.

The discoveries in Davenport generated great excitement. However, the fact that such a concentration of apparently conclusive finds regarding the moundbuilder controversy had been discovered by a single individual within a radius of a few miles of one Iowa town caused many to question the authenticity of the discoveries.

Cyrus Thomas launched an in-depth investigation of the tablets. Evidence from Gass's excavation indicated pretty clearly that the tablets had been planted only recently in the mound. Also, Thomas believed that he had identified the source of the bizarre, multiple-alphabetic inscription: *Webster's Unabridged Dictionary* of 1872 presented a sample of characters from ancient alphabets; all of the letters on the tablet were in the dictionary, and most were close copies. Thomas (1894, 641–42) suggested that the dictionary was the source for the tablet inscription.

Marshall McKusick (1991) reports a confession by a Davenport citizen, who alleged that the tablets and the other artifacts were **frauds** perpetrated by a group of men who wished to make Gass appear foolish. Though there are some significant problems with the confession (most notably the fact that the confessor was too young to have been an active participant in the hoax), the Davenport Tablets were certainly fraudulent.

More recently, McKusick has discerned the presence of lowercase Greek letters on the second Davenport Tablet—but lowercase Greek letters were not invented until medieval times. McKusick has also identified Arabic numbers, Roman letters, musical clefs, and ampersands (&) on the tablet. Their presence is clear proof of the

The Davenport Tablet shown here is one of a handful of artifacts discovered in the Cook Farm Mound by Reverend Jacob Gass in 1877. It is covered with characters from a number of Old World alphabets. (Proceedings of the Davenport Academy of Natural Sciences, 1876–1878)

fraudulent nature of the stone. In fact, no genuine artifacts containing writing in any Old World alphabet have ever been found in any of the mounds.

Further Reading

The definitive work on the Davenport Tablets is the book *The Davenport Conspiracy Revisited* by archaeologist Marshall McKusick (1991).

Dawson, Charles

Charles Dawson (1864–1916) was a country lawyer whose heart and intellectual inclination led him to his preferred pursuits as an amateur natural historian in England (Russell 2003). Dawson spent much of his time wandering the rural countryside of the south of England searching for fossils, interesting geological specimens, bones, artifacts, and anything else that captured his imagination.

Dawson had already gained a certain amount of notoriety—and professional respect—as an amateur scientist before he happened upon a gravel pit on Barcombe Manor in Sussex, near Piltdown, in 1908. His apparently extraordinary luck at finding scientifically significant specimens—he had already had three fossils named after him: a dinosaur, an ancient mammal, and a plant—led some to call Dawson "the Wizard of Sussex." Though an amateur with no formal training in any of the sciences, Dawson had already been named to two prestigious British scientific societies: the Geological Society and the Society of Antiquaries of London. Dawson hobnobbed with the scientific elites of Great Britain, who apparently treated him with a measure of respect.

Once again, in 1908 Dawson seemed rather serendipitously to be at the right place at the right time to make an important paleontological discovery. With the assistance of the workers in the gravel pit, he discovered a cranial fragment that appeared to be that of a primitive human ancestor unlike any found previously in Europe and the first such discovery made in the British Isles. Returning to the site in 1911, and with the assistance of Arthur Smith Woodward (an enormously well-respected scientist whose title was "Keeper of Geology" at the Natural History Museum in London) and Jesuit priest Père Teillard de Chardin, additional cranial fragments, a part of the mandible (lower jaw), a canine tooth, and numerous other animal bones and artifacts were discovered in the gravel pit.

The so-called **Piltdown Man** fossil became a cause célèbre in paleoanthropological circles, not the least because it was the first human ancestral fossil found in England and because it seemed to contradict the morphology of other ancestral human fossils, particularly Java Man and Neanderthal Man, found in Asia and Europe, respectively. Specifically, Piltdown seemed to lend support to a favored view of human evolution called the "brain-centered paradigm," and its existence called into question the significance of all of the other ancestral human fossils found previously. If Piltdown was legitimate, all the other specimens must have been evolutionary diversions, minor, short-lived, and insignificant side branches off of the main trunk of human evolution with only Piltdown at the base of the main line.

Piltdown was, however, a complete fabrication, a clumsy **fraud** that fooled so many professional scientists because they wanted to believe it and embraced its implications about human evolution.

Dawson's precise role in the Piltdown forgery is unknown. It is unclear whether he had sufficient expertise and the necessary access to bones and artifacts to pull off the hoax on his own. A biographer (Russell 2003) points to other apparent fabrications on Dawson's part as well as the fact that he was the only person present at each discovery, including a second, very similar-looking human cranial fragment (Piltdown II), to support his thesis that, at the very least, Dawson was an active co-conspirator in the hoax. Dawson may have been the only one involved, an active co-conspirator, or merely a "useful idiot" who unknowingly discovered specimens planted by someone else entirely—a some-one else who wished to embarrass colleagues he felt had slighted him, or even someone outside of science entirely who hoped to embarrass the scientific com-munity generally. The truth may never be known.

Further Reading

The best place to go for the complete story of the life of Charles Dawson is the fasci-nating biography by Miles Russell, *Piltdown Man: The Secret Life of Charles Dawson and the World's Greatest Archaeological Hoax* (2003).

Diffusionism

Diffusionism was a perspective that characterized the British school of anthro-pology in the early years of the twentieth century. An underlying view of this school of thought was, put most simply, that human beings were, in general, dull, unimaginative, and uninventive; most ancient human groups were culturally static and, if left on their own, would have changed very little through time. Of course, it was well known that humanity had, nevertheless, undergone vast cultural changes since the Paleolithic. Diffusionists explained these changes as the result of exceptions—or perhaps a single exception—to the above characteri-zation of human groups as culturally inert: one "genius" culture, or at most a very few such cultures, that had developed in antiquity. The cultural precocity of such a group or groups was ascribed by some to their superior genetic endow-ment and by others to their location in a privileged habitat.

One of the chief architects of diffusionism was Grafton Eliot Smith, a pro-fessor of anatomy at Victoria University in Manchester, England. For Smith, the single genius culture was that of pharaonic Egypt. Smith hypothesized that, before 6,000 years ago, people all over the world were living in a natural, primi-tive, and more or less fixed state. At about this time, a group of humans settled along the Nile and, as the result of an incredibly rich subsistence base made pos-sible by the fertile valley soil, were afforded time free from the requirements of subsistence production. Using that free time to their advantage, Smith believed that the ancient Egyptians singularly produced most, if not all, of the key inven-tions that made civilized life possible: agriculture, animal domestication, ceramic technology, writing, monumental construction, and urban settlements.

From the diffusionist perspective, these inventions spread like waves on a still pond, emanating from Egypt and moving across the face of the Earth. For Smith, though the Egyptians alone had independently evolved a complex civilization, several other world areas—including a number located across the Atlantic Ocean in the New World—became civilized by contact with and through their adoption of the inventions of ancient Egypt. The proverb may state that all roads lead to Rome, but as Smith saw it, all *intellectual* roads led from the Nile Valley.

(The intellectual legacy of Grafton Eliot Smith will, perhaps, forever be tainted by his association with the **Piltdown Man** hoax. Though almost certainly not materially involved in perpetrating this paleontological **fraud**, Smith became one of the false fossil's strongest proponents precisely because its morphology matched his expectation of a human ancestor with a modern-looking cranium, an apelike jaw, and, by inference, an apelike body.)

Though a cultural font for many diffusionists, not all embraced Egypt as the ultimate source of civilization. Some diffusionists supported the notion that, instead of Egypt, a civilization now lost in the clichéd "dim mists of antiquity" had been the source of all human progress. Certainly, writer and unsuccessful vice presidential aspirant **Ignatius Donnelly**'s vision of the Lost Continent of **Atlantis**, as articulated in his book first published in 1882, *Atlantis: The Antediluvian World*, qualifies as an alternative source conforming to the general diffusionist perspective.

In his *Timmaeus* and *Critias* dialogues, the Greek philosopher **Plato** told the story of Atlantis, a materially wealthy, militarily powerful, technologically advanced, but spiritually lacking society. Today, Atlantis is viewed by many as little more than a plot device, a seemingly insurmountable adversary invented by Plato to put to the test an equally mythical ancient Athens—a perfect society that by a convenient coincidence was a close match politically and socially to the hypothetical perfect society laid out by Plato in his work *The Republic*.

Donnelly, however, believed that Atlantis was no literary invention but a veritable place. In the late nineteenth century—and, therefore, presaging Smith—Donnelly believed that agriculture, writing, metallurgy, and monumental architecture had been invented just once—in his construct, not in Egypt but on Atlantis—and spread out from there, inspiring development of the historically known civilizations of the Old and New Worlds.

In the years since Donnelly presented his argument, evidence for an Atlantean source for all world civilizations has not been forthcoming. His argument was, after all, based on little more than general similarities among ancient civilizations: many built pyramids and used the arch in construction; many possessed a writing system and practiced agriculture. Donnelly proposed a common, Atlantean source for all of these. Upon close inspection, however, one can see vast differences in the expression of these features in various ancient cultures, supporting an interpretation of their independent invention rather than diffusion from a single, common source. For example, cultures on either side of the Atlantic may have built structures that we call pyramids, but the use of a common term results from an imprecision in our language and not in detailed similarities. Differences between **Egyptian pyramids** and those of the **Maya** or the Aztec and their predecessors in terms of their raw materials, engineering techniques, construction methods, and purpose should convince us that there could not have been a common source for them. In another example, though ancient complex societies on both sides of the Atlantic possessed agricultural subsistence bases, the crops and animals were entirely different, and archaeological evidence shows long and independent developmental sequences from foraging to agriculture in a number of regions in both the Old and New Worlds. The most parsimonious explanation for this is independent invention, not diffusion from a common source.

In the 1960s another iteration of the extreme diffusionist perspective was presented, to be sure a weirder and wilder version than that of Smith or even Donnelly. Instead of pointing a finger toward Egypt or out to a spot in the middle of the Atlantic, Swiss writer **Erich von Däniken** pointed up to the heavens, electing to find a source for human civilization and technological achievement in the cosmos. Von Däniken's is a space-age application of the diffusionist view; if intrinsically dull, uninventive, and unimaginative human beings had, in deep time, exhibited remarkable technologies, marvelous architectural skills, and mathematical sophistication, it must have come from somewhere else. For von Däniken, human beings did not develop such things but adopted them, through the assistance of extraterrestrial interlopers. Once again, in what is clearly an extreme version of an already extreme paradigm, the ability of most or even all groups of humans to develop independently is rejected or, at least, downplayed. In this application, we don't even need to find a single genius culture, at least not among humans and at least not on our planet.

This brings us to the writings of **Graham Hancock**. One cannot help but be struck by the similarities between the outlook exhibited in his books and in the writings of Smith, Donnelly, and von Däniken. Here again, we encounter a writer who is perplexed that we find evidence of truly wondrous achievements in the ancient world: remarkable monumental structures with **astronomical alignments**, incredibly precise stone masonry, accurate calendrical systems—all issues that Hancock addresses in his book, *Fingerprints of the Gods*. This perplexity originates in the same assumption that underpinned the diffusionist perspective of the late nineteenth and early twentieth centuries: a viewpoint that rejects or at least is extremely skeptical of the possibility that people all over the world were capable of and responsible for such accomplishments by the sweat of their own brows and the application of their own intellectual abilities.

Like the extreme diffusionists who preceded him, Hancock's argument is circular and contradictory at the same time. Hancock must show that the archaeological record of ancient civilizations exhibits, simultaneously, incredible technological and intellectual sophistication and primitive simplicity. He argues from this that the simplicity represents the true state of these ancient peoples and that the sophistication was introduced by a lost civilization.

Consider the following. In *Fingerprints of the Gods*, Hancock refers to the great sophistication of the calendar used by the ancient Maya and maintains that we should be greatly surprised by it among this ancient people. He is so skeptical of the ability of ancient Mesoamericans to have developed this calendar that he proposes they *didn't* develop it, but instead "inherited" it from a much older, super-sophisticated **lost civilization**.

To support his thesis that a lost civilization must have been responsible, Hancock must show that the Mesoamerican calendar is inexplicably, even shockingly, out of character with the rest of Mesoamerican culture; otherwise, no hypothesis of an outside source is warranted. Here he has painted himself into a tidy methodological corner and has no choice but to characterize the noncalendrical achievements of one of the most impressive and awe-inspiring ancient civilizations as "generally unremarkable" and to characterize their way of life as being only "semi-civilized." He *must* maintain this, because an objective analysis of the remarkable achievements of the Maya and their Olmec antecedents in architecture, agriculture, artwork, and so on indicates that their calendar is not out of character at all, but was just one marvelous achievement in a long list. The sophistication of the Mesoamerican calendar is not surprising at all when one fairly assesses the sophistication of the rest of their culture. Any hypothesis of an external source for the calendar for no given reason other than the fact that it is sophisticated presupposes that which it is attempting to test.

Hancock admits regularly in his books that ancient people could have developed sophisticated calendars, built magnificent monuments, and so on, independent of outside help, but he just as regularly suggests that it more likely was otherwise. That Hancock points to Antarctica rather than Egypt, Atlantis, or Proxima Centauri as the homeland of the lost civilization and source for cultural development is interesting but beside the point in this discussion. Of greater relevance here is the fact that Hancock's argument is, at its core, based on an underestimation of the abilities of ancient human beings, at least those not lucky enough to be members of the lost civilization that was the source of all cultural development. In other words, it is diffusionism all over again, with the same long-ago-discredited philosophical underpinnings.

Dighton Rock

Dighton Rock is a large boulder currently housed in a small museum (open to the public only by appointment) located in Dighton Rock State Park in the town of Berkley in eastern Massachusetts. The 40-ton boulder was originally located along the banks of the nearby Taunton River, but was removed from that location and placed in a museum building for its protection.

Dighton Rock is covered with a plethora of petroglyphs and graffiti. Some claim it bears a message of Portuguese sailors who may have made landfall in Massachusetts in 1501 and 1502. Others claim it was inscribed by ancient Norse or even Chinese explorers. (K. Feder)

Dighton Rock has at least one if its broad, flat surfaces covered with engraved images or **petroglyphs**—primarily lines, geometric shapes, and schematic drawings of people, along with writing, both verified and not. The earliest extant record of the petroglyph-covered boulder dates to 1680, when an English settler, Rev. John Danforth, produced a drawing of the images. Unfortunately for those who believe that the marks on Dighton Rock represent the equivalent of graffiti left by ancient European (or African or Asian) seafaring visitors to America's shores, it should be pointed out that Danforth's drawing of the markings he saw on Dighton Rock bear very little resemblance to what others have reported and look virtually nothing like what can currently be seen there today.

Ten years after Danforth drew the markings, the famed Rev. Cotton Mather noted the existence of the marked stone and said about the petroglyphs:

> Among the other Curiosities of New-England, one is that of a mighty Rock, on a perpendicular side whereof by a River, which at High Tide covers part of it, there are very deeply Engraved, no man alive knows How or When about half a score Lines, near Ten Foot Long, and a foot and half broad, filled with strange Characters: which would suggest as odd Thoughts about them that were here before us, as there are odd Shapes in that Elaborate Monument.

Speculation has been rife, since these first seventeenth-century reports, concerning the source of the carvings. Certainly, local Natives were fully capable of engraving a rock face with various designs. Though petroglyphs are not terribly common in New England (in the United States, they are far more common in the Southwest), there are some; the Bellows Fall Petroglyphs located along the Connecticut River on the eastern border of Vermont is a prime example of a New England petroglyph. In fact, the schematic face seen on the right-hand side of the Dighton Rock panel bears a striking resemblance to the Bellows Falls faces.

Several other sources for the Dighton Rock petroglyphs have been cited, all of which depend on the assertion that European, Asian, or African explorers were present in New England at some point before the arrival of English settlers in the seventeenth century. A long-standing suggestion is that the markings were left by the Portuguese explorers Gaspar and Miguel Corte Real. Brown University professor Edmund Burke Delabarre became convinced that among the admitted hodgepodge of scratches, *X*'s, lines, circles, geometric shapes, and whatnot, there was an actual written message in Portuguese: "Miguel Cortereal by will of God, here Chief of the Indians."

Gaspar and Miguel were real people. According to reliable historical accounts, in 1501 Gaspar was outfitted by his father with three ships and dispatched to the New World in search of the fabled "Northwest Passage" by which navigators hoped to travel beyond the newly discovered North American continent and reach Asia. Gaspar's brother Miguel was aboard one of the ships. The three ships, apparently, reached Labrador and Newfoundland, whereupon Gaspar continued exploring the North American coast while Miguel and two of the ships returned to Portugal with a bunch of captive Indians, who were sold into slavery back in Europe. Apparently the plan was that Gaspar would meet up with Miguel back in Portugal once he was done searching for the Northwest Passage, but Gaspar did not show up at the appointed time.

Fearing the worst, Miguel launched what ultimately was a doomed expedition for his brother the following year, in 1502. Sadly, Miguel's search-and-rescue expedition also disappeared, and neither of the brothers was ever seen again. Delabarre's assertion was that at least Miguel made it to the shores of what was to become Massachusetts and inscribed the message he (Delabarre) believed was on Dighton Rock. In one interpretation of the supposed message, Miguel survived and was living with an Indian tribe in Massachusetts at the time he made the inscription.

Others look at the same rock and see completely different messages in completely different languages. Danish writer Carl Rafn saw the name of Thorfinn Karlsefni, whose name also shows up in the Norse sagas about the discovery of Newfoundland.

Gavin Menzies (2002, 333–35) looks at exactly the same series of markings and proposes that they were left by **Chinese** world explorers. Menzies—to either his credit or his detriment—doesn't attempt to coax a message written in ancient Chinese from the existing petroglyphs (it's unclear in his book whether he's actually seen Dighton Rock in person). Instead, he claims, on the basis of no evidence whatsoever, that there may have been a message in Chinese in there somewhere at sometime in the past, but that the Chinese characters were destroyed accidentally by people who, in the past, scrubbed the rock to better expose the writing. Menzies also asserts that there was a petroglyph of a typical Chinese sailing vessel among the markings on Dighton Rock. It's an interesting claim, but one might as well assert that the rock originally bore inscriptions in ancient Hebrew, Sanskrit, or, for that matter, ancient Martian. There simply is no evidence that any such message, in Chinese or any other language, ever existed on Dighton Rock.

To be sure, Dighton Rock is a significant artifact, with clear evidence of Indian "rock writing" already present when historically known seventeenth-century European settlers entered Massachusetts. Most people, however, see no message on the rock at all, just a series of lines and curves, elements of Indian ceremonial designs, settler graffiti, and even intentional attempts to fool researchers. Unfortunately, none of those who claim the presence of anything other than Indian drawings can even come to a consensus on what's there (their drawings of the petroglyphs differ so greatly, it is sometimes astonishing that they are supposed to be of the same rock).

Discovery of America

The year 1992 marked the 500th anniversary of the first voyage of Christopher Columbus in search of a western route to the Orient. Though he never made it to Cathay or Cipangu (China or Japan), his accidental, but certainly auspicious, encounter with a "new world" was commemorated with a world exposition in Seville, Spain, in that anniversary year.

As part of a decade-long preparation for that celebration, in 1982 a resolution was proposed by a group of Latin American representatives to the United Nations to officially honor the great navigator for his achievement in discovering the New World and changing the course of history.

It was a simple and symbolic gesture in a body with certainly more concrete concerns. Nevertheless, it caused quite a stir. Initially, Ireland's ambassador objected, claiming that a sixth-century Irish monk actually had discovered America before Columbus. The representative from Iceland chimed in, asserting that the Viking Leif Erikson had sailed to the New World 500 years before Columbus. Next, African delegates asserted that prehistoric African navigators had also traversed the Atlantic, discovering the Americas long before Columbus. Though part of the debate was tongue-in-cheek, it can be said that even in the 1980s, even in the United Nations, and even in terms of a purely symbolic gesture, controversy erupts when the question is posed: "Who discovered America?"

The irony of this is that the answer to that question is quite clear. Who discovered America? The ancestors of modern Native Americans did. There should be little argument on this often-ignored point. Even by the most conservative estimate, ancestors of modern American Indians first entered the New World more than 13,000 years ago, thousands of years before any of the European, African, or Chinese contenders for the title "America's Discoverer."

The pre-Columbian discovery of America is a common theme in speculative archaeology. An entire journal, *Ancient American*, is dedicated to exploring these claims. A number of organizations are dedicated to exploring such possibilities (e.g., the **New England Antiquities Research Association**). Several entries in this encyclopedia address specific claims: that the New World was the stomping ground of ancient:

- Celts (see *America B.C.*; **America's Stonehenge**; **Celt Discovery of America**; **Fell, Barry**; **Ogham**)
- Irish monks (see **Brendan, Saint**; *Navigatio*)
- Africans (see **African Inspiration of the Olmec**; **van Sertima, Ivan**)
- Chinese seafarers (see **Chinese Discovery of America**; **Fusang**; **Palos Verdes Stones**)
- Israelites (see **Bat Creek Stone**; **Newark Holy Stones**)
- Scottish knights (see **Westford Knight**)
- Welsh kings (see **Madoc, Prince**)
- Portuguese explorers (see **Dighton Rock**)

To be sure, the possibility of ancient transatlantic and transpacific interaction between cultures in the Old and New Worlds is intriguing. Professional archaeologists, however, tend to be skeptical that such contacts occurred in antiquity or, at least, that they occurred regularly and had a profound effect on the visited as well as the visitors. This entry explains the reasons for such skepticism (see Feder 2010 for a more detailed version of what follows).

Archaeology Is Garbology

In 1980, the PBS science series *Odyssey* broadcast a film about archaeology. Its title puzzled many, but is an accurate and concise description of what archaeologists mostly study: *Other People's Garbage*. Fabulous grave goods, remarkable hoards of gold coins, pyramids, mummies, and mysterious inscriptions are exceptional in much of archaeology. The common currency of our discipline tends to be, instead, mostly mundane objects that people made, used and used up, lost, discarded, or secreted away for safekeeping, and that have fortuitously been preserved.

Herein lies one of archaeology's axioms, a fundamental rule that resides at the core of our discipline: Wherever people go, wherever they visit, explore, walk about, colonize, or reside, they leave behind a mess. This "mess" is what constitutes the bulk of the archaeological record.

It also should be noted that we are a peripatetic species, and wherever we go, we bring along with us, as comedian George Carlin characterized it, a bunch of our "stuff." And, as the archaeological record clearly shows, people leave some of that stuff behind wherever they travel. This "left-behind stuff" constitutes archaeological evidence for the presence of people in the places they colonized or passed through.

There is another important rule in archaeological reasoning: Everybody's stuff is unique. Practitioners of different cultures do things in different ways. They may make functionally equivalent tools, but the styles are different. They may produce similar ceramic vessels, but use dissimilar procedures, with clays from different sources, and they may apply different kinds of surface treatments—slips and glazes—and employ a vast combination of different etched, incised, painted, or built-up design elements. They may produce very different kinds of structures or monuments. They likely have their own, culturally prescribed ways of burying their dead. Archaeological sites reflect the unique material and spatial patterns of each culture.

The styles of pottery, types of hunting weapons, ways trash is disposed, and so forth, are culture specific. The material patterns and, therefore, the archaeological sites left behind by the Navajo, by seventeenth-century Dutch settlers of Manhattan, by the builders of **Stonehenge**, by West African farmers, or by **Egyptian pyramid** builders are each different. The unique patterns these and myriad other archaeological manifestations left behind by these different groups are recognized by archaeologists and can be used to identify the presence of particular cultures in a given region.

When a foreign group enters into a new territory, it brings along and then leaves behind elements of its unique material culture. The sudden, stratigraphically intrusive appearance of a new brand of stuff in the archaeological record is precisely the way archaeologists detect the presence of intruders in the territories of other people. This certainly is the case for any one of a number of documented, historical forays of explorers to the New World. We can readily recognize the presence of these known travelers in the archaeological record because each group left a trail of unique and recognizable physical evidence. The objects made, used, and discarded by fifteenth- and sixteenth-century Europeans journeying to and through North America are distinguishable from those made by Native Americans from the same time period. Their stuff is recognizably "alien," different from the stuff made, used, and discarded by native people.

The Archaeology of Columbus

Consider this: Suppose the voyages of Christopher Columbus to the New World were not historically verifiable. Suppose his log disappeared, that no maps existed, and there were no memoirs. In other words, suppose the story of Columbus's voyages to the New World was little more than oral tradition and perhaps nothing more than a legend, much like the Viking Sagas were initially—or like the legend of the Welsh prince Madoc. Would the archaeological record allow us to state with certainty that the Columbus voyages took place?

The answer is a qualified yes. We certainly would know, based solely on the archaeological record, that Europeans, most likely Spaniards, were present in the Caribbean in the late fifteenth and early sixteenth centuries. Archaeologist Charles Hoffman (1987) has recovered European artifacts at Long Bay on Watling Island that date to Columbus's first expedition. Archaeologist Kathleen Deagan's work has focused on La Navidad on Haiti, a colony established by Columbus on his second expedition, and on La Isabela, a settlement he founded sometime later. At La Isabela, there is an abundance of early sixteenth-century European stuff, unlike any of the aboriginal stuff traceable to the native people of the Caribbean: pieces of chain mail armor, pieces of metal swords, and cannons, along with an enormous quantity of glazed pottery (the natives made only unglazed wares), including readily recognized Spanish majolica. Even without extensive documentary evidence, archaeologists would surely recognize the presence of European foreigners in the Caribbean in the late fifteenth and early sixteenth centuries.

Martin Frobisher: A Model of Untidiness

Consider Martin Frobisher, an English navigator who sailed to the New World in 1576, 1577, and 1578 with companies of 36, 145, and 397 men, respectively (Fitzhugh and Olin 1993). Frobisher sailed from England along a northerly route, reaching Labrador and Baffin Island in northern Canada in his quest for a northwest passage past the Americas to Asia. Finding no passageway to the west, Frobisher attempted to recoup his sponsor's investment in the expedition by prospecting for gold. He found none, but during the search, he and his men left physical traces of their presence in the form of readily identifiable, late sixteenth-century English artifacts and features, particularly on Kodlunarn Island (Fitzhugh 1993). These remnants include raw and partially processed iron "blooms" (made while smelting iron, a technology not practiced by the native people of Kodlunarn), an iron nail, fragments of broken ceramic crucibles, bricks, ceramic roof tiles, and the remains of several structures built by the explorers. The artifacts and features left behind by Frobisher and his men are identifiable as belonging to the English Elizabethan age

(1558–1603) and represent physical evidence of an English presence in northeastern Canada in the 1570s. Even had there been no *documentary* record of Frobisher's voyages to the New World, we would still have known from the *archaeological* record on Kodlunarn Island that people bearing typical, western European artifacts and practicing sixteenth-century western European metallurgical methods had been in northeastern Canada in the late sixteenth century.

The model provided by the Frobisher expedition would seem to apply to instances in which Old World people might have traveled to the New World in antiquity, especially if they remained for a period of sufficient length to teach the locals how to build pyramids or plant crops, or even to score some coke. In such cases, substantial archaeological evidence—the "stuff" brought along and then lost or discarded by the visitors—should be present. But has such evidence been found?

Most archaeologists would answer in the negative, and the lack of such standard archaeological evidence cannot be attributed to a lack of research. Consider the intensity with which archaeologists have conducted surface and subsurface surveys of various places in North America where the mundane traces of pre-Columbian and pre-Norse explorers might reasonably be expected, had they made the trip. I will use the example of my own bailiwick, southern New England, where various claims have been made concerning the visitation and settlement in antiquity by Vikings, Celts, and Hebrews.

Absence of Evidence

Much of the archaeology currently conducted in New England can be characterized as "compliance archaeology," in which states, local municipalities, developers, and private land owners contract for archaeological site surveys to comply with government regulations regarding the preservation of endangered archaeological resources. Most of the archaeological site survey reports required by these regulations and produced in my own state of Connecticut are submitted to archaeologist David Poirier at the Connecticut Historical Commission, the state agency that administers historic preservation regulations. Poirier estimates that in *each* of the years of the 1990s, paperwork describing about 10,000 individual test borings excavated by archaeologists in Connecticut was submitted to his office. This does not include the test pits dug in university field schools or by avocational archaeologists in the state archaeology society, which likely would add a few thousand more. Even if we confine ourselves just to the test pit reports submitted to the Historical Commission, a minimum of 100,000 test pits were excavated by archaeologists in Connecticut in that 10-year period.

I also spoke to Paul Robinson at the Rhode Island State Historic Preservation Office, a colleague with a job equivalent to Poirier's. Posed with the same question, and again recognizing that this relates only to test excavation reports that were submitted to his office, Robinson estimated that from the late 1980s up until about 1997, between 4,000 and 6,000 test pits were excavated by archaeologists in Rhode Island each year. In the period between 1997 and 1999, that number declined to between 1,000 and 2,000. Using the lower numbers provided by Robinson, we come up with an estimate of about 31,000 test excavations in Rhode Island in the 1990s.

Brona Simon, whose official title is state archaeologist of Massachusetts, was next on my list. According to her records, during the course of the 1990s, there was a mean of about 7,500 test pits excavated on a yearly basis in the projects that fall under her jurisdiction. So 75,000 test pits in Massachusetts is probably a fair minimum estimate for the decade.

For the three relatively small states just surveyed, in the 1990s, archaeologists excavated more than 200,000 test pits in federally or state-mandated archaeological site searches. Thousands of sites have been found in these test pit surveys including very rare, very ancient sites. Yet, in none of the 200,000 or so test pits excavated by archaeologists in this small sample of just three states, did any archaeologist report the discovery of even a single artifact attributable to a non-native group in the dim mists of antiquity.

This leaves us with the obvious question: Why not? There are several possible explanations we should consider:

1. Perhaps these ancient visitors were here in such small numbers and their visits were of such short duration that they are virtually invisible in the archaeological record. This certainly is possible. Though still an interesting phenomenon, this scenario also suggests that such visits would probably have been of limited potential cultural impact or significance.
2. Perhaps American archaeologists are so ignorant of the material culture of ancient Europeans, Africans, or Asians that, though they find evidence of their presence, the archaeologists simply don't recognize it. This might be the case, but not for long. The odds are good that I would not immediately recognize a mundane African, Celtic, or Hebrew artifact if I encountered it in a test pit, but I certainly would know I had found something alien and unexpected in pre-Columbian stratigraphic context and would find someone who *could* identify it. I think that goes for all of the archaeologists I know.
3. Perhaps archaeologists actually *are* finding and recognizing such evidence and, through some peculiar conspiracy, are covering it up—I have actually heard this and been accused of being part of this conspiracy. Anyone who can say this doesn't hang out with the crowd I do. As a group, archaeologists talk too much, drink too much, and are far too contrary to pull off a conspiracy of silence of that magnitude.

4. Perhaps archaeologists are finding such evidence, but they simply are afraid for their careers and unwilling to admit their discoveries of Celtic, African, or Hebrew artifacts. Perhaps. Some likely might be cowed by the near certainty of very careful and, to be frank, potentially acrimonious scrutiny that such a claim would generate. But tenure is a wonderful thing; few tenured academic archaeologists would feel so threatened by the skepticism of their colleagues that they would conceal important evidence like this. In fact, the discovery of conclusive evidence for such contact would likely represent a watershed in an archaeologist's career with benefits that would far outweigh any initial unpleasantness. The Ingstads (Helge and Anne Stine) didn't cover up their discovery of the tenth-century Norse settlement in Newfoundland—and they got a book deal and funding from the National Geographic Society.

5. Perhaps the ancient visitors were fastidious, picking up all the ordinary stuff that would diagnose their presence. That seems unlikely in the extreme and contradicts the fundamental archaeological axiom mentioned previously about people leaving a mess. Archaeologists might be surprised to find evidence of ancient Old World visitors in North and South America, but they would be stunned if these visitors had been here and left no mundane evidence of their presence.

6. Perhaps professional archaeologists have been, collectively, looking in all the wrong places and, therefore, not finding the kind of evidence that would show definitively that such visits were common. For this to be the case, someone will have to explain what process is at work in creating such a disturbingly nonrepresentative sample of the archaeological record. We are finding lots of other sites. How and why are we missing only the locations of ancient Old World visitors (apart from the possibility raised in point 1 above)?

7. Recognizing that an absence of evidence cannot always be interpreted as evidence of absence, perhaps, on this issue, it means exactly that. We don't find the kinds of archaeological evidence we would expect for the simplest reason imaginable: these proposed visitors *weren't here*.

Whichever of the myriad and nameless explorers of various ethnic and cultural backgrounds who are claimed by some to have visited America and to have communicated, traded, and shared technology with native people in antiquity, archaeological evidence like that available for the presence of documented visitors in the sixteenth century should be there. That such evidence has not been found presents a challenge to the supporters of such scenarios to explain why.

Further Reading

I devote an entire chapter in my book *Frauds, Myths, and Mysteries: Science and Pseudoscience in Archaeology* (Feder 2010) to the issue of the possibility of a pre-Columbian discovery of America, with a special focus on the kinds of evidence archaeologists expect to find if any of those proposed instances of contact between the Old and New Worlds actually took place.

Donnelly, Ignatius

More than anyone else in science or literature, Ignatius Donnelly (1831–1901) is responsible for our modern fascination with the story of the Lost Continent of **Atlantis**, as a result of his book *Atlantis: The Antediluvian World*, published in 1882.

Donnelly is a fascinating historical figure. Born in Pennsylvania in 1831, he became a lawyer in 1852 and moved to Minnesota in 1857, where he entered the political scene after helping establish a utopian community and cooperative farm (the community was a financial disaster and folded rather quickly). Despite the failure of the commune, Donnelly was fairly successful in local politics—in Minnesota, he served as lieutenant governor and state senator—as well as national politics; he was one of Minnesota's representatives in Congress for three terms and was nominated for the position of vice president of the United States in 1900 by the People's Party, a short-lived political party of the populist movement. Donnelly was remarkably progressive; he contributed to the formulation of the People's Party platform, which included a progressive income tax and an eight-hour workday.

Donnelly was a voracious reader apparently and had an active mind and, perhaps, an overactive imagination. Along with his major work presenting a hodge-podge of evidence for the historical validity of **Plato**'s Atlantis, Donnelly wrote a number of other books presenting equally extraordinary claims, though the success he experienced with *Atlantis: The Antediluvian World* was never equaled in his subsequent works. For example, just a year after his Atlantis book, Donnelly wrote *Ragnarok: The Age of Fire and Gravel*, in which he proposed that the impact of a comet was the cause of the destruction of Atlantis. Transcending his interest in ancient catastrophes, in his book *The Great Cryptogram: Francis Bacon's Cipher in Shakespeare's Plays* (1888), Donnelly claimed to have discovered a secret code in the plays ostensibly written by British playwright William Shakespeare that proved, in fact, that Francis Bacon was the actual author of those plays. None of Donnelly's arguments in any of his books have withstood scientific scrutiny.

Dorak Treasure

The Dorak Treasure is a difficult issue for any archaeologist to consider because it involves an admittedly controversial but nevertheless respected colleague who either was intimately involved in a grand hoax or, for various reasons, was readily duped by a hoaxer.

The esteemed colleague was British archaeologist James Mellaart, whose most significant contribution to the field was the excavation of Çatalhöyük, a 10,000-year-old village located in southern Turkey. Though ancient and dated to the cusp of the agricultural revolution, Çatalhöyük was anything but a community of simple, early farmers. The village consisted not of a broad distribution of huts, but, instead, was a sprawling, self-contained, monumentally scaled, continuous structure of interconnected apartments. The size of the structure, its population—estimated to have been in the thousands—its antiquity, and evidence that hunting and gathering as well as agriculture contributed to the inhabitants' subsistence altogether fascinated archaeologists because the combination was so unexpected. Adding the mystery was the preponderance of what Mellaart (1965) labeled "shrines." These were rooms that, in his estimation, were not residences but places of worship, having walls adorned with three-dimensional sculptures, usually images of bulls or rams, along with paintings of hunters in leopard-skin pelts, more wild bulls, stags, and, especially, vultures.

Though many of Mellaart's interpretations have been questioned as the result of subsequent excavations at the site (Balter 2005), Mellaart's contribution to archaeology is acknowledged by his colleagues. This makes the Dorak affair so painfully vexing. The facts behind the story are murky (I have relied on Suzan Mazur's [2005] compelling account of the affair).

Mellaart first announced the discovery of a fabulous "royal treasure" in the November 28, 1959, issue of a popular magazine, the *Illustrated London News*, accompanied by his own drawings of some of the most impressive pieces. The treasure included a fabulous array of gold and silver objects, including bracelets, drinking cups, and human figures. One of the figures, which Mellaart identified as a queen, was made of electrum, an ancient alloy of gold, silver, and copper. There also were daggers covered in jewels and marble axes with lapis lazuli, obsidian, and amber decorations affixed to their surfaces. Finally, Mellaart was able to fix the Dorak Treasure in time; a flat sheet of hammered gold was covered with Egyptian hieroglyphs that mentioned the pharaoh Sahure, whose reign occurred from 2487 to 2473 BCE. If this artifact had been a gift from Sahure to the person buried in the tomb, as Mellaart contended, the Dorak Treasure was nearly 4,500 years old.

According to his account, Mellaart had not excavated the so-called treasure, but had been shown the fabulous collection of objects by Anna Papastrati, a Greek woman he met on a train in 1958. According to Mellaart, their meeting was entirely accidental. He approached her on the train because she was wearing a beautiful gold bracelet that, she ultimately told him, was part of an astonishing hoard of gold and silver objects plundered between 1919 and 1922 from two tombs of the Yortans, a previously little-known ancient culture.

It's a fascinating tale: a beautiful woman on a train wearing an ancient gold bracelet, a brilliant scholar, a plundered treasure, an accidental encounter. But is it more than a story? Here's the crazy part: No one other than James Mellaart claims to have actually seen *any* of the Dorak Treasure artifacts. That's right—more than just a little ink has been spilled by writers pondering the historical significance of the Dorak Treasure and the role played by the Yortan culture in antiquity, but it has been based *entirely* on Mellaart's *Illustrated London News* drawings. That's it.

I suppose we could add one additional eyewitness to the Dorak Treasure: Anna Papastrati. But there's a problem with that, too. The only person who claims to have seen Anna Papastrati is James Mellaart! As far as anyone knows, Ms. Papastrati doesn't exist.

It is entirely bizarre. Mellaart is an accomplished scholar, famous in his field, though, admittedly, not a household name and not well enough known to be ensconced in the pantheon of such archaeologist-heroes as **Howard Carter** of King Tut fame or Heinrich Schliemann, who discovered ancient Troy. In terms of public celebrity, the Dorak Treasure did put Mellaart, however briefly, on the map as a "famous scholar." But would fame have been an adequate motivation to make up the Dorak Treasure story? It seems unlikely to those who know him as a brilliant, if a bit eccentric, scholar—although there *are* curious elements to his biography, and he ran afoul of the authorities in Turkey and was forbidden to dig in the country for a time in the 1960s.

Did the Dorak Treasure ever exist? Are the artifacts real, but illegally obtained from one or a number of sites? Did Papastrati exist, or is this name a pseudonym of another person? In a bit of detective work, Suzan Mazur (on whose work this entry is largely based) has analyzed the one document we have that is supposedly traced to Papastrati, a typed letter to Mellaart granting him permission to publish his drawings of the Dorak Treasure in the 1959 *Illustrated London News* article. Mazur sees some idiosyncratic stylistic commonalities between that note and a series of notes she examined that had been typed by James Mellaart's wife, Arlette. For example, Arlette Mellaart and Anna Papastrati both used the capital letter "I" for the numeral 1. Many old typewriters lacked the numeral "1" as a space-saving strategy, but the vast majority of people used the lower-case "l" as a substitute for the number 1. It's not a smoking gun, to be sure, but it is suggestive.

The Dorak Treasure remains an annoyingly unsolved mystery. Mellaart is about 85 years old as I write this, and without his clarification of the story, we may never know the solution.

Further Reading

The most comprehensive summary of the Dorak Treasure mystery has been written by Susan Mazur (2005).

Dowsing

Dowsing for subterranean water is a venerable tradition. Using a Y-shaped stick, a pendulum, or two metal wires with a 90-degree bend in each, some claim the ability to walk over the ground and, depending upon the motion of the device, identify the location, depth, and even the flow rate of underground water.

While "water witching" goes back hundreds of years—the first recorded reference is in 1568 (Chambers 1969, 35)—its application to the discovery of archaeological artifacts or buried structures is more recent (Schwartz 1978 [108–35] details the alleged abilities of Maj. Gen. James Scott Elliot in Britain; Noel Hume 1974 describes its use at Williamsburg, Virginia; Bailey 1983 details the use of dowsing in medieval church archaeology in England; and Goodman 1977 discusses "map dowsing," where sites are supposedly discovered by using a dowsing technique on maps).

For some (Schwartz and Goodman, for example), dowsing is simply a method for enhancing or facilitating the psychic abilities of the user. Others maintain that the dowsing device simply allows them to locate, through some unknown but normal process, magnetic anomalies caused by the buried objects (General Elliot, as cited in Schwartz 1978, eschews the "psychic" label; Noel Hume [1974] uses dowsing to find only metal objects as a result of their magnetism).

Small but discernable magnetic effects, indeed, are known to result from human activity and have been used in locating archaeological artifacts or features. In a related approach, the electrical resistivity of soil has been measured and used to locate buried foundations and walls. In the former case, a device called a proton magnetometer can be used to locate anything displaying magnetism that differs from the background magnetism of the earth: iron objects, fired clay, or even ancient pits (pit fill is more loosely packed than surrounding soil, resulting in differences in what is called "magnetic susceptibility"). In the latter case of electrical resistivity surveying, soil resistance to an electrical current varies depending on the compactness of the soil or medium (rock, brick) through which the current is passing. Buried walls and pits, for instance, exhibit different resistivity to the current than the surrounding soil. These differences can be mapped, and the buried objects or features causing the differences in resistivity can be investigated.

So, measurable phenomena do exist. But can people detect these without the thousands of dollars of equipment ordinarily considered required?

A number of experimental tests of water dowsing have been performed by skeptics; in one case, the president of the American Society of Dowsers was involved (Randi 1979, 1984; Martin 1983/1984); a test was even performed on the ABC television news program *20/20*. In each case, the self-proclaimed dowsers agreed to the scientific controls imposed and the design of the experiment. All maintained that they could easily detect flowing water under test conditions (water flowing in randomly selected routes, through buried or covered pipes).

In all cases here cited, the dowsers failed utterly. They simply could not detect flowing water using their rods, sticks, or pendulums, even when a prize of $110,000 was at stake.

If you believe everything you read on the Internet (not a good idea), it is easy get the impression that dowsing rods are a regular part of the archaeologist's tool-kit and that dowsing is commonly used both to find sites and to select the most promising areas within sites to excavate. You might further believe that you don't read or hear much about this simply because we archaeologists don't like to admit that we employ the technique for fear of ridicule from our colleagues.

Though I do know archaeologists who think that dowsing actually works in finding buried objects, in fact, not many do. I conducted a survey in 1983 of teaching archaeologists in the United States, only about 13.5 percent of whom (anonymously) responded positively to a question regarding the efficacy of dowsing in archaeology (Feder 1984). The vast majority of archaeologists don't use dowsing, because they don't believe it works.

Martin Aitken (1959), a pioneer in the use of the proton magnetometer and electrical resistivity surveying in archaeology, tested dowser P. A. Raine of Great Britain. Raine could not successfully dowse the location of an archaeologically verified buried kiln that had been initially identified by magnetometry (it had produced extremely high readings). Aitken concluded from this that dowsing for archaeological remains simply did not work. Though practitioners of dowsing hold quite strongly to their beliefs, they seem to be unable to produce under scientifically controlled conditions. Until they do, dowsing cannot reasonably become a part of the archaeologist's repertoire.

Perhaps the most support for dowsing comes from British archaeologists, where the procedure has been tested in a number of investigations of old churches (Bailey, Cambridge, and Briggs 1988). As researcher Martijn van Leusen (1999) has pointed out, however, the consistency and predictability of church architecture makes them a poor choice for an objective testing of the efficacy of dowsing. As van Leusen shows, when accurate predictions of the locations of buried architectural features are made by dowsers, it is impossible to distinguish between those actually based on dowsing and those based on a simple knowledge of how churches were built.

Then why, it might reasonably be asked, do some people swear by the ability of dowsers to find water and/or archaeological sites in the field? An answer can be found in a simple statistic. The regional government of New South Wales, Australia, keeps very accurate records of the several thousand water wells drilled in its territory, including those located by local dowsers. According to these records, the dowsers have been very successful, with about a 70 percent hit rate; about seven out of every 10 wells they directed drillers to, produced water (Raloff 1995, 91). This sounds impressive—until you compare the dowsers' success rate with that of all other (nondowsing) methods for locating wells. For these, the hit rate was 83 percent (Raloff 1995, 91).

That dowsers seem to be almost as successful as geologists and others at finding water is not so surprising. As Robert Farvolden of the Waterloo (Ontario) Centre for Groundwater Research pointed out in an interview (Raloff 1995, 91), "In most settled parts of the world it is not possible to dig a deep hole or drill a well without encountering groundwater." So, you will be right more often than not, whether you locate a well by dowsing, geological and hydrological principles, ESP, tea leaves, or anything else.

Like their success at locating water, dowsers (as well as psychics—and even psychic dowsers) will often be right in locating archaeological sites. This might sound provocative, but really means little. Archaeological remains are not nearly as rare as many nonarchaeologists assume. In some favored locales, buried archaeological materials may be virtually continuous (see **Alexandria Project**). There are some places where, even along lengthy transects, it is almost impossible to dig a test pit without exposing archaeological remains. In such places, a dowser might direct an archaeologist to dig in a particular spot and artifacts will be found; but anyone using any technique could have accomplished the same feat in these archaeologically rich zones. So, without success in the lab, under controlled conditions, the efficacy of dowsing cannot be upheld and will not become part of the archaeologist's repertoire.

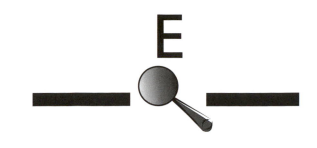

Easter Island Moai

The Easter Island moai are iconic monuments of the ancient world (van Tilburg 1994). For some, the 887 megalithic sculptures produced by the native people of Easter Island symbolize the spectacular abilities of human beings to accomplish remarkable feats when they coordinate the labor of a large number of committed individuals. For others, such as **Erich von Däniken**, the moai represent a great historical mystery, an achievement that would have required the intervention of extraterrestrial aliens, though precisely what would motivate aliens from space to erect monumental statues in a distinctly Polynesian style is not addressed in these fantasies.

Undeniably, the moai are amazing. The vast majority (some 95 percent) were sculpted out of the local tuff, a solidified volcanic ash that is ubiquitous on the island dominated by the cones of three extinct volcanoes. A sizable aboriginal quarry is located on the flanks of the island's central volcanic cone, Rano Raraku, where a large number of partially finished statues, never fully extracted from the bedrock, can still be found (all but 54 of the 887 moai were crafted from the tuff found on Rano Raraku). A large number of completed, erected moai stand close by the Rano Raraku quarry. Including unfinished and erected moai, a total of 397 of the total 887 statues are found in the quarry area. The rest of the statues are scattered across the entire extent of the island, most along its coastal margins, positioned as if gazing out to sea. Archaeological evidence indicates that the islanders' primary tools for quarrying and then sculpting the statues were axes and chisels made out of basalt, another volcanic rock, harder and denser than the tuff.

Sometimes mistakenly called "stone heads," the moai actually are stylized sculptures of the bodies of people or spirits in a Polynesian style. Though the heads do dominate most of the sculptures, there are arms and legs on most of them, if only suggested by incision or light relief on the bodies.

The moai range widely in size and proportions. Archaeologist Jo Anne van Tilburg (1994) breaks them down into four forms: short and squat; medium-size and vertically rectangular; tall and vertically rectangular; and tall, vertically rectangular, and gracefully slender. The moai on the flanks of Rano Raraku reflect the fourth category and are among the most impressive of the moai.

There are 887 so-called moai on Easter Island in the eastern Pacific. Sometimes mistakenly characterized as "heads," most of them are stylized, whole body sculptures with a mean weight of 12,500 kilograms, the vast majority having been made out of the island's local volcanic rock. (Sonja Gray)

Even the smallest moai weigh several thousand pounds and would have been a challenge for people to have transported from the quarries to the spots where they were erected. The mean height of the statues has been calculated to be about 13 feet (4 meters) from the top of the head to the base. The mean weight is about almost 14 tons (12,500 kilograms). The largest moai weighs an astonishing 82 tons (74,000 kilograms) and is 32 feet (9.8 meters) long. Many of the statues were topped off with large blocks of red tuff, serving as a stylized hairdo or headdress. Though the statues currently have only hollow sockets for eyes, originally the builders fixed dramatic, precisely shaped, white coral eyes with round red scoria (another soft rock) for the eyeballs, in those sockets. Some of the statues were positioned together on artificial platforms of stone called *ahu*.

That the moai are a monumental and astonishing achievement is undeniable. That their existence is so shocking to some that they feel compelled to suggest scenarios involving the agency of extraterrestrial aliens is a testament to their ignorance, on the part of those who suggest such nonsense, of the capabilities of human beings, including those ordinarily described with the too often racially based pejorative adjective "primitive." Please remember that the residents of

Easter Island were descended from a hardy people whose navigational skills allowed them to discover, explore, and then migrate to a tiny, isolated speck in what is effectively the middle of the Pacific Ocean. Von Däniken was so perplexed by even just the navigational ability of the native people of the Pacific that he suggests (I'm not making this up) that "the earliest Polynesians could fly" (1973, 133).

Such lunacy aside, Polynesians were and are demonstrably a remarkably intelligent and capable people. The archaeology of Easter Island has revealed the existence of quarries with partially finished statues, the presence of thousands of the hard basalt axes and chisels used to quarry the stones, and dozens of statues on their backs and sides along the pathways toward the coast, broken or abandoned during transport—all of which reflect a typically human project, replete with trial-and-error attempts, mistakes, improvement, and, eventually, successful completion of the task. Experiments in replication of the process of quarrying the statues, transporting, and then erecting them have produced a number of possible methods the islanders were fully capable of employing to accomplish these tasks. In one experiment by **Thor Heyerdahl** (1958), just six quarriers in a few days were able to rough out a statue a little bigger than the mean size of the moai (their replica was about 16 feet/5 meters long). A larger group of workers, using ropes and levers, transported that statue along a remnant of one of the ancient roadways used by the islanders clearly for this purpose and erected it, all in the course of just a few weeks. More recently, using computer simulation procedures, van Tilburg came with another set of specific techniques, including the use of a sled made of wooden beams, for transporting the statues.

Between the actual archaeological evidence on Easter Island and the efforts (both on the ground and by computer simulation) to experimentally replicate the processes the native people might have used to quarry, transport, and erect the moai, archaeologists have a pretty good handle on how it was accomplished. There is no need to fall back on hypotheses that involve flying Polynesians or extraterrestrial aliens with a fetish for carving statues of volcanic tuff.

Further Reading

The best work on the archaeology of Easter Island with a focus on the moai is Jo Anne van Tilburg's *Easter Island: Archaeology, Ecology, and Culture* (1994).

Egyptian Pyramids

The pyramids of Egypt are iconic. They symbolize all that is remarkable and mysterious about the ancient world. Even the smallest were gigantic undertakings

Though iconic, the ancient Egyptians constructed just a little more than 100 pyramid burial monuments. Pictured here is the pyramid of the pharaoh Khafre, who ruled between 2558 and 2532 BCE. (M.H. Feder)

that required a substantial investment in terms of time and labor, a huge social and economic investment in the production of a monument whose primary purpose was to house the body and the spirit of a dead leader. The largest of the Egyptian pyramids, the triad of monuments located at Giza, are among the most impressive structures ever built by human beings—their construction would pose a challenge even today, with mechanized assistance that the ancient Egyptians did not have at their disposal.

But, as impressive as the pyramids were and are, they should not lead us to surrender to unsupported speculations about the role played in their construction by supernaturally advanced Atlanteans or extraterrestrial aliens. Following **Occam's Razor**, we should first consider how the pyramids reflect the amazing capacity of people of any era, when they are motivated and their labors efficiently coordinated, to communally produce wonders. When we consider the history of pyramid construction in ancient Egypt, we see a predictable and painfully human pattern of the slow development of a new practice, perfected only through a process of trial and error that would make no sense had the pyramids been introduced by an advanced civilization.

There are, altogether, only a little more than a hundred pyramids in all of Egypt (the latest pyramid census puts the figure at 118). The earliest construct in this group isn't even a geometrically true pyramid—that is, a form with four

The triad of pyramids at Giza, in Egypt, were the burial chambers of three generations of pharoahs: Khufu, Khafre, and Menkaure. These pyramids are the only surviving monuments of the Seven Wonders of the Ancient World. (M.H. Feder)

isosceles triangular faces meeting at a common apex—at all; it is a stepped structure, vaguely triangular in outline, and is little more than an elaborate version of the mastaba burial chamber form seen in the royal burial ground at Abydos, Egypt. A *mastaba* is an aboveground, rectangular-block, mud-brick structure and the most common burial building built for the elites of Egyptian society. Not content with merely a larger, more impressive, and more elaborate mastaba, however, the pharaoh Djoser (who ruled Egypt from 2668 to 2649 BCE) had his royal architects and builders innovate, building him an impressive monument of six mastabas of diminishing size, one on top of the other, producing the appearance of a stepped pyramid about 197 feet (60 meters) in height. It is an impressive monument, to be sure, but it was an evolutionary step in Egyptian burial monument construction—the kind of advance in size, sophistication, and elaboration typical of the development of human practices and nothing that would have required the assistance of extraterrestrials to help the Egyptians along. We even know the name of Djoser's architect, the man who designed the structure of superimposed mastabas: his name was **Imhotep**, and though we don't know much about him, he is depicted as an ordinary Egyptian man, not a strange alien.

Following Djoser, the form of pharaonic burial monuments changed, and here, definitively, we see a typically human pattern of trial and error at work.

The pharaoh Snefru, who ascended to the throne in 2613 BCE, was determined to construct a burial monument larger and more impressive than his predecessor Djoser—this time a true pyramid with flat, massive faces, arching up to the heavens in an unbroken surface. But Snefru's architects, designers, and engineers attempted too large a leap, beginning the construction of a monument that was too tall, too massive, and too steep (the faces of the pyramid presented a slope of over 70°) for their abilities. The project was abandoned in midbuild, after the facing of the structure cracked and became unstable. All that is left today is the more or less intact pyramid core surrounded by the rubble of its collapsed facing. It is, in fact, called the **Collapsed Pyramid**.

I'm not sure I would have wanted to be Snefru's royal architect or designer when the pharaoh had to be informed that his prized burial monument project, on which tens of thousands of laborers likely had worked for years, would have to be abandoned and it was back to the drawing board. But back to the drawing board they went, attempting a structure with its faces at a gentler angle, this time only 54.5°. Frustratingly for the builders, even at this gentler slope, the weight and stresses produced on the base of the structure were too great and cracks and fissures developed that might have proved disastrous had they continued with the original plan. Compounding the problem, while three of the corners of this pyramid were built on immovable, solid bedrock, the fourth corner was situated on a much less stable, compressible foundation: gravel. As a result, the gravel-based corner settled far more than the corners on bedrock causing external cracking and internal deformation of the pharaoh's burial chamber (Brier and Houdin 2008).

As a seat-of-the-pants attempt at a fix, the builders of Snefru's second attempted burial monument reduced the slope of the sides of the pyramid about two-thirds of the way up to 43.5°. Their reasoning—and hope—was that a lesser angle for the top third of the building would ease the pressure on the bottom two-thirds, and the structure would remain intact. They were right, for the most part, and the pyramid remained intact. Their strategy, however, gives the pyramid an odd, crooked appearance, as well as its modern name, the **Bent Pyramid**. Its strange shape apparently did not satisfy Snefru, who rejected it.

The third try was the charm. Beginning the third attempt at the same angle the builders of the Bent Pyramid applied at the top third of that monument, the so-called Red Pyramid was a success from start to finish, and its form became the model for all subsequent pyramids, including the acme of pyramid construction, **Khufu**'s massive monument at Giza, the largest pyramid built by the ancient Egyptians.

The point of this discussion is this. Writers like **Erich von Däniken** and **Graham Hancock** claim that Egyptian technology in general, and the pyramids in particular, appeared instantly, fully developed, perfect in form and construction, and therefore are inexplicable. In von Däniken's (1970, 74) fantasy, "the pyramids sprung out of the ground." For Hancock (1995, 135), in the case of Egypt, "Technological skills that should have taken hundreds or even thousands of years to evolve were brought into use almost overnight—and with no apparent antecedents whatever." This is cited as proof that they could not have been developed by the Egyptians but must have been introduced from the outside.

Such claims betray a stunning misapprehension of the history of the iconic Egyptian burial monument. The pattern exhibited in the archaeological record is clearly one of slow, painful, even dangerous, development of pyramid construction, filled with fits and starts, trials and errors, mistakes and fixes, last-minute responses to problems, work-arounds, and, finally, success. And this process took place over the course of close to a hundred years. It is a stereotypically human pattern and requires no surrender to foolish and uninformed speculations about the involvement of **Atlantis** or extraterrestrials in the process.

Further Reading

For the best source of reliable information on how the pyramids were built, see Dieter Arnold's book, *Building in Egypt: Pharaonic Stone Masonry* (1991). For the source that best places the pyramids in historical context, see Egyptologist Mark Lehner's *The Complete Pyramids* (1997).

Electromagnetic Photo-fields

Archaeologists are always on the lookout for innovative procedures that might render the labor-intensive and time-consuming processes of site survey (the search for archaeological sites) and site excavation (where buried remains are revealed and recovered) more effective and efficient. One such proposed method, though its efficacy has never been proven, involves the detection and interpretation of so-called electromagnetic photo-fields or EMPFs.

EMPFs have been defined by their discoverer, Karen A. Hunt, as invisible, electromagnetic imprints that result from the presence of buildings and surface features such as roads or walls. According to Hunt—a researcher with no discernable training in physics but possessed of a master's degree in anthropology—EMPFs are naturally produced when aboveground structures or features absorb or block the "minute particles from outer space" (Hunt 1984, 2) that constantly bombard the Earth. Again according to Hunt, EMPFs can be detected long after the structures or features have been removed or destroyed. An EMPF is supposed to be, in essence, a sort of eternal electromagnetic shadow of a building, wall, road, gravestone, or other structure. EMPF practitioners examine an area in order to detect these remnant photo-fields and then use the spatial patterns they ostensibly find to determine the form and size of such features.

How Do EMPFs Work?

It sounds intriguing. If such a procedure were effective, it would make an enormous contribution to archaeological research, allowing us to discern the layout of no-longer-visible houses, temples, walls, and roads at a site without having to engage in the time-consuming but widely accepted practice of excavation for actual remnants of those structures or features.

But, though intriguing, don't bother looking up "EMPF" in a high school or college physics textbook or, for that matter, in any publication other than those authored by Karen A. Hunt. EMPFs are not a scientifically recognized phenomenon and have never been shown to exist; on the contrary, their very existence has been labeled an impossibility by physicists who have examined Hunt's claims.

No electrical meter or detector is used in an EMPF survey, as these cannot, apparently, actually detect the photo-fields. In fact, an EMPF survey in practice sounds suspiciously like **dowsing**. As in dowsing, the EMPF investigator walks over the ground, interpreting the movements of bent wires held in his or her hands. The movement of the wires, it is claimed, occurs as the investigator encounters the photo-fields. Tracing out the photo-fields supposedly reveals the configuration of the aboveground archaeological structure or feature.

EMPF Application in Australia

In the mid-1980s, a local government in Australia was sufficiently intrigued to pay Hunt $1,600 in expenses for her to come to Australia and divine the layout of a now-destroyed historic homestead located in a public park. Walking over the ground with her bent wires, Hunt claimed to have detected the EMPFs left behind by more than a hundred structures, fences, and pathways, 25 burials, and a number of Aborigine huts, all of which she then located on a map. The complete lack of scientific rigor employed in this experimental application of EMPF surveying is reflected in this simple fact: in no instance did Hunt or anyone else attempt to confirm the existence of any of the alleged structures, features, or burials with physical, archaeological evidence (Money 1985). It would have been easy enough to excavate in the footprint of those locations where Hunt had determined there had been aboveground features. Buried foundations, burials, or house footings found in the places where Hunt's EMPF study indicated such things should exist would have gone a long way toward validating the technique. No such subsurface testing was conducted, however. Thus, all we are left with is Hunt's say-so that these electromagnetic imprints were present, which renders the entire process about as meaningful as conducting a séance at the site in an attempt to contact the homestead's long-dead inhabitants (as in **psychic archaeology**).

After 16 days of fieldwork, Hunt submitted her report. Her benefactors were said to be quite pleased and felt they got a good deal; a traditional archaeological and historical investigation of the old homestead would have included an extensive subsurface study, involving test excavations and the employment of such sophisticated remote-detection techniques as electrical resistivity surveying, proton magnetometry, and ground-penetrating radar—all of which have the advantage of being based on known, physical phenomena and have shown their utility in numerous archaeological investigations, but would have cost upwards of $10,000.

Hunt's rather cluttered EMPF map of the homestead was assessed by Michael McIntyre, director of a local archaeological survey project in Australia. McIntyre stated that Hunt's drawing of the site based on the EMPF analysis looked nothing like an Australian settlement, but did resemble a nineteenth-century Midwest American town (Bryce, Eng, Harris, and Wheeler 1985). Perhaps not coincidentally, Hunt is from the American Midwest, specifically Missouri—which is, ironically, the "Show Me" State.

Hunt's EMPF research, in fact, showed nothing of value for archaeological methodology, but it did reveal the cynicism of government officials more interested in saving money than in conducting a proper archaeological and historical investigation. EMPF analysis, such as it is, has not become part of the repertoire of techniques employed in archaeological site survey or excavation; it is purely fantasy.

Further Reading

For a detailed discussion of tested and proven remote-sensing techniques that allow archaeologists to investigate sites without excavation, see, for example, *Ground-Penetrating Radar for Archaeology* by Lawrence B. Conyers (2004).

Eoanthropus Dawsoni

Eoanthropus dawsoni is the official taxonomic classification of the **Piltdown Man** fossil. *Eoanthropus* is the genus to which the type specimen (the original fossils found in the gravel pit on Barcombe Mills manor located in Piltdown, Sussex, in the south of England) were assigned, while *dawsoni* is the species. Just as anatomically modern human beings are assigned the taxonomic name *Homo sapiens*, chimpanzees are classified as *Pan troglodytes*, and the ancient human ancestor Lucy is called *Australopithecus afarensis*, the cluster of cranial fragments initially found by workers in Piltdown in 1908 and then added to by **Charles Dawson**, Arthur Smith Woodward, Père Teillard de Chardin, and others during formal excavations over the next few years was labeled *Eoanthropus dawsoni*.

As is often the case in the practice of taxonomic classification, the name given in this case has a specific meaning related to the presumed implications of the specimen as well as honoring the discoverer. In this case, *eoanthropus* means, literally, "dawn man" (*eo-* is the Greek prefix for "dawn," while *anthropus* comes from *anthropo*, which, again, is Greek, for anything related to human beings). The *eo-* prefix has been used frequently in taxonomy, as well as in geology, to signify anything especially old; for example, the eohippus is an early horse, and the Eocene is a very early geological epoch. The species name applied to the specimen, *dawsoni*, is a way of recognizing the role of Charles Dawson in bringing the supposedly significant fossil to the attention of scientists.

The Piltdown fossil was, however, a fake, fairly characterized as one of the most damaging in the entire sordid history of archaeological and paleontological fakery. Though those who named the fossil after Dawson did so as a way of honoring their friend and colleague, in the end it attached his name forever to a hoax. Whether or not Dawson deserves that opprobrium is uncertain, although it seems probable that he played a significant role in perpetrating the Piltdown Man **fraud**.

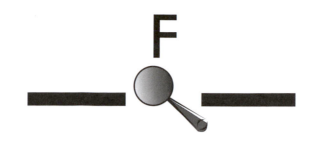

F

Fantastic Archaeology: The Wild Side of North American Prehistory

Fantastic Archaeology: The Wild Side of North American Prehistory was written by Steven Williams (1991), an archaeologist and curator of North American archaeology at the Peabody Museum of Archaeology and Ethnology at Harvard University. He currently is retired and professor emeritus. Williams's book is a valuable contribution to the regrettably short list of publications by professional archaeologists examining, responding to, and debunking extreme claims made in the name of the discipline.

Williams's book focuses on **frauds** and misrepresentations about North American prehistory, with chapters on the earliest human settlement of the New World, the **moundbuilder myth**, **psychic archaeology**, the **Norse** discovery of America, assorted other claims of pre-Columbian **discovery of America**, **Atlantis** and catastrophism, the Mormon view of American prehistory, and an especially detailed and valuable chapter on one fraud in particular, the **Walam Olum**. The book is currently out of print, but used copies can be found and should be in the library of anyone interested in frauds, myths, and mysteries in archaeology.

Fell, Barry

Born in the south of England, Barry Fell (Howard Barraclough Fell; 1917–1994) grew up in New Zealand and moved to Scotland for his graduate studies. Fell's primary training was in invertebrate zoology, and he became a professor at Harvard University.

Along with his professional research—he was best known among his fellow zoologists as an expert in fossil sea urchins—Fell displayed a lifelong interest in epigraphy (the decipherment of ancient written languages) and an attendant interest in the possibility that ancient writing could be used to trace the movement of human groups across the face of the Earth in antiquity.

Fell's interest in epigraphy can be traced back to at least 1940, when he analyzed and published on **petroglyphs** in Polynesia. What made Fell famous—and, it should be told, infamous among most archaeologists—was his assertion that there was a substantial body of epigraphic evidence for the ancient presence of explorers and colonists throughout the New World. In Fell's scenario, substantial numbers of visitors and migrants from Iberia (Spain and Portugal), northern Africa (Phoenicians and Egyptians), Israel (Hebrews), Greece, and Scandinavia traveled to and colonized the Americas beginning close to 4,000 years ago. Fell provided the ostensible proof for his claims in a series of three popular books: *America B.C.* (1976), *Saga America* (1980), and *Bronze Age America* (1982).

Virtually all of Fell's proof consisted of artifacts that he interpreted as genuine examples of ancient Old World writing in pre-Columbian contexts in the New World. Unfortunately, the majority of professionally trained linguists disputed Fell's interpretations on a number of grounds. First, many of the artifacts that Fell cited in his works had been proven to be **frauds** (for example, the **Davenport Tablets** and the **Bat Creek Stone**). In addition, Fell's translation of ostensible inscriptions in **Ogham** has been judged to be delusional by archaeologist Ann Ross and historian Peter Reynolds. Fell dates New World Ogham inscriptions to before Ogham was even invented in Europe. Further, without any supporting evidence, Fell asserts the New World Ogham was written without vowels; the reader supplies those. This, according to Ross and Reynolds (1978), allows Fell to "translate" any marks on stones, including simple tally marks or even parallel lines accidently left behind by a plow blade scraping over a piece of bedrock or glacial stone. Ross and Reynolds characterize Fell's epigraphic evidence as "a semantic phantasy of the wildest nature" (106).

Just as importantly, Fell cannot point to very much in the way of standard archaeological evidence for the presence of all of these scads of Old World interlopers in the New World. Though Fell makes reference to vast kingdoms of **Celts** and such scattered across the New World landscape, these folks left nothing behind—other than the purported written messages—to alert us to their presence.

Flint Jack

The forging of archaeological specimens to support a cherished hypothesis about the past, to prove a point, to get publicity or fame, or just to be obnoxious has a long and ignoble history, but perhaps the most common purpose for archaeological fakery is simply and plainly the desire to make money. There is no better example of this than the case of Edward Simpson (or was his actual name John Wilson? or Jerry Taylor? he went by a number of aliases), who, based on his propensity for finding ancient stone implements, was commonly referred to as "Flint Jack."

Simpson apparently began his archaeological career honestly enough in the mid-nineteenth century as a fieldworker in legitimate archaeological excavations. According to an article published in the London *Times* in March 1867, with his experience in and knowledge of archaeology in Great Britain, Simpson began forging specimens and selling them in order to support his drinking habit. As Flint Jack, he traveled widely across England, Ireland, and Scotland selling fake antiquities to museums, which, it must be assumed, merely thought he was an extremely diligent and lucky collector of local artifacts. Among the items he produced were **fraudulently** ancient coins, rings, bits of armor, necklaces, Roman urns, and, perhaps most extensively, stone implements. It is believed that to this day, more than 140 years after the fact, small museums throughout Great Britain still unknowingly possess antiquities forged by Flint Jack.

Pictured here with his stone toolmaking equipment, Flint Jack (his actual name was Edward Simpson) was one of the best known nineteenth-century forgers of ancient stone tools.

Simpson confessed to his forgeries in 1859 when confronted by a Professor Tennant. Interestingly, at least for a time, Simpson capitalized on the revelation of his activities and gave lectures in which he showed his methods for making fraudulent Paleolithic tools; he even signed the tools "Flint Jack" in order to distinguish his now legitimately produced "replicas" from real artifacts. Signing or otherwise marking modern replicas has become standard operating procedure among modern replicators, again to insure that their replicas are never mistaken for legitimate, ancient artifacts.

Ultimately, the lecture circuit was not as remunerative as the forger's profession, and Simpson ended up in prison in 1867. He passed into obscurity at that point, although, in a way, he lives on in the doubtless hundreds of forgeries that are still on view in various British museums.

Forbidden Archaeology: The Hidden History of the Human Race

Forbidden Archaeology: The Hidden History of the Human Race (1993) was the first and most significant monograph (all 900-plus pages of it) published by the **Bhaktivedanta Institute** in its apparent attempt to proselytize for the Hindu religion or philosophy. The authors, Michael A. Cremo and Richard L. Thompson, reject evidence of evolution and, much like Christian creationists, maintain that human beings, in our present form, can be traced back essentially to the beginning of time.

Cremo and Thompson's underpinning approach can be summarized in the following way:

- They reject utterly the consensus view of human evolution, including the divergence from a common ancestor with the apes at sometime between 5 million and 7 million years ago; a bipedal ancestor with an apelike brain dated to this same time period; descendants of that biped with a larger-than-ape-size brain by about 2.5 million years ago; and the development of anatomically modern human beings by close to 200,000 years ago.
- They allege that there is a conspiracy (the authors call it a "knowledge filter") designed to ignore or keep hidden any evidence that contradicts the prevailing evolutionary paradigm.
- They further claim that there is evidence in the form of incised bones, stone tools, and even modern-appearing human skeletal remains that date to long before traditional anthropology maintains even the most ancient ancestral human forms are supposed to have appeared. This evidence shows that "beings quite like ourselves have been around as far back as we care to look—in the Pliocene, Miocene, Oligocene, Eocene and beyond" (Cremo and Thompson 1993, 525; in standard geological chronology charts, the Eocene begins more than 55 million years ago). The authors even point to the discovery of "humanlike footprints" in Kentucky dating to about 300 million years ago (p. 456).
- They dispense with all evidence of human evolution from an apelike ancestor as being suspect at best and explaining these as the fossil remains of nonancestral hominids or even extinct apes. They interpret Bigfoot, the Abominable Snowman (yeti), and other creatures whose existence has not been proven as the descendants of these animals whose skeletal remains they reject.
- Where archaeologists and historians trace the earliest complex societies— "civilizations" characterized by the appearance of cities, monumental construction projects, a writing system, social stratification, and the development of specialist classes (of artists, scribes, architects, engineers, and military officers)— to less than 10,000 and closer to 5,000 years ago, Cremo and Thompson assert that there is evidence of anomalously advanced civilizations extending back millions of years into the past.

Forbidden Archaeology is a relentless hodgepodge of discredited data and unsupported interpretation, much of it collected in the nineteenth century and fraught with speculation about the depth of human antiquity long before accurate dating methods had been developed and applied to archaeological specimens. Cremo and Thompson either ignore the fact that archaeologists and paleoanthropologists working in the twentieth and twenty-first centuries, with a suite of far more sophisticated dating and analytical techniques at their disposal, simply don't find any evidence to support any of the nineteenth-century claims they use to buttress their anti-evolutionary argument, or they are reduced to claiming that such evidence is in fact found all of the time, but we archaeologists and paleoanthropologists have conspired to hide the awful truth from you all, for reasons they never make especially clear and which completely mystify me.

It likely is significant that Hindu literature is essentially nonevolutionary. To Hindus, time is cyclical, with each cycle or *kalpa* lasting 4.32 billion years. Each *kalpa* is further broken down into 14 *manvantaras*, each of which lasts 300 million years. After each *manvantara*, the world is created anew, as are human beings, fully formed in our modern state, with no need for evolution. In short, what *Forbidden Archaeology* presents is a version of Hindu creationism supported by outdated and discredited data from the nineteenth century.

Frauds

There are several archaeological frauds or hoaxes highlighted in this encyclopedia. These range from the ridiculous, with little or no impact on archaeology (for example, the **Cardiff Giant**), to hoaxes that had an enormous impact on our scientific understanding of the human past (the evolution of modern human beings, as in the case of **Piltdown Man**, or the numerous hoaxes perpetrated by **Shinichi Fujimura**).

It is important to ask how frauds such as these and the others discussed in this work were so successful, why they convinced so many people, and why a healthy dose of skepticism seems to have been so lacking in so many of these cases.

How to Perpetrate a Successful Fraud

Successful archaeological hoaxes have several things in common. The most important of these is that the hoaxers have provided a version of the human past that is appealing to a sizable segment of the population.

As a counterexample, because of my access to prehistoric ceramic artifacts found in New England and as a result of my expertise in excavating such objects, I probably could create a pretty convincing hoax involving a sample of those ceramics. Fleshing out my "planned" hoax, you should know that the oldest pottery sherds found in Connecticut date to about 3,000 years ago. We know this based on stratigraphy—the context of the lowest natural soil layers in which those ceramics have been found—as well as the radiocarbon dates derived from organic remains found in spatial proximity to those ceramic artifacts, especially when found in the same stratigraphic layer. Now, suppose I were to plant some ceramics in a stratigraphic layer alongside some charcoal that I knew radiocarbon-dated to, say, 3,500 years ago, 500 years older than the oldest pottery heretofore found in Connecticut. Then, suppose I held a press conference to announce this momentous discovery. Would anybody show up? In fact, such a discovery would interest a very small number of people—essentially, only the archaeological community in southern New England, at most, a few hundred people. The National Geographic Society would not exactly be banging down my door with grant money in hand and a contract for a 13-part series on my storied discovery of pottery that was unexpectedly old by half a millennium. Such a hoax would not have much potential to attract the interest of the general public, funding organizations, cable documentary makers, or Oprah.

Successful and historically significant hoaxes involve what, essentially, is marketing research. Successful hoaxers figure out what people *want to believe* about the past, what they would be interested in reading about, watching on TV, and so on—and then give the public what it wants. With the **Scarith of Scornello**, for instance, Curzio Inghirami concocted a fabulous history with intellectually precocious Etruscans that seventeenth-century Tuscans craved. Fujimura fabricated a time depth to Japanese prehistory that rivaled that of mainland Asians and produced a degree of pride among his Japanese countrymen. **Charles Dawson**, working alone or perhaps with co-conspirators, gave scientists a human ancestor more in line with their hopes and expectations. At the same time Dawson's "discovery" lifted Britain's sense of evolutionary inferiority by giving it a player in the evolutionary story of humanity that not only rivaled the specimens previously found in France and Germany but even knocked them off their pedestals and elevated the English to the people with the oldest human lineage. As any magician will tell you, it is far easier to fool people who don't want to disbelieve, who want to experience something that would truly be wonderful, if only it were true.

There is no clearer case of charlatans and hoaxers exploiting a wish to believe than that of Sir Arthur Conan Doyle. Doyle, who created Sherlock Holmes, the most rational and deductive mind in literature, was himself an entirely credulous believer in all things occult, even becoming a major supporter of the transparently absurd claims of two young girls that fairies regularly appeared to them in their garden and that they photographed their antics.

The evidence they provided Doyle was laughable, but Doyle accepted it all—precisely because he wanted to. His son had been killed during World War I, and Doyle hoped beyond all reason that by delving into the paranormal, he might find proof that life transcends death and that he might be able to communicate with his deceased son. The exploitation of Doyle by spiritualists is based on the same underlying theme of archaeological fakery: find out what people want to believe and give it to them, and they won't look too closely for the trick or hoax.

Another rule underlying a successful hoax is often broken by fakers greedy for wealth or hungry for fame: never appear to be *too* lucky. Luck breeds suspicion and resentment. Suspicion and resentment, in turn, breed skepticism, which then leads to a level of attention that most hoaxes cannot withstand. Dawson was incredibly lucky, or so it seemed, at finding archaeological, paleontological, and geological specimens and even historical documents, gaining the nickname "the Wizard of Sussex." Trumping Dawson, Fujimura appeared to be so singularly gifted at discovering ever-older evidence of a human occupation of the islands of Japan that his countrymen referred to him as "God's Hand." Though it might be personally validating to be known as a wizard at finding archaeological sites or to have a nickname that implied that you had godlike abilities to find ancient artifacts, that level of recognition is actually not a good thing, because it inspires questions about why and how, exactly, it's always *you* finding the Etruscan scrolls or the Paleolithic artifacts or the human remains. Such questions inspire a closer examination of the artifacts and the way they were discovered, and those are never good things if you're attempting to pull off a successful fraud.

Some of the frauds discussed in this work inspired vigorous debunking by professional archaeologists (or geologists or sculptors or whatever). Now, one might think that having knowledgeable individuals deconstruct a clumsy fake would be detrimental to the faker, but this does not have to be the case. In a number of instances, in fact—for example, the **Michigan Relics** and the **Newark Holy Stones**—rather than dispiriting the perpetrators of archaeological frauds and their gullible supporters, debunking has served the valuable purpose, from the perspective of the fakers, of providing them with a primer on what they did wrong the first time and how to improve the quality, character, and authenticity for their next attempt. Once it was pointed out that unbaked clay artifacts like those initially found as part of the Michigan Relics assemblage could not have been preserved for any length of time in the damp soil of Michigan, prospectors began finding only *fired* clay objects. Once experts in Hebrew concluded that the first of the Newark Holy Stones bore an unmistakably modern variety of the written Hebrew language, the next of the Holy Stones, found just weeks after the discovery and debunking of the first, bore a form of Hebrew far more in keeping with the time period of the mound in which they were "found."

In summary, a good archaeological faker follows three cardinal rules:

1. Give the people what they want. Tell them what they want to hear, provide them with archaeological evidence that supports something they already believe or that they want to believe.
2. Do not go to the well too frequently. Don't appear so lucky as to engender suspicion, resentment, or envy among those who might be skeptical about your discovery in the first place. Envious people are more likely to look closely at your claims.
3. Archaeological fakery involves a learning curve. Expect to make mistakes the first time around that professionals will be able to sniff out quickly. Then use their criticism to construct more convincing frauds the next time you attempt it.

Motives for Frauds

There likely are as many specific motives for archaeological hoaxes as there are hoaxers, but we can consolidate these into four discrete categories.

1. *Money.* The ability to make money through the agency of archaeological fraud provides a rationale for many archaeological hoaxes. For example, museums have paid enormous sums for convincing frauds. Alternatively, Stub Newell and George Hull made a great deal of money very quickly with their fraudulent Cardiff Giant because people wanted to see a specimen that seemed to confirm the biblical stories about giants.
2. *Fame.* Scientists usually toil in obscurity, at least as far as the general public is concerned. The average Nobel Prize winner (if there can be such a thing as an "average" Nobel Prize winner) is unknown by the public, and only a handful of scientists, like **Carl Sagan**, for example, become household names. Most scientists are content with that and are happy that they and their work become known among their colleagues.

   But fame can be seductive, to scientists and nonscientists alike, and archaeological fakery can be a ticket to a sort of stardom for people who crave attention. After all, Dawson would have died an obscure British lawyer but for his role in the "discovery" of Piltdown Man; now, he is immortal, and not just because authors like me write about him nearly a hundred years after his death. The Piltdown specimen itself preserves Charles Dawson's name; its taxonomic label is ***Eoanthropus dawsoni***, or "Dawson's Dawn Man." You simply can't get much more famous or immortal than that in paleoanthropology. Archaeological fakery may just be a way in which those hungry for fame find an avenue to their goal.

3. *Nationalism.* The roots of nationalism often run deep into antiquity. Most of us define ourselves ethnically or nationally or by some combination of ethnicity and national identity. We are proud of who we are and of where we came from (geographically and metaphorically). This sometimes leads to competition among various groups and arguments about who showed up in a region first (Palestinians or Jews?), who was more culturally sophisticated or advanced in the past, and so forth. The misapplication of the archaeological record or even the fabrication of fake artifacts may be a reflection of the use of archaeology to prove or support a nationalistic or even racist view of the past.

It should surprise no one that the Nazis used archaeology in an attempt to prove the superiority from deep antiquity of the so-called Aryan people (Arnold 1992). Toeing the party line, Nazi archaeologists in the 1930s and 1940s interpreted artifacts outside of Germany as representing the formerly more widespread appearance of Aryan people. There even was the belief that, somehow, the Aryans were descendants of the people of **Atlantis**.

4. *Religion.* Unfortunately, religion has contributed to the record of archaeological frauds. Of course, many people have a strong emotional investment in their religion and, while most religions do not require physical proof for the existence of God or for the historical accuracy of any of the events enumerated in their holy books or oral traditions, the possibility that any of that may be supported by physical evidence provided in the archaeological record is alluring. Pieces of **Noah's ark**, evidence of giants like those mentioned in the Old Testament (the Cardiff Giant), bones of the saints, pieces of the One True Cross, and a miraculous image on the burial shroud of Jesus Christ (the **Shroud of Turin**) are all artifacts that, if valid, would lend support of Bible stories or even the existence of miracles. Artifacts like this might be worth quite a bit of money (the Shroud of Turin was used almost from when it first turns up in the thirteenth century as a way to get donations), so religiously significant artifacts may have the money motive at their core.

However, some religiously oriented hoaxes are perpetrated not for nefarious or pecuniary reasons, but with the goal of saving souls. That is to say, fraudulent artifacts may be used as a tool by well-meaning people to bring others to God. Consider what Martin Luther, leader of the Protestant Reformation, had to say about lying: "What harm would it do if a man told a good strong lie for the sake of the good and for the Christian Church . . . a useful lie, a helpful lie, such lies would not be against God; he would accept them" (Arthur 1996, 88).

Further Reading

For a more detailed discussion of the motives that drive archaeological frauds, see my book *Frauds, Myths, and Mysteries: Science and Pseudoscience in Archaeology* (Feder 2010).

Fujimura, Shinichi

Shinichi Fujimura's (1950–) educational background was in electronics, working essentially at the Japanese equivalent of Radio Shack. His heart wasn't in it, though. His true calling, it seems, was not in consumer electronics but in Japanese prehistory. In that regard, he began serving as a volunteer on archaeological digs in his native country. Then, in 1981, the amateur volunteer stunned the archaeological community by finding artifacts that appeared to be almost twice as old as the previously presumed oldest artifacts in Japan.

When Fujimura began volunteering as an archaeological fieldworker, conducting the scut work of archaeology—troweling back ancient soil layers, sifting soil matrix through hardware cloth screening, and washing and cataloging artifacts back in the lab—the time depth of Japanese prehistory was relatively shallow. While mainland Asian nations could boast of a prehistoric record that stretched back hundreds of thousands and even upwards of 1.5 million years, the oldest sites in Japan were little more than 30,000 years old. Japan consists of a series of islands and has been separated from the mainland for millions of years. Human beings reached Japan's shores only upon the development of a seafaring capability, and for northern Asia and specifically Japan, this appears to have occurred sometime after the aforementioned 30,000 years ago.

Though accepting this established chronology and culture history and their place as relative latecomers to the story of Asian prehistory, the idea that the Japanese people were derived from other parts of Asia—Korea, for example, or China—never sat well with them, and the fact that this derivation was so relatively recent was even more disappointing. Fujimura's discovery in the 1980s of artifacts not 30,000 but 60,000 years old was embraced by archaeologists and the prehistory-interested Japanese public alike. Sixty thousand years was still late in the broad chronological sequence of Asian antiquity, but it seemed much better—maybe twice as good—as 30,000.

Fujimura's apparent luck was just beginning, and in the ensuing years, he seemed always to be at the right place—the right archaeological site—at the right time and was responsible for discovering a sequence of ever-older artifacts, almost single-handedly pushing Japanese antiquity back, to 80,000, then 100,000, then 200,000 years. His great skill—and astonishing luck—convinced the archaeological community in Japan that Fujimura's time would be better spent not in selling Play Stations or fixing computers but in devoting his energies full-time to archaeology. They made him an offer he couldn't refuse and presented him—a man wholly untrained in archaeology, geology, paleontology, paleoanthropology, or in fact in any related field—with the directorship of an archaeological institute where trained scientists would take their marching orders from him.

A cardinal sin many archaeological hoaxers are guilty of consists of being too lucky (for instance, Curzio Inghirami, he of the **Scarith of Scornello** infamy, just couldn't resist "finding"—that is, fabricating—an ever greater number of **fraudulent** Etruscan scrolls). Fujimura's singular luck at finding more and more—and progressively more ancient—archaeological artifacts on Japanese soil made him famous and led to his nickname, "God's Hand." It might sound great to have such an exalted sobriquet—I mean, what archaeologist wouldn't like to be thought of as possessing the hand of God when it comes to finding fabulous archaeological treasure?—but when you seem to be uniquely, almost supernaturally, lucky in that regard, you are bound to generate resentment, jealousy, and skepticism, and that's exactly what happened to Fujimura after playing the role of God's hand for 20 years.

At least one of Fujimura's colleagues in the small community of Japanese archaeologists, Takeoka Toshiki of Kyoritsu Women's University, shared his suspicions with journalists and the *Mainichi Shimbun* newspaper (others may have been suspicious, but none have come out after the fact to admit it). In the best tradition of private detectives checking on the marital fidelity of a spouse who is acting suspiciously or of those endless stings on *60 Minutes* or *To Catch a Predator* on television, *Mainichi Shimbun* set up a hidden camera at the site where Fujimura was working in 2001. Fujimura did not disappoint—well, he didn't disappoint the journalists; he certainly did disappoint the archaeological community of Japan and, ultimately, of the world. The hidden video was clear enough; Fujimura arrived at the site early with a bag of specimens which, he later admitted, were genuinely ancient artifacts he obtained on the Asian mainland. He can then be clearly seen digging a hole and planting the artifacts in sufficiently old layers. *Mainichi Shimbun* held its fire, but didn't need to wait long. The planted artifacts were "found" within days, inspiring Fujimura to hold a joyous press conference in which he announced the discovery of artifacts in Japan dating to in excess of 600,000 years ago—older, in fact, than most archaeological sites on the Asian mainland.

Fujimura did not have long to revel in his new achievement. The newspaper held a press conference the following week exposing his turpitude. Fujimura was busted, but confessed, at least initially, to only two incidents in which he had planted old artifacts at his site. He rationalized his behavior by maintaining that he felt a heavy burden of the expectations of his countrymen to find ever older artifacts, pushing back the glory of Japanese antiquity. He was sorry, but he only did it to uplift his country, and he would never do it again. We all know what happens in all of those police dramas when the dope dealer or child molester or tax evader or whatever finally gets caught but maintains, by some fascinating coincidence, the incident that led to their arrest was, cross-my-heart, the first and only time I've ever done something like that. Right. Further investigation revealed that Fujimura had planted artifacts not just once, as he initially maintained, but at least 42 times. Ultimately, none of the more than 180 sites Fujimura worked on during his 20-year tenure as God's Hand could be trusted.

When Fujimura began finding increasingly ancient artifacts in his native Japan, it was common for archaeologists to assert that "now we will need to rewrite the textbooks." Unfortunately, those rewrites were based on a complex web of deceit. Ironically, after Fujimura's confession and after the additional investigations spawned by his incomplete accounting of his fakery, those textbooks had to be rewritten yet again. They now convey a cultural history that begins not 600,000 years ago but, again, 30,000 years ago. In other words, Japanese antiquity is right back where it started from when Shinichi Fujimura burst onto the scene in 1981.

Fusang

Fusang (sometimes written Fu-Sang) is a place name provided by Hui Shen, a peripatetic fifth-century CE Buddhist missionary who wrote about his travels in 499 (Frost 1982). Hui Shen's discussion of geography is not entirely clear and depends on how you interpret the starting point of his statistics and which definition you accept for the Chinese measure of distance, the *li* (which varied through time). Fusang is 20,000 *li* east of China, which might be anywhere from 4,500 to 6,000 miles (7,000 to 10,000 kilometers).

Hui Shen describes the land of Fusang in great detail: though there was no iron in Fusang, there was plenty of copper; the people had domesticated or at least tamed deer, raising them for food and milk; they had horses and used them for personal transportation; other large animals like buffalo were used to pull carts; and they made a kind of paper from local plants and fruit was a major source of food for the Fusang. They cremated their dead, had a sophisticated, advanced civilization, and had converted to Buddhism when they were visited by missionaries sometime in the mid-fifth century.

Some scholars believe that Fusang is an entirely mythical place and any attempts to identify it with an actual piece of real estate would be the equivalent of trying to situate Middle Earth, Oz, or Shangri-La—an interesting literary exercise, but not a pursuit of real geography. Others disagree and identify Fusang as a muddled description of Japan, which, though not nearly the distance from China that Hui Shen maintains, might nevertheless be the ultimate source for his vague but fascinating account of a country that was not very well known to the Chinese in the fifth and sixth centuries.

Another possibility, if Fusang is not entirely mythical and if we accept its distance from China as presented by Hui Shen, places Fusang in the New World; some would say the coast of California, others British Columbia.

A significant problem with taking any of Hui Shen's descriptions literally rests in the fact that none of them bear any relationship to what we know about New World cultures in the fifth and sixth centuries. There were no horses in the Americas between their extinction here at the end of the Pleistocene (the Ice Age) or the beginning of the Holocene (the modern epoch), around 10,000 years ago, and their reintroduction by the Spanish in the sixteenth century. Though many groups of native people in the New World hunted various species of wild deer, there is no evidence anywhere that they raised, tamed, tended, or domesticated them or that they milked them (in fact, even modern efforts to domesticate deer for meat and hides have been universally unsuccessful). As far as the Buddhist conversion, perhaps it doesn't need saying, but I'll state it anyway: in the ethnohistorical descriptions of the culture of America, there are none that suggest Buddhist beliefs or practices were endemic to the New World in antiquity. Hui Shen's other descriptions of the culture of Fusang's people are so vague and general that they are useless in attempting to identify an actual historical source for his stories.

So we're stuck here. If you are to associate Fusang with any known place, you are forced to ignore significant parts of Hui Shen's story. For it to be Japan, you must ignore the distances he supplies. For it to be the New World, you can accept the distances, but must ignore the cultural descriptions, which don't come close to matching any New World societies. Indeed, it would seem that the most sensible course of action here is to assume that the country of Fusang is essentially mythical.

Large stone anchors found through dredging off the Palos Verdes Peninsula in California in 1975 excited some historians, as they were quite similar to anchors used by Chinese seamen as long ago as 500 CE. As inconclusive as Hui Shen's descriptions had been, maybe these anchors would provide the direct physical evidence needed by archaeologists to support the hypothesis that equated Fusang with California. Perhaps these were the anchors of the ships of Chinese Buddhists who, Hui Shen reports, visited Fusang to convert the natives.

A careful analysis of the **Palos Verdes Stones**, as they were called, however, showed that the rock from which they were made had not originated in China but was, instead, Monterey shale, a rock native to California. The anchor stones were culturally Chinese, but date to Chinese sailors living in California who used traditional sailing vessels—and, it just so happens, traditional stone anchors—in the nineteenth century. Ultimately, no convincing archaeological evidence has been found in North America (California, British Columbia, or anywhere else) for a Chinese Buddhist presence here in the fifth or sixth century.

Further Reading

For a nice summary of the Palos Verdes Stones, see the article in *Archaeology* by Frank Frost, "The Palos Verdes Chinese Anchor Mystery" (1982).

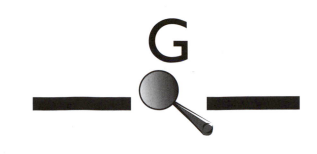

G

Gordon, Cyrus

Cyrus Gordon (1908–2001) was a brilliant university professor and a prolific scholar, especially as an expert in ancient languages, Middle Eastern antiquity, and the Bible. Gordon ventured into controversy when he publicly supported the authenticity of various artifacts ostensibly found in pre-Columbian archaeological contexts in the New World that depicted messages in a number of Old World scripts. Based on Gordon's acceptance of (and translations of) the **Bat Creek Stone** from Tennessee, the Paraiba inscription found in Brazil, and the **Los Lunas Decalogue Stone**, Gordon concluded that the New World had been repeatedly visited and settled by Jews and Phoenicians long before the voyages of exploration by Christopher Columbus in the late fifteenth century and even before the **Norse** excursions to the New World in the late tenth century.

Unfortunately, there is no archaeological evidence to support the assertion that ancient Israelites or Phoenicians voyaged to the Americas in antiquity—no mundane artifacts traceable to these ancient cultures have been found here, no colonial settlements diagnostic of these people exist here, none of their recognizable human remains have been discovered here. Along with the fact that the artifacts that Gordon translated have been shown to have been faked, his conclusions about a Jewish and Phoenician **discovery of America** in antiquity cannot be supported.

Gosford Glyphs

Never known for being particularly peripatetic, it would be remarkable indeed if there was genuine archaeological evidence for the presence of ancient Egyptian travelers in, of all places, Australia. Nevertheless, if the so-called Gosford Glyphs are genuine, the implications would be staggering, proving absolutely that Egyptians had visited Australia in antiquity. However, the Gosford Glyphs are transparent fakes, poorly done and providing further proof for the assertion that an archaeological **fraud** need not be well conceived, well thought out, or well executed to garner a following among the gullible who wish to believe in its legitimacy.

Pictured here is one of the panels of fake Egyptian hieroglyphs found in about the most unlikely place for genuine ancient Egyptian writing: Australia. (Steve Spillard)

First noticed in 1975 in Kariong, a rural district about 37 miles (60 kilometers) north of Sydney (on the southeast coast of Australia), the Gosford Glyphs are a series of about a hundred Egyptian hieroglyphs in an area replete with Aboriginal **petroglyphs** of giant kangaroos and men with spears. Some of the hieroglyphs appear to be genuine in the sense that they appear to be fairly true copies of actual Egyptian written symbols, but none of them are authentically ancient. None were seen before 1975 despite the fact that a local surveyor, Alan Dash, had been visiting the region since 1968. Dash further reports that, after his first encounter with the hieroglyphs in 1975, for the next five years, each time he visited the area new glyphs had appeared. During a visit in 1984, Dash actually discovered the culprit (or perhaps he was one of several) inscribing hieroglyphs into the rock face. Though within the boundaries of an Australian national park and blatantly illegal, the perpetrator was not arrested, as he appeared to be mentally ill.

One might have thought that Dash's eyewitness testimony would have put the nonsense entirely to rest. It hasn't. Claims have been made that the glyphs exhibit too much erosion to be recently made, for example—though geologists deny this, pointing out that the local sandstone is a very soft rock that, in fact, erodes very quickly. The visible weathering of the hieroglyphs belies any notion of great age when compared to the 250-year-old Aborigine petroglyphs in the same area, the erosion of which is far more substantial than is the case for the faux hieroglyphs.

The hieroglyphs themselves, though some look like actual Egyptian writing, make no sense at all, according to Prof. Nageeb Kanawati, the head of the Macquarie University Egyptology department in Sydney. Some of the glyphs are reversed, and some in the same panels are from entirely different periods of Egyptian history. Then there are the entirely un-Egyptian hieroglyphic carvings that include bells, a dog's bone and, it pains me to report, what look suspiciously like flying saucers.

The Gosford Glyphs are a transparent fraud, at least some of which were produced by a mentally handicapped man whose motives are obscure, and others of which have been recently produced by people whose time might be better spent in other pursuits. Ancient Egypt was a remarkable culture, very advanced in architecture, construction, and engineering, but there is no evidence that they made any transoceanic voyages at all and certainly not to Australia in particular. The only conclusions that can be drawn from the Gosford Glyphs are that some folks need to find a better outlet for their creative expression and that the gullibility of some people is boundless.

Grand Canyon Lost Civilization

On April 5, 1909, the *Phoenix Gazette* published an astonishing article based on the testimony of a G. E. Kincaid concerning the discovery of evidence of an ancient Egyptian outpost, represented by an enormous, underground citadel carved into the sandstone of a wall within the Grand Canyon in Arizona. The discovery, or at least its investigation, had been done, according to Kincaid, by Prof. S. A. Jordan of the "Smithsonian Institute." According to the newspaper article, Professor Jordan had explored a vast underground network of interlinking tunnels and gigantic, artificially carved chambers deep within the walls of the Grand Canyon, some nearly a mile underground. Kincaid claimed that, after extensive investigation of the subterranean world, Jordan estimated that as many as an astonishing 50,000 people could have inhabited the complex.

Within this subterranean world, according to the article, Jordan encountered an enormous assemblage of remarkable artifacts, all of which reflected the source of their makers—most likely ancient Egypt—and the great sophistication of their technology. Jordan found copper weapons as hard as steel, enameled and glazed ceramic vessels (the native people of the New World did not apply glaze to their ceramics), and objects made of a gray metal scientists could not identify, though it was similar to platinum.

One of the subterranean passageways led to a room that appeared to be a shrine housing a large idol resembling not any known Egyptian god but, instead,

Buddha, replete with the requisite lotus flower in each hand. Within the shrine, Professor Jordan is alleged to have found walls and urns covered with hieroglyphs—although, to continue the unbounded weirdness of Kincaid's report, the writing was not that of Egypt but most resembled writing of the **Maya** region of the Yucatan Peninsula of Mexico. Finally, Jordan located a great crypt filled with mummies, but only those of adult men; there were apparently no women or children in this rather odd and improbable alternate universe.

So, let's review: A highly sophisticated ancient civilization constructed a huge and elaborate, mile-deep underground complex capable of housing 50,000 people, at some time in the distant past. These people were technologically sophisticated, wrote in a language that resembled Maya, were Buddhists, and consisted entirely of men. Oh my.

If you'd like to examine any physical evidence of this mysterious, fascinating, **lost civilization** of the Grand Canyon, you're going to need a vivid imagination. There is absolutely no evidence for any of this fevered nonsense (Colavito 2005). Not a single artifact, hieroglyph, mummy, copper weapon, unidentifiable gray metal artifact. Nothing. Zero. Zip.

Beyond the complete lack of any confirming archaeological evidence for the Egyptian-Maya-Buddhist civilization in the Grand Canyon, no one who has looked into the source of the article has ever been able to trace G. E. Kincaid (there is no evidence that he ever existed). As to Professor Jordan, there is no record of any such person actually working for or with the Smithsonian Institution or even the "Smithsonian Institute."

What is, perhaps, the most fascinating element of this hoax is the response of those who want desperately, for whatever reasons, to believe it, despite being faced with the simple fact that there is not a scintilla of direct physical evidence to prove it. For lost civilization boosters, the lack of evidence—and the inability to locate Kincaid and Jordan—is interpreted as confirmation that the story is true! How is that possible? The lack of evidence is itself interpreted as evidence of—are you ready?—a cover-up.

Please understand the significance of this interpretation, as it is a textbook case of a pseudoscience, because there is no way to falsify or disprove the claim or hypothesis. One of the hallmarks of science is falsifiability. By that I mean, in order for a hypothesis to be *scientific*, it must be testable; there must be some way of evaluating its truth or falsity, a way to prove it false if it is, in fact, incorrect. A bogus or *nonscientific* hypothesis is one that cannot be disproved, no matter what. For believers of the lost civilization of the Grand Canyon and other such fanciful theories, their belief cannot be shaken regardless of the outcome of any scientific investigation. Either there is direct, archaeological evidence of the discoveries reported by Professor Jordan or, if there is no evidence (and no Jordan), then it must be the result of a vast conspiracy to hide the truth. Do you see the madness of this mode of reasoning? The hypothesis can never be proven wrong. This method of reasoning is intrinsically, irredeemably, and irrevocably nonscientific. Belief in the lost Grand Canyon civilization by writers like David Hatcher Childress, who wrote *Lost Cities in North and Central America*, is in fact far more like a religion then a science-based hypothesis.

Further Reading

You can read the 1909 *Phoenix Gazette* article about the Grand Canyon lost civilization at http://grandcanyontreks.org/fiction.htm. Then check out Jason Colavito's thorough debunking of the hoax, titled "Archaeological Coverup?" at http://jcolavito.tripod.com/lostcivilizations/id8.html.

Grave Creek Stone

There are a number of entries in this book in which I present the stories of fraudulent artifacts on which messages of various and sometimes multiple ancient Old World written languages were ostensibly discovered within the soils of ancient American earthworks in the nineteenth century (e.g., the **Bat Creek Stone**, the **Davenport Tablets**, **the Michigan Relics,** and the **Newark Holy Stones**). In each of these instances, until their fraudulent nature was exposed, the artifacts were viewed by some as valuable contributions to a possible solution of the **moundbuilder** mystery, important data that would allow the revelation of who the true moundbuilders had been, where they had come from—Europe, Asia, or Africa—and when they had constructed their elaborate earthworks in North America.

Because the moundbuilder mystery generated so much interest—and acrimony—in nineteenth-century America, and maybe especially because so much seemed to be riding on its solution, there were those who felt justified in concocting fake artifacts that would seem to substantiate their favored hypothesis concerning the origins of the North American earthworks. To be sure, proof of who the perpetrators were in each case is extremely hard to come by; I'm not sure, concerning any of those suggested in this work, that there is evidence—nothing "beyond a reasonable doubt"—sufficient to convict any of them in a court of law today. Without knowing definitively who the perps were, it's impossible to prove definitively what their motives were. However, whether it involved proof of monogenesis (**Newark Holy Stones**) or of a Jewish connection with the mounds (**Newark Holy Stones, Bat Creek Stone**), those motives likely involved swaying thinkers toward a particular solution to the mystery of who built the mounds—a lie, to be sure, but a white lie that would bring people to the truth, at least the "truth" as the hoaxers viewed it.

The Grave Creek Stone is a forged inscription found in a mound located in West Virginia. Like a few of the other fake inscriptions ostensibly found in American burial mounds in the nineteenth century, the Grave Creek inscription reflects an impossible mash-up of a number of Old World scripts. (Grave Creek Mound Archaeological Complex, West Virginia Division of Culture and History)

At the same time, it seems to be the case, among scientists and nonscientists alike, that there were people who, when confronted with artifacts that seemed to support their favored explanation as to who the moundbuilders were, checked their skepticism at the door and embraced specimens that, with a little application of common sense, they should have realized were highly questionable and likely fraudulent. **Cyrus Thomas**, for example, should have been a lot more skeptical about the Bat Creek Stone and the relationship of its inscription to the Cherokee syllabary developed only in the nineteenth century. Thomas, however, seems to have been a victim of his own desire to find archaeological validation for his hypothesis that Cherokee Indians were responsible for the construction of at least some of the mounds of the American Southeast and mid-South.

I tell you all of this to set the stage for discussion of the Grave Creek Stone. The most likely motive for the Grave Creek **fraud** is different. Instead of providing proof for a favored explanation of the mounds, the motive was far simpler and baser: money. As shown by the fascinating bit of detective work conducted by anthropologist David Oestreicher (2008), the motive behind the Grave Creek Stone was simply to make a pile of cash by exploiting the desire of so many to solve the moundbuilder mystery, especially in a way that showed that Native Americans had not been responsible for their construction.

The story of the Grave Creek Stone as revealed by Oestreicher begins with Dr. James W. Clemens in Wheeling, West Virginia, in 1838. Though a successful physician, Clemens apparently wanted do something more significant with his life than heal the sick and, at the same time, was experiencing significant financial difficulties. Killing two birds with one stone, Clemens, it seems, became involved in a scheme to excavate Grave Creek Mound in order to reveal and make money from the riches he was convinced lay within.

Grave Creek Mound was located in the far western margin of West Virginia, near that state's border with Ohio, on private property. It is a substantial earthwork, a conical burial mound measuring 69 feet (21 meters) in height and a diameter of some 295 feet (90 meters) at its circular base. According to Oestreicher, the owners had resisted previous attempts by diggers to excavate the mound, but that changed in 1838 when the owners signed a contract with a number of men to allow excavation; the contract also stipulated the way in which any treasures revealed would be distributed. A group of amateur archaeologists—really just a bunch of folks with shovels acting essentially like artifact miners—had convinced the landowners that the mound on their property would produce a trove of valuable objects sufficient to make them all—owners and diggers—fabulously wealthy and nationally famous. It is entirely unclear on what this extremely optimistic prediction was based.

Contracts between landowners, diggers, investors, and excavation underwriters were fairly common in archaeological excavations in the nineteenth and even into the early twentieth century. For example, Lord Carnarvon, the British earl who funded archaeologist **Howard Carter**'s excavation of **King Tut's** tomb, had just such a contract drawn up between himself and Carter, specifying ownership of the artifacts discovered during digging.

Though there is no direct linkage between Clemens and the signatories of the Grave Creek Mound excavation contract, Oestreicher suggests that similarities in the wording of an anonymous newspaper article trumpeting the incredible riches—historical, cultural, and economic, that almost certainly lay within the mound—and a speech Clemens gave at Franklin College about the moundbuilder mystery strongly suggest that Clemens was the author of the article and intimately connected to the excavation project. Oestreicher also found that Clemens had borrowed $2,600 around the time of the mound excavation contract signing. One way in which money was to be made was by soliciting investments in the excavation; investors were told they would reap financial benefit from the sale of the fabulous treasures that were sure to be found. It seems likely that Clemens was one of those investors.

The anonymous newspaper article likely written by Clemens was a model of moundbuilder mystery speculation, predicting that within its soil, diggers would discover "relics which would establish without a doubt a wonder of the world." The author of the piece asserted that Grave Creek Mound had been built by a people present in the New World before the Indians and that the artifacts found within would prove this fact and settle the question of who built the mounds for once and for all.

The actual excavation of Grave Creek Mound—the process bore little relation to archaeological excavation and had far more in common with mining—indeed revealed objects wonderful from the perspective of an archaeologist. The dig unearthed two human skeletons, some copper bracelets, and a handful of shell beads, but the hoard of hoped-for treasures did not materialize. Examination of the artifacts by modern archaeologists reveals the mound to belong to the Adena culture, likely dating to more than 2,000 years ago.

Before long, it became clear that no one was going to get rich off of Grave Creek Mound, there would be no great museum built there that would attract thousands of tourists from the world over, there would be no solution to the moundbuilder mystery—at least not one that involved non-Indians—and there would be no assemblage of artifacts rivaling those found in the tombs of Egyptian pharaohs.

Clemens, for one, must have been devastated. His participation in the Grave Creek Mound dig would not make him famous, represent an enormous contribution to science or history, or secure a place for him in the pantheon of major archaeologists; it would certainly not make him rich. Clemens or whoever had written the newspaper article had wildly oversold the archaeological and economic potential of Grave Creek Mound, and there was a host of at least disappointed and at worst extremely angry investors to contend with.

Though there was no Tut's tomb secreted within the soil of Grave Creek Mound, Clemens apparently did have a "plan B." Returning to the mound after discovering a second burial chamber at its base, Clemens personally made a spectacular and curious discovery. It wasn't gold or lapis lazuli, no pharaoh's treasure, to be sure, but there was, according to Clemens, something equally significant and maybe just as valuable: a small (just two inches/five centimeters in diameter) oval disc exhibiting 22 inscribed hieroglyphs. As the local Indians were not known to have a writing system and the hieroglyphs appeared to be a mash-up of a number of ancient scripts, including Egyptian, Phoenician, Celtic, and Norse, the Grave Creek Stone, as it was called, seemed to reflect evidence of an Old World origin for the mound in which it had been discovered.

Perhaps all was not lost. Even though there wasn't gold or silver, ivory or brass, diamonds or emeralds in the mound, something of enormous historical value—and, perhaps, of inestimable monetary value, as well—had been found in Grave Creek Mound, an object that would solve the moundbuilder mystery or, at least, prove that it wasn't Indians who had built the mounds.

The hieroglyphs on the Grave Creek Stone did not match the writing on other inscribed tablets found in mounds in the nineteenth century. The Grave Creek Stone's writing wasn't consistent with that found on the Davenport Tablet, the Newark Holy Stones, or the Bat Creek Stone; the jokers who produced these stones obviously didn't coordinate their frauds. The Grave Creek Stone has even less to recommend its authenticity than does the Bat Creek Stone or the Newark Holy Stones; at least those were internally consistent, presenting messages in a single consistent language. The individual elements on the Grave Creek Stone (like the Davenport Tablets and the inscribed Michigan Relics) were from a number of different ancient Old World scripts, so, of course, it can't be read, any more than you could coax out a sensible message from a random series of characters taken from the Roman, **Chinese**, Sanskrit, and **Mayan** alphabets.

Researcher Oestreicher puts the final nail in the coffin of the Grave Creek Stone's authenticity when he points out that the individual hieroglyphic elements seen on the Grave Creek Stone can all be found in a 1752 book written by a Spanish historian, *An Essay on the Alphabets of the Unknown Letters That Are Found in the Most Ancient Coins and Monuments of Spain*. Oestreicher found instances where the same nonsensical sequences of characters printed in the book turn up on the Grave Creek Stone. He concludes from this that Clemens must have had a copy of the book in his possession—it is known that he had a large collection of books in his personal library—and used it as a source for the Grave Creek Stone, grabbing random bits of various languages as presented in the book.

Adding insult to injury, though the Grave Creek Stone had its supporters, it did nothing to save Clemens's reputation or his financial condition. He ended up selling his home to pay off his personal debts. The artifact itself disappeared just 30 years after its discovery and may have been sold to the British Museum, where it may still be hidden away in storage. Fortunately, a cast was made and a replica is on display at the Grave Creek Mound Museum, a new, state-of-the-art facility that opened in 2008.

Further Reading

To get the full story of the Grave Creek Stone, read the article by David Oestreicher (2008). The Web site of the Grave Creek Mound Archaeological Complex is www.wvculture.org/museum/GraveCreekmod.html.

Great Sphinx

Along with **Stonehenge** in England and the trio of **Egyptian pyramids** at Giza, there is no ancient monument more iconic of human antiquity than the Great Sphinx (actually located next to the Giza pyramids). With the recumbent body of a lion and the head of a man, the Great Sphinx is the largest of a series of

The Great Sphinx was the largest, but by no means the only, Egyptian depiction of a creature with the body of a lion and the head of a man. The Great Sphinx is part of the pharaoh Khafre's funerary complex and likely dates to 2550 BCE. (M.H. Feder)

similarly carved man-lion chimeras. Carved in what is usually referred to as "living rock," meaning it was sculpted from an in-place limestone bedrock deposit, the Great Sphinx is 240 feet (73 meters) long from the end of its front paws to its hindquarters, and 66 feet (20 meters) high at its tallest point, the top of its human head.

The limestone from which the sphinx is sculpted was left in place while the rock from around it was quarried away for use in construction of the nearby pyramids and ancillary structures. The limestone occurs in horizontal bands of lighter, soft rock and harder, darker stone. These alternating bands can be seen quite clearly in the body of the sphinx, where the softer rock has eroded to a greater degree than the harder layers. The head of the sphinx is made up almost entirely of a thicker layer of the hard, dark limestone. As a result, the face is better preserved than the body; the sculptors may have chosen the rock for exactly that reason, knowing that the face would withstand the natural processes of erosion. During its lifetime, parts of the Great Sphinx were sheathed in stone masonry; this brickwork can be seen most clearly today on the front paws, sides, and rear end.

The style of the sculpted face of the Great Sphinx matches that seen in Egypt during the 4th dynasty of the Old Kingdom, the same period during which the Giza pyramids were constructed (2575 to 2467 BCE). Its location, along a causeway leading back to the pharaoh Khafre's pyramid, and a comparison of the face seen in the Great Sphinx and in known and identified sculpted depictions of Khafre have led Egyptologists to ascribe the Great Sphinx to Khafre's reign, the sculptors depicting the great pharaoh as a monumental lion.

Three essential myths and mysteries surround the Great Sphinx today. The first is perhaps the easiest to dispense with. You will commonly read and hear that the Sphinx's nose was shot off at the order of the visiting French general, Napoleon Bonaparte. This is not true. The nose was already gone when Napoleon visited the region in 1798–1801.

The second legend states that there are hidden chambers beneath or within the monument in which spectacular secrets of the ancient world were housed, perhaps left behind by residents of the Lost Continent of **Atlantis**. Such a **Hall of Records** was noted during his trances by **Edgar Cayce**. Explorers and archaeologists have identified three real chambers at the base of the Great Sphinx; these are historically known and contain no records or, for that matter, anything else.

Remote-sensing technologies have been applied to the issue of hidden chambers in or around the Great Sphinx. Specifically, in the late 1970s, partially funded by the Edgar Cayce Research Foundation, researchers conducted an electrical resistivity survey of the soils around the Sphinx. An electrical resistivity survey is a tried-and-true method in archaeology where an electric current is passed through a medium (soil, for example), and areas where there are differences or anomalies in the medium's resistance to the flow of the electrical current are assessed for the possibility of being buried artifacts or features like interments, hearths, or trash pits. The sphinx survey worked exactly as researchers hoped it would, revealing genuine electrical resistance anomalies in the bedrock beneath the monument's rear paws. However, no Hall of Records was found; drilling into the anomalies revealed that they were natural pockets in the limestone from which the Sphinx was constructed (Jordan 1998). In the early 1990s, again funded by the Edgar Cayce Research Foundation, additional electrical anomalies were found, this time on the side of the Sphinx and under its front paws. The Egyptian authorities have denied permission for any additional digging or drilling to test the significance of these anomalies, fearing, I suppose, that damage to the monument will occur in a fruitless search for a nonexistent chamber beneath it.

Myth number three has to do with the age of the sphinx. Geologist Robert Schoch has examined the degree of erosion of the Great Sphinx and suggests that the form and degree of erosion of the monument is more in keeping with weathering caused by water, as opposed to the standard explanation of windblown sand. The area of Giza, however, has not seen the kind of climate capable of producing that degree of water erosion since the commonly accepted date of construction, that is, about 2500 BCE. Schoch therefore suggests, instead, that the Great Sphinx was more likely built in a far earlier period, before 5500 BCE and perhaps as much as 7500 BCE (almost 10,000 years ago).

Schoch's geological argument is rejected by the vast majority of Egyptologists for a number of reasons, including:

1. The positioning and style of the Great Sphinx match it perfectly with the culture and time period of the Giza pyramids, about 2500 BCE. In other words, the Great Sphinx is not a surprising monument for that time period.
2. The Great Sphinx appears to be an integral part of the funerary complex of the pharaoh Khafre.
3. Though admittedly a subjective impression, the face of the Great Sphinx is a pretty close approximation of other artistic depictions of Khafre.

The final and primary reason for rejecting an earlier period for the construction of the Great Sphinx, however, is that there is no evidence whatsoever for a culture capable of building the Great Sphinx much before the traditionally accepted date. A large and impressive monument like the Great Sphinx cannot have built itself; there must have been a social and practical infrastructure in place to accomplish that task. In other words, only a culture with a pattern of social stratification and the capability to enlist the labor of a large pool of workers would have been capable of building the Great Sphinx, and for the period predating 2500 BCE, there is no evidence at all of such a culture—no complex settlements with substantial populations, no social hierarchy reflected in inequality in housing or burials. There is no sign at all of an infrastructure necessary to support a large population of workers, no sign of the ability to produce a large agricultural surplus to feed the construction workers, no evidence of dormitories for housing them, no huge storage facilities for food, no great bakeries, no cemeteries in which to bury the workers who would have died during the construction project. These kind of infrastructure elements *are* found dating to 2500 BCE to support the vast workforce called upon to build the pyramids. Almost certainly, that same workforce built the Great Sphinx, probably as a tribute to their pharaoh Khafre. No archaeological evidence supports the hypothesis of a substantially older date for the monument.

Further Reading
The best work focusing on the Great Sphinx is Paul Jordan's 1998 book *Riddles of the Sphinx*. Paul Jordan is a terrific researcher and a marvelous writer. I highly recommend this book.

Gungywamp

Gungywamp is a site located in Groton, Connecticut, that consists of a complex of stone walls, foundations, stone chambers, and a stone circle. Some have claimed

The Gungywamp site is located in southeastern Connecticut. A fascinating place, some suggest that it was constructed by pre-Columbian, seafaring explorers from the Old World, claiming that the circular feature (left) reflects a non-native ceremonial practice. However, the stone ring is almost certainly the remains of a bark mill like the one shown in the photograph on the right. (K. Feder)

that the site is ancient and was built by pre-Columbian European settlers to the New World, most likely **Celts**. Archaeological excavations, however, have never revealed even a single artifact diagnostic of the styles that typify ancient Celts, and no artifacts have been found at the site in a pre-Columbian context made of raw materials whose source is in western Europe, which, from an archaeological standpoint, precludes the presence of a population of ancient Celts (see **Discovery of America**). The stone chambers found at the site are similar to cold storage facilities usually used as root cellars in colonial farmsteads. Assertions that these storage facilities are **astronomically aligned**—and therefore reflective of an ancient Celtic pattern, like that shown at **Stonehenge**—are partially true: as storage facilities for root crops, the chambers were intentionally aligned with their openings to the rising of the winter sun in the southern sky in order to avoid too hard of a freeze, as eighteenth- and nineteenth-century publications for farmers (not ancient Druids) advised.

Perhaps the most interesting and, for some, provocative feature at Gungywamp is a double circle of low lying, curved stones. Some have suggested this feature was ceremonial and reminiscent of the ancient stone circles of western Europe, although the stones in the double circle at Gungywamp are not upright, like the megalithic stone circles, but recumbent. In fact, the Gungywamp circle likely is the remnant of an animal-powered bark mill, a small, typical, colonial facility for extracting tannin from bark to be used in leathermaking. An upright mill wheel would have been set into the double circle with a horizontal axle running through it to a central, vertical post. When draft animals were harnessed to the horizontal axle and walked in a circle, they would cause the mill wheel to turn and move around within the double circle of stones, crushing whatever was placed on the ground in front of it. Similar mills were used as the first step in a two-step process of apple cider production (Quinion 2008). In the first step, apple pulp was produced by turning the vertical mill wheel over the apples placed in the trough between the stone rings. The pulp was then transported to a cider press bedstone (like the so-called sacrificial table at **America's Stonehenge**) where the juice was extracted in the second step in cider production.

That the remnant of an animal-powered bark mill or a mill used in the production of apple cider can be mistaken for a Celtic ritual site is a product of cultural amnesia. In the twenty-first century, we are far removed from a time, a culture, and a technology that utilized things like bark or apple pulp mills (or lye stones or cider press bedstones; see **America's Stonehenge**). When confronted by the archaeological remains of such things, we make up stories based on our ignorance. To be sure, an ancient Celtic temple in the woods of southeastern Connecticut may seem to reflect a more romantic scenario than a colonial bark or cider mill. But **Occam's Razor** and the extant evidence lead us to a conclusion that involves not goddess-worshipping Celts, but frugal and industrious nineteenth-century farmers.

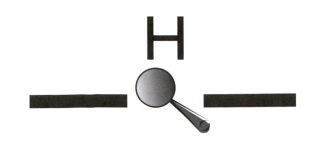

Hall of Records

The Hall of Records, in the context of this book, is a reputed place or structure (or places or structures; in some accounts, there is more than one Hall of Records), ostensibly located in Egypt, within which secret records of the ancients were stored. When these records are finally located and revealed, our traditional understanding of human history will need dramatic revision.

In the version of a story told by the so-called sleeping prophet **Edgar Cayce**, around 10,500 BCE escapees from the Lost Continent of **Atlantis** arrived in Egypt with a library of records that represented the greater part of their cultural heritage. According to Cayce, the Hall of Records is the repository of these Atlantean records. He explained that the remnant population of Atlanteans built the largest of the **Egyptian pyramids**, **Khufu**'s at Giza, as well as the **Great Sphinx**. While Cayce never placed the Hall of Records in a hidden chamber within or underneath the Sphinx and it's not entirely clear where he thought it was located, others have read the sphinx's location into Cayce's story.

Crews supported in part by the Edgar Cayce Research Foundation have searched for the Hall of Records near the Great Sphinx. Using remote-sensing equipment in an attempt to peer through the limestone from which the sphinx was sculpted, researchers have found pockets of lower densities, but when these have been investigated by drilling into the rock, no great voids have been found, only natural pockets in the rock. No geological or archaeological evidence has been found to support the notion of a great room within or beneath the Great Sphinx.

Cayce also is purported to have asserted that there were additional Halls of Records, one associated with Atlantis itself (and, therefore, located under the waters of the Atlantic) and another associated with the **Maya**, somewhere in the Yucatan Peninsula. However, Cayce also predicted that the Hall of Records would be discovered, opened, and its material revealed to the world in 1998. Its revelation was to usher in a new world order and presage the Second Coming of Christ.

The bottom line: There isn't any evidence that supports the claim that there is a Hall of anything, much less a hall of ancient Atlantean records, under the Great Sphinx in Egypt or anywhere else, for that matter. In that sense, the Hall of Records has something very significant with its source, Atlantis: they are both entirely fictitious.

Hancock, Graham

Graham Hancock (1950–) is a British writer, with no background or training in archaeology, who has written several best-selling books with the underlying theme that orthodox archaeology has it all, or at least mostly, wrong. Hancock suggests that a **lost civilization** far more ancient than Egypt or Mesopotamia stands at the root of human cultural evolution. The ancient Egyptians, Mesopotamians, **Maya**, and others, in Hancock's estimation, all developed not as the result of their own trajectory of cultural evolution or development but, imperfectly, as inheritors of the great lost civilization that he asserts dominated the world in the distant past, but was destroyed 10,500 years ago in some sort of cataclysm.

Hancock's books are, essentially, works of fiction. Throughout his works, he points to the achievements of ancient people and questions the idea that they would have been capable on their own, without assistance, of accomplishing the great feats reflected in the archaeological record. Among his more egregious allegations, in *Fingerprints of the Gods*, Hancock (1995) questions the sophistication of the ancient Maya and expresses doubt that they were able to develop the very sophisticated calendrical systems they clearly used. Hancock betrays his ignorance of the achievements of the Maya, calling them "semi-civilized" and "generally unremarkable." This is terrible nonsense and bears no relationship to the actual culture and achievements of the Maya. In any event, there isn't a shred of evidence to back up Hancock's claims.

Harmonic Convergence

On August 16 and 17, 1987, all over the world, people congregated in various special locations to mark the beginning of a new age. The geographical foci chosen were supposed "sacred sites," including **Mystery Hill**, **Serpent Mound**, and Cahokia (Peterson 1988). The moment was one apparently resonant with earthshaking possibilities, for it heralded the beginning of a change in the trajectory of human evolution and history.

This was not because August 16, 1987, was the tenth anniversary of the death of Elvis Presley, though that irony (or perhaps it was a joke after all) seems to have been lost on the true believers. No, those days had been singled out in a very popular book, *The Mayan Factor: The Path beyond Technology*, by Jose Arguelles. He called that two-day period (conveniently on a weekend so the celebrants wouldn't have to take a day off from work) the Harmonic Convergence (1987, 170).

In that book, Arguelles argues that the **Maya** weren't just regular folks but were, instead, intergalactic beings who visited the Earth. They were not the crude, high-tech types of **Erich von Däniken**'s fantasy, cruising the universe in spaceships. Instead the Maya were beings who could "transmit themselves as DNA code information from one star system to another" (59). Their purpose on Earth, again according to Arguelles, is rather obscure (to me, at least):

> The totality of the interaction between the Earth's larger life and the individual and group responses to this greater life define "planet art." In this large process, I dimly perceive the Maya as being the navigators or charters of the waters of galactic synchronization. (37)

If that doesn't quite clear it up for you, Arguelles adds that the Maya are here on Earth "to make sure that the galactic harmonic pattern, not perceivable as yet to our evolutionary position in the galaxy, had been presented and recorded" (73). Well, there you go.

Apparently, the Maya, who are actually from the star Arcturus in the Pleiades cluster, materialized in Mesoamerica a number of times as "galactic agents." They introduced writing and other aspects of civilization to the Olmec as part of some quite vague plan to incorporate humanity into some sort of cosmic club.

Arguelles should be given credit (or, rather, the blame) for being one of the first authors to claim that the end of the Maya cycle of time that began in 3113 BCE—the current *baktun*—will end on December 21, **2012** CE. Arguelles is not one of the doomsayers who claim that the world will come to a catastrophic end on that date, though. Instead, he states that the Maya are on their way back to Earth via "galactic synchronization beams," traveling by way of "chromo-molecular transport" (169). The Maya will arrive on December 21, 2012, not to witness the destruction of Earth but to usher in a new age related to, in Arguelles's incomprehensible and utterly meaningless phrasing, the "re-impregnation of the planetary field with the archetypal harmonic experiences of the planetary whole" (170). Of course.

Surprisingly (not), there is no reference to archaeological evidence or any sort of scientific testing for the speculations of Arguelles. There are no insights concerning the Maya and their civilization. The Harmonic Convergence ultimately was little more than a rather silly exercise based not on a scientific understanding of the ancient Maya but on some vague hope that the world will improve if we just wish it would.

Heavener Runestone

Located in the rather improbable location of eastern Oklahoma, the Heavener Runestone is an ostensible record of the visit of a group of **Norsemen** to the American Midwest. The stone itself is about 12 feet (3.7 meters) tall and 10 feet

This short runic inscription was found on a stone located in Oklahoma, not the most likely place for a band of seafaring Norsemen to leave their mark. (Lyle Tompsen)

(3 meters) wide. The runic inscription is positioned on the bottom third of the stone and consists of a short string of eight characters called *runes*.

Runes were a form of writing in Germanic languages, including Norse. The earliest runic writing samples found date to as early as the first century CE, but most are from after the third century. Runic writing was largely replaced by Latin during the medieval period, but there are authentic runes that date to as late as the eighteenth century.

All of the indisputably authentic runes—all 6,000 or so of the extant examples—are located in Europe. An estimated 100 runic inscriptions, at approximately 50 sites, have been reported in North America (primarily in New England and eastern Canada) and have been used to support the hypothesis that ancient Norse travelers visited the New World before Columbus, leaving a written record of their presence (Fitzhugh and Ward 2000). None have been validated by runic experts, but the significance and authenticity of at least some have been vigorously debated. Perhaps the most significant of these "runestones," with its rather long and detailed inscription, is the **Kensington Stone** in Minnesota.

The presence of the Heavener Runestone with its purported ancient Viking inscription was reported to the Smithsonian Institution in 1923, although there may be references to the stone nearly 100 years before this.

Seven of the eight characters on the stone are identified as a form of runic writing called Elder Futhark; the eighth inscribed mark cannot be accurately characterized. The precise form of Elder Futhark used in a runic inscription is an indication of its age. Unfortunately, because the Heavener inscription is short and some of the runic forms are a bit ambiguous, the particular version of Elder Futhark used cannot be precisely determined. A detailed examination of the details of the Heavener runes suggests a date of either sometime between the third and fifth centuries or else a bit later, between the seventh and ninth centuries (Tompsen 2008, 14).

Could the Heavener runic inscription be genuine, evidence of a Norse presence in Oklahoma at least 700 years before Columbus made landfall in the Caribbean? It seems unlikely. In contrast to the Kensington Runestone, which presents the translator with a cogent and meaningful statement, the Heavener runes, as researcher Lyle Tompsen states in his master's thesis, are in "no coherent sequence and appear somewhat nonsensical" (2008, 18). It should be further pointed out that, just as was the case with the Kensington Stone and as even supporters of that inscription's authenticity admit, there is no archaeological evidence whatsoever for a Norse presence in the vicinity of the Heavener Runestone specifically or in Oklahoma or the American Midwest generally. There are no Norse artifacts, no Norse settlements, nothing in the form of material archaeological evidence that would certainly have been left behind by a band of Vikings traveling through the region and stopping long enough to leave an apparently meaningless runic inscription along the way. Such evidence *has* been found in eastern Canada and proves a Norse presence there; it seems unlikely that the Norse would get significantly more fastidious about leaving any evidence behind of their presence in Oklahoma.

In the end, there is very little to recommend the authenticity of the Heavener Runestone. Tompsen (2008, 21) points out that the letters are too large; the diagonal strokes in individual runes are discontinuous, unlike all other reported runes; the distance between individual runes is greater and less regular than seen in authentic inscriptions; and if the stone was used to mark a territory, as has been suggested by some authenticity supporters, it would be unique among runestones. Thompsen concludes his analysis of the Heavener Runestone by admitting that there is no definitively damning evidence of it being a hoax, but he leans toward the interpretation that it is most likely a nineteenth-century **fraud**.

Heyerdahl, Thor

Thor Heyerdahl (1914–2002) was a Norwegian adventurer with an abiding interest in anthropology and archaeology. He had a particular fascination with the people and cultures of the Pacific. He also had a special interest and expertise in the seafaring abilities of ancient people and became convinced that eastern

Polynesia, specifically, Easter Island (called Rapa Nui by the native Polynesians who live there), was initially populated by migrants not from islands to the west, as most anthropologists thought, but by Native Americans living to the east, on the coast of South America.

Heyerdahl's primary claim to fame was a replicative experiment in transpacific transportation he organized in order to test his hypothesis that the Easter Islanders were actually South American Indians. He oversaw the construction of a raft he called the ***Kon-Tiki***, built of appropriate materials, including light and buoyant logs of balsa wood, ostensibly based on artistic depictions by European visitors to South America of local Indian watercraft.

No one should question Heyerdahl's courage or his singular dedication to testing a hypothesis. He was also a bright, articulate, fascinating individual and possessed an abiding respect and admiration for the native people of Polynesia. However, because of significant problems with the specific construction of the *Kon-Tiki* itself (it was not, in fact, an authentic replica of any native South American Indian watercraft) and the fact that Heyerdahl and his crew brought canned food and used modern navigation instruments—and because the archaeological, linguistic, and biological records simply didn't support his hypothesis that Easter Islanders were really South American Indian migrants into the Pacific—he never garnered the acceptance of professional anthropologists or archaeologists. More recent DNA analysis shows conclusively that the natives of Easter Island, like the rest of the people of Polynesia, came from Southeast Asia and not South America.

During the time he spent on Easter Island, Heyerdahl conducted valuable research on the **Easter Island moai**, the famous megalithic statues that are so iconic of the ancient culture of Rapa Nui. He oversaw a replicative project on the island in which natives quarried, carved, transported, and erected a moai. Heyerdahl showed conclusively in the experiment that, with a bit of ingenuity, the application of a little muscle, and the coordination of the labors of a group of dedicated people, the statues were completely within the abilities of the people who lived on the island. He even participated in a deconstruction of **Erich von Däniken**'s **ancient astronaut hypothesis**, belittling the notion that the moai must have been made by extraterrestrial aliens.

Heyerdahl tried to replicate his success—at least the success he experienced in terms of fame and public interest in his work—with two attempted transatlantic crossings in papyrus boats, the *Ra* and the *Ra II*. Like the *Kon-Tiki*, the *Ra* craft were ostensibly based on an aboriginal boat design, in this case of ancient Egypt. With the *Ra* boats, Heyerdahl's goal was more general than it was for the *Kon-Tiki*. Primarily he wanted to show that ancient watercraft were seaworthy, not necessarily that Egyptians had visited the New World in antiquity. The first *Ra* ended up sinking like a stone. The second was not based on an Egyptian design, but was built by Bolivian Indians based on their native boats on Lake Titicaca. The *Ra II* was much more seaworthy and survived the Atlantic crossing. But it is unclear exactly what it proved to sail a Bolivian Indian style of boat from Africa to the New World.

Heyerdahl's main contribution to archaeology and anthropology rests primarily in his popularizing the fields by organizing and conducting interesting and exciting projects.

Holly Oak Pendant

Like the **Lenape Stone**, with its apparent depiction of an animal that had become extinct in North America more than 10,000 years ago, the Holly Oak Pendant was accepted as authentic by many when it was discovered in the middle of the nineteenth century. The pendant, found in Delaware, appeared to be an incised drawing on shell of a prehistoric woolly mammoth. It reminded many of the Paleolithic cave paintings and carvings of the Europe of 20,000 years ago, convincing some of the existence of a similar—and similarly ancient—artistic tradition in North America.

While the Lenape Stone cannot be dated directly and therefore cannot be shown definitively to be of the correct age to be genuine, the shell in the Holly Oak pendant itself has been analyzed using the technique of radiocarbon dating (Griffin, Meltzer, and Smith 1988). In this procedure, the remains of once-living things (bones, wood, seeds, antlers, hide, nuts, shell, etc.) can be dated by reference to the amount of a radioactive isotope of carbon, carbon-14, left in the object. Carbon-14 decays at a regular, known rate and thus serves as a sort of atomic clock. It is quite useful to archaeologists when dating objects more than a few hundred and less than 60,000 years old.

The Holly Oak Pendant, if genuine, should have dated to more than 10,000 years ago, since that is about the time that woolly mammoths became extinct— obviously, people would not have been drawing mammoths long after they had disappeared. In fact, the shell turned out to be only about 1,000 years old. The artifact was a fake, though cleverly carved on an old piece of shell. Certainly, there is no reason why an ancient American could not have carved the image of a woolly mammoth on a shell (or, in the case of the Lenape Stone, a piece of slate), but the evidence shows definitively that the Holly Oak Pendant is a fake.

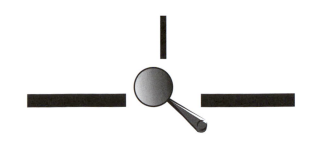

Ica Stones

The Ica Stones represent one of the most transparent and absurd archaeological hoaxes ever perpetrated. In the case of the other fakes discussed in this encyclopedia (e.g., the **Bat Creek Stone**, **Newark Holy Stones**, and **Holly Oak Pendant**), an effort was made to render them at least minimally plausible. Not so with the Ica Stones. They're simply inane (Carroll 2003).

The ostensible story begins in 1961 with a Peruvian doctor, Javier Cabrera, who claims that he received as a gift a hard, dense andesite cobble (a volcanic rock) with a stylized engraving of a fish. According to Cabrera, the engraved stone appeared to be an artifact produced by one of the ancient peoples of Peru. There are plenty of genuine artifacts on the antiquities market in South America, so there was nothing terribly peculiar about getting something like the stone as a gift. The odd part about the object was the fish image. Made with a sharp tool by incising lines through the hard, dark oxidized surface of the stone, exposing its lighter interior, the fish seemed to be a very ancient, extinct species, unlike anything that would have been known to a prehistoric people; the extinct species had only been identified recently by scientists.

Fascinated by the stone, Cabrera sought out its source and became obsessed with purchasing more of them. Not surprisingly—and certainly not coincidentally—once word got out that a wealthy doctor was throwing money around in search of engraved stones, they started turning up all over the place. At first, a couple of local artifact collectors sold him more than 300 of the stones. Then, a local peasant, Basilio Uschuya, contacted Cabrera and soon became his major source for what became known as the Ica Stones, after the town that seemed to be ground zero for the engraved volcanic stones.

Perhaps in an attempt to keep Cabrera's interest piqued—and his money flowing—the engravings became increasingly extraordinary, bizarre, and hallucinatory. One stone shows what looks like a doctor performing a heart transplant. In another, an observer appears to be gazing at the stars through a telescope. Other stones depict maps of unknown territories. On my favorite stones, images of human beings are seen alongside and sometimes in pitched battles with dinosaurs or, in far more tranquil scenes, with the dinosaurs appearing to be habituated to people. People are riding dinosaurs in some of the depictions and seemingly going into battle

Among the many reasons not to take the Ica Stones seriously are examples like this one depicting a virtual menagerie of cartoonish dinosaurs, ostensibly drawn by an artist who actually saw them hanging around in his backyard. (Jennifer Davis)

against other dino-riders. Perhaps these dinosaurs have been domesticated, sort of like Dino the dinosaur pet of the Flintstones.

Having caught the Ica Stones bug, Cabrera abandoned his medical career and has devoted his life to their study and display, going so far as to open his own museum in Ica, the Museo de Piedras Grabadas (Museum of the Engraved Stones). He has thousands of the things (perhaps as many as 15,000), identifying the source as a cave that, rather remarkably, no one else has ever seen, in which, he claims further, there are more than 100,000 more stones yet to be recovered.

What do the stones mean? Cabrera has an opinion, which he has shared with the world in a book, *The Message of the Engraved Stones of Ica*. The stones, in his view, were manufactured and left behind by an ancient extraterrestrial civilization that sent emissaries to the Earth from their home in the Pleiades about a million years ago. Apparently our standard chronologies about the dinosaurs (including the fact that they became extinct 65 million years ago) are wrong, because the Gliptolithic people from the Pleiades interacted with dinosaurs on Earth far more recently than that. At some point in the distant past, the Gliptolithic people left for another planet, using the **Nazca** lines as a sort of spaceport for departing flights.

It should not surprise you in the least that **Erich von Däniken** is a supporter of this hypothesis of Cabrera's. In fact, in his book *Gold of the Gods*, von Däniken clearly states that Cabrera took him to the cave and showed him the spectacular items secreted within, including more of the Ica Stones and a plenitude of gold objects. When Cabrera himself disputed this, von Däniken admitted that he made it all up, defending his story as the result of a sort of poetic license.

There is, I hope needless to say, not a shred of evidence for any of this positively crazy stuff. Although he has been very difficult to pin down and while he has recanted just about every version of the story he has told, Cabrera's major source for the Ica Stones, Basilio Uschuya, has admitted to being not the discoverer of the stones but their fabricator. Basing the images on photographs, drawings, and illustrations in magazines and books, he engraves the images onto and through the dark surface of the stones using metal knives, chisels, and a dental drill. Then, to add a patina of age to the stones, he bakes them in donkey and cow dung, which seems poetically appropriate. The Ica Stones clearly are not the most sophisticated of the archaeological hoaxes discussed in this book, but they certainly rank up there as the most preposterous.

Imhotep

Imhotep was a remarkable individual: a physician, a poet, a priest, an advisor to the pharaoh, and, most significantly in this context, the architect who, more than any other individual we can name in ancient Egypt, designed the pyramid burial monuments for pharaohs. Living between 2650 and 2600 BCE, Imhotep is recorded as the designer of the pharaoh Djoser's Step Pyramid, considered the earliest of the **Egyptian pyramids**. Imhotep's full title was "Chancellor of the King of Egypt, Doctor, First in Line after the King of Upper Egypt, Administrator of the Great Palace, Hereditary Nobleman, High Priest of Heliopolis, Builder, Chief Carpenter, Chief Sculptor, and Maker of Vases in Chief." Robert Brier and Jean-Pierre Houdin (2008, 23) call Imhotep "the Leonardo da Vinci of Egypt." Those who assert that the pyramids were inspired by an extraterrestrial technology ignore the fact that the Egyptians themselves credited Imhotep as its architect and designer. Statues of Imhotep depict him as an ordinary human being.

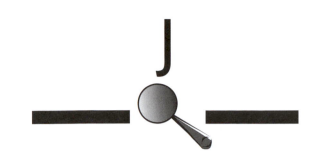

Jesus Ossuary

Of course you're going to gain the attention of the media when you announce that you've found an ossuary, a traditional burial box, with the inscription "Jesus, son of Joseph." That's exactly what happened in 2007, even though, apparently, the burial box had been discovered 27 years previously, in 1980. Other boxes in the same crypt bore the inscribed names of Joseph and Mary. And that's not all. Another box ostensibly found in the same crypt bore the remarkable inscription "Jude, son of Jesus."

Do these ossuaries represent physical, archaeological evidence of the existence of Jesus Christ and the *Da Vinci Code*–like scenario in which Jesus survived long enough to be married, let's say to Mary Magdalene, and have a son whose name was Jude?

It's a fascinating possibility, but not so fast. The inscription found on a previously announced ossuary, reading "James, son of Joseph, brother of Jesus," was shown conclusively to be a fake. Israeli archaeologist Yuval Goren demonstrated that the inscription was modern, having broken through the weathering rind or patina on a genuinely old ossuary. He showed further that, aware of this, the forger painted over the recent inscription with a false patina made of a mixture of water and ground chalk.

The "James, son of Joseph, brother of Jesus" ossuary continues to be a flashpoint of controversy. At least one of the men involved with bringing the ossuary to the public's attention, Oded Golan, has been charged with running an antiquities forgery ring. And several of the claims made in support of its authenticity as presented in a documentary about the ossuaries (directed, by the way, by James Cameron, the director of *Titanic* and now *Avatar*) have been disputed by the very people supposedly quoted in the documentary. Meanwhile allegations fly, millions of dollars are involved (Golan, or at least someone believed to be speaking for him, at one time was reportedly offering to sell the James ossuary for more than $2 million), and Golan's trial has become stalled.

Ossuaries, or "bone boxes," are common in ancient Israel. What makes this one so controversial is the inscribed reference to Jesus. (AP Photo/Eyal Warshavsky)

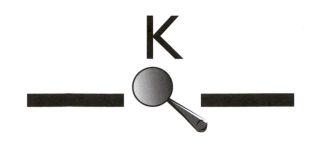

K

Kensington Stone

The Kensington Stone (or Kensington Runestone) is an artifact found in Kensington, Minnesota, with an inscribed message written in runes, a form of writing used by the Norse (Vikings) during the medieval period. The message on the Kensington Stone can be translated:

> 8 Swedes and 22 Norwegians on a discovery voyage from Vinland westward, we had anchored by 2 rocky islets one days voyage north from this stone. We had fished a day, after we came home [we] found 10 men red with blood and dead. AV(E) M(ARIA) deliver from evil. We have 10 men at sea to look after our ship 14 days voyage from this island. Year 1362.

If the stone and inscription, found by local farmer Olof Ohman while clearing his land in 1898, are genuine, it would prove that Norse travelers were in Minnesota as early as 1362, 130 years before Columbus made his first landfall in the Caribbean. As we already know that the Norse were in eastern Canada a little earlier than 1000, the possibility that they made forays farther into the interior of North America sometime thereafter is not unreasonable.

An assessment of authenticity of the Kensington Stone, however, takes more than an argument about the plausibility of a Norse presence in Minnesota more than 600 years ago. It takes an analysis of the inscription itself and actual archaeological evidence of a Norse presence in the region, the everyday stuff that people invariably leave behind and that constitutes the majority of the archaeological record everywhere (see the discussion under **Discovery of America**). Archaeological evidence of the pre-Columbian presence of the **Norse in America** has been found elsewhere, so it must be found in direct association with the Kensington Stone, or at least in its general vicinity, to buttress the claim that the runestone is a genuine artifact of a Norse expedition to the American upper Midwest in the fourteenth century.

There probably are as many opinions about the possible authenticity of the Kensington Runestone as there are scholars who have examined it. Frustratingly, small errors or inconsistencies in the runic writing have been used to support both the argument that the artifact is a fake (the mistakes betray the ignorance of

The Kensington Stone, if genuine, notes the presence of 30 Norsemen—"8 Swedes and 22 Norwegians"—in Minnesota in the year CE 1362. (Runestone Museum, Alexandria, Minnesota.)

a hoaxer unschooled in the particulars of runic inscriptions) and the argument that it is genuine (a faker would make sure to get the runes perfect, but a *real* fourteenth-century Norseman would likely make mistakes). However, skeptics point to a number of features of the inscription that seem to indicate an origin far more recent than its fourteenth-century date stamp would imply. For example, the Swedish term *opthagelse farth* found on the stone, meaning "discovery," appears to be not just a mistake but an anachronism. The term has not been found on any other Norse document and could not date to before it was borrowed from the French in the sixteenth century. Intriguingly, however, and perhaps not coincidentally, the term was used frequently by a nineteenth-century Norwegian historian and author, Gustav Storm, in articles he wrote for a Norwegian-language newspaper that was available in Minnesota. Perhaps a forger, conceivably Ohman, saw the term, assumed it was the correct form for a fourteenth-century runestone, and incorporated into his forgery.

Anthropologist Alice Kehoe (2005) has written a valuable summary of the Kensington Stone controversy. Citing geological analysis of weathering on the stone and linguistic analysis of the runes, she comes out on the side of authenticity. She recognizes, however, the fundamental problem presented by the lack of any confirming artifactual evidence in support of a Norse presence in the area in the time period specified by the runes on the Kensington Stone.

Wherever human beings live or work, they inevitably leave behind a material record of their presence. But there is no such confirming evidence in association with the Kensington Stone. As Kehoe reveals, there have been excavations where the runestone was found in 1899 and then again, more thoroughly, in 1964. A wide archaeological survey was conducted in Kensington in 1981, and there was additional testing in 2001. Nothing was found in any of these studies that could be related to the 30 hardy Norsemen who, had they genuinely traveled through the area, would have camped, eaten meals, thrown away trash, discarded broken tools, or lost objects before, during, or after carving their message in runes on a chunk of local sandstone. Nor were the skeletal remains or burials found of any of the 10 men killed, presumably by local Indians, as mentioned in the runic inscription. In fact, no diagnostic fourteenth-century Norse artifacts were recovered in any of the excavations Kehoe cites that might support the assertion that a contingent of Norsemen was present there more than six centuries ago.

Compare this to L'Anse aux Meadows (see Norse in America), where archaeologists found an assemblage of demonstrably Norse, demonstrably ancient artifacts, including a soapstone spindle whorl, a ring-headed bronze pin, and iron boat rivets. Pieces of chain-mail armor, a bronze trader's balance, and spun yarn were found in well-dated contexts in eastern Canada. The Norsemen who carved and erected the Kensington Runestone, on the contrary, are archaeologically invisible. From an archaeological perspective, it is extremely unlikely that a group of people moving through a territory could leave a detailed message in the form of the Kensington Stone without also leaving an unintentional, archaeological trail of their journey. As a result, most archaeologists conclude that the Kensington Runestone is a forgery.

Further Reading

Though I disagree with her conclusion about the Kensington Runestone (she leans toward accepting its authenticity), I highly recommend Alice Kehoe's book *The Kensington Runestone: Approaching a Research Question Holistically* (2005) for her fair and dispassionate presentation of the evidence.

Khufu

Khufu is the Egyptian name for the pharaoh the Greeks called Cheops. Khufu's father was the pharaoh Snefru, whose reign spans the period 2613–2589 BCE. Snefru was the first pharaoh of the 4th pharaonic dynasty. There are no records for the second pharaoh of the 4th dynasty—he apparently reigned for only a very short span—and Khufu became the third Egyptian king in the 4th dynasty of pharaohs. We know little about what he accomplished during his 23- or 24-year reign, from 2589 to 2566 BCE. There is evidence that he initiated or continued military excursions to the east, into the Sinai Peninsula, where, it is assumed, Egyptian forces were needed to maintain the flow of Sinai turquoise into the pharaoh's coffers. There is additional evidence during Khufu's reign of an Egyptian presence far to the south, at Aswan where Egyptian builders obtained the fine red granite available there.

Khufu's sons, first Djedefre (2566–2558 BCE) and then Khafre (2558–2532 BCE), ruled as pharaohs, as did his grandson, Menkaure (2532–2504 BCE). The pharaohs Snefru, Khufu, Khafre, and Menkaure are best known today for the monuments constructed to house them in death. Altogether, though they are emblematic of their ancient civilization, the **Egyptian pyramids** number just a little more than a hundred (the tally changes as the ruins of smaller pyramids are found, but the last enumeration I read counted 118 of the monuments).

Snefru was the first pharaoh buried in a true pyramid. Following in his footsteps, Khufu, Khafre, and Menkaure were each buried in their own pyramids, each located in proximity to one another at Giza. The triad of family pyramids at Giza reflects one of the most amazing sets of construction projects in the ancient world and is the one surviving element of the renowned Seven Wonders of the Ancient World.

Among the three pyramids at Giza, Khufu's is the largest and most impressive. The statistics of Khufu's pyramid are amazing:

	Metric	English
Height	146.6 meters	481 feet
Sides	230 meters	755 feet
Area of base	52,609 square meters	566,280 square feet (13 acres)
Average weight of stone blocks used in construction	2,268 kilograms	2.5 tons (5,000 pounds)

The footprint of Khufu's pyramid was incredibly precisely made. The four sides of the base are very close to being exactly the same length with a maximum deviation of about 8 inches (20 centimeters) or only about 0.09 percent. Certainly that's remarkable, but not so precise that it required a technology unknown to ancient Egyptians.

Lest anyone wonder whether the ancient Egyptians were capable of a construction feat such as Khufu's pyramid, consider the following incontrovertible facts:

1. Located just a few hundred yards from Giza is a quarry bearing witness to the Egyptian method of extracting large blocks of stone. The bases of quarried stones, the marks left behind by the quarrying process, and stone blocks only partially carved out of the quarry and left in place are all visible. The gash in the earth left behind is almost exactly the correct volume for the workers to have extracted all of the stones for Khufu's pyramid from that one quarry.
2. In an experiment in replicative history, an American archaeologist (Mark Lehner), a stonemason, a sculptor, and a dedicated and experienced crew of Egyptian construction workers were able to build a fairly impressive, small-scale pyramid replica (it was about 21 feet/6.4 meters tall), in about three weeks'

time. Most of the procedures used were those ancient Egyptians might have employed, based on archaeological evidence, artistic depictions by ancient Egyptians of their construction projects, the written record, and trial-and-error, seat-of-the-pants, common-sense techniques used by builders everywhere. This experiment proved conclusively, if not necessarily exactly how the ancient Egyptians built the pyramids, certainly how they *might* have. Though an enormous project, the experiment showed that even the most enormous undertaking can be broken down into a series of manageable components.

3. Like workers everywhere, the people on the front line of Egyptian pyramid-building felt the need to leave their mark on the work they were performing. Hidden high up in an interior chamber of Khufu's pyramid, in a place where overseers and foremen would never see it (so the workers were unlikely to get in trouble), one group of workers left a bit of graffiti, proudly announcing their role in building the pharaoh's eternal home: "We did this with pride in the name of our great King Khnum-Khuf [another name for Khufu]" (Jackson and Stamp 2003, 78).

The point is this: Khufu is a known figure in Egyptian history. He was a powerful pharaoh, reigning in a well-known and important dynasty early in the history of the empire. His pyramid is spectacular, to be sure, but certainly not out of line in the context of Egyptian history, architecture, construction, and religion. The Great Pyramid is a story of human achievement, not the result of the intervention of extraterrestrial aliens or mysterious members of a **lost civilization**.

Further Reading

There are lots of terrific sources available about Khufu and his pyramid. The best place to read about Khufu's historical context is in Peter Clayton's *Chronicle of the Pharaohs* (1994); for his pyramid's historical context, see Mark Lehner's *The Complete Pyramid* (1997). In terms of the actual construction of Khufu's pyramid, two great books are *Building the Great Pyramid* by Kevin Jackson and Jonathan Stamp (2003) and *How the Great Pyramid Was Built* by Craig B. Smith (2004). For an interesting, new idea about the construction of Khufu's pyramid, see *The Secret of the Great Pyramid* by Bob Brier and Jean-Pierre Houdin (2008).

King Tut's Curse

Tutankhamun was only nine years old when he ascended to the throne of ancient Egypt, becoming what he was later to be called, the "boy king." Tut became pharaoh at such a young age during a time of great internal turmoil in

Egypt. His father, the pharaoh Akhenaten, died in 1334 BCE under mysterious circumstances, possibly the result of an assassination plot concocted by the priests of Amun Re, the most powerful god in the Egyptian pantheon.

Akhenaten was responsible for the Amarna revolt, an attempt to wrest some of the growing power away from the Amun Re priesthood. Akhenaten attempted to depose Amun Re and his priests from their exalted position and to elevate Aten, a previously insignificant deity, into the role of a god so powerful and unique that it verged on monotheism. Needless to say, in so doing and by moving the capital of Egypt from Thebes—where the most important temples of Amun Re were located—to a newly built city, Amarna (then called Akhetaten), which became the seat of Aten worship, Akhenaten did little to endear himself to the powerful priests of Amun Re and the other Egyptian gods. When Akhenaten died unexpectedly, his new shining city of Aten was abandoned and sacked and everything returned to the way it was, with his very young son, Tutankhamun, becoming pharaoh. Tut certainly was merely a titular head during his youth, with the power behind the throne—generals, regents, as well as Nefertiti (Tut's father's principal wife, but not Tut's mother)—calling the shots.

Tut's death at the tender age of 19 has long perplexed historians and Egyptologists. A number of scenarios have been sketched out proposing that Tut's death, just as he was approaching a stage in his life when he likely expected to actually wield the power of the throne, like his father's, was the result of an assassination by those who wanted to keep that power for themselves. A detailed examination of Tut's remains conducted in 2005 showed a teenager in the apparent bloom of youthful health and vigor, well nourished, with no sign of disease or infirmity and, more to the point, no evidence of a mortal blow to the head, as had been suggested by some. There was an indication that Tut had suffered a broken leg—perhaps the result of a fall from a chariot—sometime soon before he died, and it has been suggested that such a serious break could have resulted in infection and ultimately, in a period long before the development of antibiotics, death.

Though it was common practice in ancient Egypt to prepare for a pharaoh's ascension to the afterlife very early in his reign by the initiation of tomb construction, Tut's death was so unexpected and early that those preparations were not nearly well enough along to accommodate the now deceased boy king. A tomb being prepared for another Egyptian official was appropriated for the purpose, and Tut was laid to rest in the Valley of the Kings, in a chamber prepared not for a pharaoh but for a minor official. As a result, the spectacular treasure produced to accompany Tut to the afterlife was jammed into a far too small space. Tut's tomb ended up looking like someone's garage, attic, or even a rented storage locker.

The irony here is that Tut was an insignificant pharaoh who merely got caught up in the intrigues wrought by historical, religious, and political factors over which he had little or no control. His tomb was one of the few pharaonic burial chambers not robbed of its riches, at least in part because he was unimportant and forgotten. That detracts not even a little from the magnificence of the discovery of the tomb by Egyptologist **Howard Carter** in November 1922.

After finding a mysterious staircase filled in with stone rubble, Carter believed that a long-sought-after unplundered tomb might be within his grasp. His hopes were buoyed when, upon removing the rubble, his excavators found a sealed underground doorway at the stairway's terminus. At this point, Carter drilled a hole through the door, just large enough to pass a lantern and his head through. Describing his reaction to what he saw, Carter intoned what have to be some of the best-known words spoken by an archaeologist. All was silent and the heavy desert air was thick with anticipation as Carter eased his head through the now breached doorway. The assembled crowd waited for Carter's pronouncement:

> At first I could see nothing, the hot air escaping from the chamber causing the candle flame to flicker. But presently, as my eyes grew accustomed to the light, details of the room within emerged slowly from the mist, strange animals, statues, and gold—everywhere the glint of gold. For the moment—an eternity it must have seemed to the others standing by—I was struck dumb with amazement, and when Lord Carnarvon, unable to stand the suspense any longer, inquired anxiously, "Can you see anything?" it was all I could do to get out the words, "Yes, wonderful things!" (Buckley 1976, 13)

Thus began what may arguably be called the excavation of the most spectacular archaeological find of the twentieth or, without very much hyperbole, any century. Gold statues and alabaster carvings, a throne carved in pure ebony, lapis lazuli jewelry—"wonderful things," indeed, and, among the most wonderful, the boy king's death mask, an exquisite artifact of gold and lapis lazuli.

Rumors began spreading almost immediately of an ancient curse placed on the tomb, of a string of terrible calamities that would afflict any and all who entered the tomb and despoiled and desecrated the final resting place of this Egyptian pharaoh. Inscribed over the entrance of the tomb, it was said, was the threat: "Death shall come on swift wings to him that toucheth the tomb of the Pharaoh."

Infamously, Lord Carnarvon, Carter's benefactor and the man who bankrolled the excavation, died suddenly, four months after the tomb was opened, of what appeared to be a mundane bug bite. The lights in Cairo, it was reported, went out at the instant of his death, and back home at his estate in England, legend has it that his seemingly healthy dog howled once and then dropped dead. Carnarvon, it has been asserted, was only the most famous of a frighteningly long list of individuals associated with the opening of the tomb who died of the dreaded curse.

Among the several problems underpinning the story of the curse is the inconvenient fact that there simply wasn't one. A version of the reputed curse, instead, originated in a letter written by novelist Marie Corelli, which she said she read in a book about tomb curses in general. In fact, tomb curses weren't all that common in ancient Egypt, although there are some—written threats to potential tomb despoilers that promise a miserable life, death by hunger and thirst, and even, in one case, the prediction that first the grave robber and then his wife will be "violated" by a donkey.

Be that as it may, there wasn't any such threat or warning written anywhere in Tut's tomb. No miserable life, no death by hunger or thirst, no randy donkeys. Nothing. But what about all those deaths? Wasn't there a rash of murders, accidents, and awful diseases that befell those who entered the tomb? Actually, no, or at least no more than one would expect by chance. Mark R. Nelson (2002), an epidemiologist—the medical specialty that studies disease and injury, patterns of health, and the statistics of death—probed the mortality statistics of those involved with Tut's tomb and found nothing out of the ordinary. In other words, the death rate, accident rate, and donkey violation rate of the population of archaeologists who entered and excavated Tut's tomb was no different from the population of those who didn't.

Though Lord Carnarvon did die soon after entering the tomb, he was sickly, and his personal physician had warned him against traveling to Egypt. At Carnarvon's side throughout his Egyptian sojourn was his daughter, who lived to the ripe old age of 80. Guards were hired to watch the tomb, actually sleeping in the chamber at night; none of them fell ill or was the victim of an accidental death during their stay. Finally, the man most responsible for finding, excavating, and, one might say, despoiling the tomb, Howard Carter, lived a long and productive life, spending much of it examining and writing about the fabulous material recovered from the tomb. Carter himself was aware of the curse and even admitted that, whenever the opportunity arose, he helped spread the tale, hoping that this would dissuade would-be thieves from disturbing his archaeological research. The solution to the mystery of King Tut's curse is a simple one: There wasn't one.

Further Reading

There are plenty of books that focus on King Tut and his famous curse, but there is none better than, and certainly none better illustrated than, *Tutankhamun and the Golden Age of the Pharaohs* by Egyptian Egyptologist Zahi Hawass (2005).

Kon-Tiki

Easter Island is one of the most remote places on Earth in terms of its distance to any other center of human population. It is 2,180 miles (3,510 kilometers) west of the coast of Chile in South America, and its nearest island neighbor to the west is tiny Pitcairn, 1,290 miles (2,075 kilometers) away, which is itself a contender in the "most remote place on Earth" sweepstakes. Essentially, if you were to look up the phrase "the middle of nowhere" in the dictionary, there should be a map with an arrow pointing to Easter Island. From whatever direction it was settled, the migrants had to be capable of a long, dangerous, and arduous deep-sea ocean voyage. Its name comes from the Dutch explorer Jacob Roggeveen, the first European to see the island, when he made landfall there on Easter Sunday, 1722. The 2,000 or so native inhabitants today call their island Rapa Nui. Their homeland is a patch of ground of only about 63 square miles (164 square kilometers), slightly smaller than the area covered by Washington, D.C.

In the standard scenario put forth by anthropologists, archaeologists, and historians, Easter Island was settled about a thousand years ago by Polynesians from the west. Though Pitcairn is the closest inhabited island to Easter Island, its aboriginal population was quite small and impermanent; there were no native Polynesians there when it became a refuge for the mutineers on the HMS *Bounty* in 1790. Far more likely possible sources for the native population of Rapa Nui would have been either the Marquesas Islands chain, located some 2,000 miles (3,200 kilometers) away, or the Gambier Islands (1,600 miles/2,600 kilometers away). Polynesians were accomplished mariners. They experienced their own "age of exploration" long before Europeans and, through a series of accidental journeys (for example, by being blown off course during a storm) and by intentional voyages of exploration searching for new lands to settle, spread their population across much of the Pacific Ocean, including remote outposts like Easter Island (Terrell 1986).

Norwegian explorer **Thor Heyerdahl** proposed a different scenario for the settlement of Easter Island. He hypothesized that Easter Island wasn't settled by the Polynesians from the west, but by Native Americans from the east. Heyerdahl based this view on his interpretation of archaeological, serological (blood typing), linguistic, epigraphic, and ethnographic evidence. Few, if any, professional archaeologists or ethnographers found much to recommend Heyerdahl's hypothesis, and recent research, especially in "molecular archaeology," shows conclusively that Easter Island was the easternmost outpost of Polynesian settlers. DNA testing shows that native Easter Islanders, along with the rest of the settlers of Polynesia, can be traced to Southeast Asia; they are not American Indians.

Heyerdahl's most significant contribution to the question of the settlement of Easter Island rested not in field archaeology, ethnography, or linguistics but, rather, in experimental replication. Heyerdahl built a raft, called the *Kon-Tiki*, out of buoyant balsa wood logs, ostensibly based on artistic depictions by European visitors to South America of local Indian watercraft. With a hardy crew of adventurers, on April 28, 1947, he attempted the deep ocean crossing from Chile to Easter Island.

Their landfall wasn't exactly elegant—they smashed the *Kon-Tiki* into the coral reef—and they ended up nowhere near Easter Island, but on Raroia atoll in the Tuamotu Archipelago in French Oceania, nearly 2,000 miles (3,000 kilometers) away! Nevertheless, we may judge the replicative experiment a success due to the fact that they showed that the *Kon-Tiki* was seaworthy and no one died during their 101 days aboard the craft.

Heyerdahl and his crew were able to navigate the eastern Pacific across a distance of 4,337 miles (nearly 7,000 kilometers)—a blistering pace of 1.7 miles per hour (2.8 kilometers per hour) during the duration of their journey. It was an admirable feat, to be sure. But, beyond the obvious bravery of the seafarers and the survival of the craft across a long stretch of the Pacific, was the *Kon-Tiki* itself and the voyage Heyerdahl and his crew took a sensible replication? Did it at least show a reasonable way in which ancient inhabitants of South America might have migrated to Easter Island or other islands in the Pacific?

The consensus answer of anthropologists and archaeologists is no. Among the most important considerations in experimental archaeology, among the rules by which the validity of an archaeological replicative experiment is assessed, is the absolute requirement that the technologies applied be appropriate for the time period of the activity being replicated. By this measurement, the voyage of the *Kon-Tiki* was a scientific failure. Some of the key technologies applied by Heyerdahl in the *Kon-Tiki* voyage—and that were instrumental in keeping the crew alive and the boat sailing, at least vaguely, in the right direction— were inappropriate and therefore invalidate any positive results. Along with bamboo canteens filled with freshwater, the *Kon-Tiki* crew brought along with them a solar still for making potable water out of seawater, canned food, radios, maps, and modern (for the 1940s) navigation equipment (Suggs 1970). Without these amenities, the *Kon-Tiki* voyage would not have achieved whatever success it did (remember, they didn't end up even vaguely near Easter Island). Therefore, the voyage of the *Kon-Tiki*, interesting as it may have been, lends no support to Heyerdahl's hypothesis that South American Indians explored and then settled Easter Island or other islands of Polynesia.

Further Reading
Heyerdahl's experiment may not have proved what he hoped to, but it's a ripping good tale. See his book *Kon-Tiki* (1968).

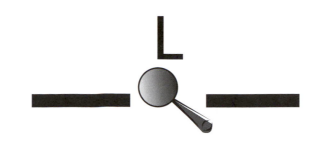

Lemuria

There may be only the thinnest whisper of evidence for the assertion that **Plato**'s story of the Lost Continent of **Atlantis** was based on an actual ancient civilization and that the Greek philosopher's story of its destruction was inspired by a folk memory of a natural catastrophe that wiped out that culture (the ostensible destruction of Minoan Crete following the massive eruption of **Thera** sometime before 1600 BCE). Be that as it may, that ephemeral whisper of evidence far surpasses any for the truly fantastic claim there was a similar occurrence in the Pacific or Indian Ocean at some point deep in time.

The Pacific or Indian version of Atlantis is called Lemuria. The existence of a now submerged Pacific continent was first hypothesized in an attempt to explain the existence of similar animal fossils found on the island of Madagascar (where live the majority of the world's species of lemurs; thus the name Lemuria) and India, but are conspicuously absent anywhere in Africa. Zoologist Philip Sclater proposed in 1864 the existence of the Lemuria landmass in an attempt to explain this distribution of fossils, proposing that India represented the eastern margin of Lemuria while Madagascar was a remnant of Lemuria's western shore. Sclater speculated that the entire center of Lemuria had been submerged, thus producing the now great separation between India and Madagascar.

Sclater was engaging in valuable and valid scientific speculation—such conjecture is often the basis of scientific hypothesis testing—however wrong he actually turned out to be. There is absolutely no evidence for any such continuous landmass in the Pacific or Indian Ocean. The correct answer was that India and Madagascar were, long, long ago, part of the same landmass (Pangea), now separated as the result of Continental Drift.

Sclater's reasonable musings about a possible submerged continent in the Indian Ocean were magnified to a point of complete absurdity by the occultist Madame Helena Blavatsky. Blavatsky was a leader in the theosophist movement of the late nineteenth century, an incomprehensible amalgam of religion, myth, philosophy, and fantasy. Blavatsky, based on nothing but her own fevered imagination, believed that all humanity was descended from a series of seven root races. According to Blavatsky, Lemuria was home to Root Race 3 (it is uncertain whether or not the members of each root race, like marathon runners, had to wear their numbers on their uniforms). Root Race 3, it is interesting to report, comprised seven-foot-tall, egg-laying, slow-witted, but spiritually advanced hermaphrodites. At some point, mammalian species appeared on Lemuria. The Root Race 3 gang, apparently, felt more warmly toward the mammals than should be discussed in an encyclopedia destined for high school libraries (that's right, Root Race 3ers engaged in bestiality with the newly evolved mammals). The gods, though which gods and where they came from are details not revealed by Blavatsky, were repulsed by the behavior of the funky Lemurians and destroyed the entire place. Those same gods then proceeded to create Root Race 4, whom they then ensconced on another continent: Atlantis.

Not all Lemurians were dispatched to eternity when their continent was destroyed by the gods, though. Some of them—at least according to Frederick Spencer Oliver, writing in 1894—survived and made it to Mount Shasta in northern California, where they constructed an underground community replete with tunnels and vast open chambers scattered throughout the interior of the mountain. If you're lucky, at least according to Oliver and a number of more recent occultists, you can catch occasional glimpses of this remnant population of Lemurians who are fond of exiting their subterranean homes, wearing flowing white robes. None of the writers have explained why they risk being revealed to the outside world in this way; perhaps it's difficult to get a good light beer inside Mount Shasta so they need to visit local convenience stores. You never know.

Sarcasm aside, the claims about seven-foot tall, egg-laying, hermaphroditic mammal lovers is just so plain silly that I think we should move on.

Further Reading

L. Sprague de Camp's splendid book, *Lost Continents: The Atlantis Theme in History, Science, and Literature* (1970), is a terrific place to start on the entire lost continents theme.

Lenape Stone

The Lenape Stone is a piece of slate about 4.5 inches (11.4 centimeters) across (actually found in 1872 as two separate but conjoinable pieces on two separate occasions more than nine years apart in the same agricultural field in Bucks County, Pennsylvania). The slate has clearly been worked into a rectangular shape, there are two holes drilled along the long axis of the object, and there is a series of images etched into both faces of the slate, including assorted animals such as turtles, snakes, fish, and birds. None of this is surprising, and similar artifacts called *gorgets* have been found in indisputable archaeological contexts and ancient soil layers throughout eastern North America. The holes found in gorgets appear to have allowed for their suspension around the necks of wearers, much in the manner of amulets.

What makes the Lenape Stone of greater interest than most gorgets is the additional, clear image on one face of an animal that seems quite recognizable as a woolly mammoth. As most gorgets have been found in archaeological levels dating to less than 2,000 years ago, while evidence points very clearly to the extinction of the mammoth in North America no later than 10,000 years ago, one of three conclusions can be drawn:

1. The Lenape Stone gorget is a genuine aboriginal depiction of a woolly mammoth and, contrary to every other gorget ever found, dates to the end of the Pleistocene or Ice Age. That would make it the first—and, until the recent discovery of a bone with the incised image of a woolly mammoth found in Vero Beach, Florida, and apparently authenticated by scientists, the only—such artifact ever found in North America, although engravings of Pleistocene animals have been found in Europe dating to a time before 10,000 years ago.
2. The Lenape Stone gorget is a genuine, aboriginal depiction of a woolly mammoth that dates to the period of all other gorgets ever found, indicating that at least some woolly mammoths survived the late Pleistocene extinction event and were still alive about 2,000 years ago when the gorget was carved.
3. The Lenape Stone gorget is a fake—or at least the mammoth carving is **fraudulent**, added to a genuine gorget to make the illustration seem much older, more important, or more interesting than it actually is.

The Lenape Stone was not excavated by a trained archaeologist and was not found in stratigraphic context. Both pieces were found on the surface of a plowed field in Pennsylvania. The stone has been roughly handled by those attempting to clean it, rendering any sort of analysis of erosion or wear of the mammoth engraving—or any comparison between the mammoth image and the others on the stone—more or less moot. Other artifacts were found on the same farm bearing stylistically similar carvings; all have been dated to the period after 2,000 years ago, but none bears any image of a woolly mammoth or any other extinct Pleistocene fauna.

A careful examination of the two different pieces of the Lenape Stone, though showing different bits of the mammoth, seem not to conjoin correctly, suggesting that the engraving was done on the already separate fragments of the stone, pretty clear evidence that the entire thing had been a hoax. Like the **Holly Oak Pendant**, the Lenape Stone is obviously a fake. The stone was sold soon after its discovery, suggesting that money had been the inspiration for the faker.

Los Lunas Decalogue Stone

The Los Lunas Decalogue Stone is a substantial flat slab of rock weighing as much as 80 tons (73,000 kilograms), located pretty far off the beaten path, about 35 miles (56 kilometers) south of Albuquerque, near the town of Los Lunas, New Mexico. The flat face of the stone shows a very sharp, crisp inscription in a

The Los Lunas Decalogue Stone, located in New Mexico, bears an inscription of the Ten Commandments in an archaic form of Hebrew. The stone is almost certainly a fake. (Brian Haines)

form of archaic Hebrew, interpreted by some to represent a version of the Decalogue, otherwise known as the Ten Commandments.

The stone was first mentioned in print in 1933, ostensibly soon after it was first seen by Frank Hibben, a well-known New Mexico archaeologist and professor. Hibben claimed that he was shown the inscription by an anonymous local man, who told him he had first seen it more than 50 years previously, in 1880.

If the inscription is authentically ancient, it would imply that ancient Jews had traveled to New Mexico and left a copy of the Ten Commandments on the face of a large boulder. Though it certainly cannot be dismissed on this basis, if it is the real deal, it certainly has significant implications concerning the history of the American Southwest.

Supporters of the authenticity of the inscription—including scholar **Cyrus Gordon**—point to the fact that the particular form of paleo-Hebrew seen on the rock wasn't known in 1880, arguing from this that no forger would have had the knowledge to produce it. Of course, the claim that the inscription existed in 1880 is based only on the eyewitness account of an unidentified individual, and we know of it only by through the account of Professor Hibben, who didn't see it until 1933. By that time, paleo-Hebrew *was* known and could have been used in a hoax.

There are a number of particular problems with any interpretation of the Los Lunas Decalogue Stone. The earliest we know it existed is 1933, so the forgery of a paleo-Hebrew inscription is a possibility. Even if it had been found in 1880, the script used is nearly identical to Phoenician, so its age isn't convincing evidence of its authenticity either. The inscription looks very sharp and crisp; it certainly does not convey the impression of an artifact that has endured wind, rain, ice, and snow for an extended period of time.

Beyond this, as is often frustratingly the case with purported ancient Old World inscriptions found in the New World, peculiarities or inconsistencies in the writing are pointed to by both supporters and detractors alike as substantiation. Some investigators have asserted that, while the writing may be paleo-Hebrew, the punctuation is modern—clinching, in their minds, that the inscription is fake; others (**Barry Fell**, for one) disagree, claiming the punctuation is appropriate for ancient times.

It doesn't help that the source of all of the information about the discovery of the Los Lunas stone is Frank Hibben. Hibben appears to have been involved in a couple of incidents with fabricated data concerning his hypothesis that the New World was inhabited at a period of greater antiquity than is accepted by most archaeologists. Though there is no evidence that he was involved in fakery regarding the Los Lunas stone, these other incidents are troubling; can we really trust his account of being taken to the stone in 1933?

As an archaeologist, I find the various arguments about the authenticity of the Los Lunas Decalogue Stone interesting, but missing the most important point. I freely admit an archaeological bias here, but seriously. Before we even need to examine closely all the intricacies of the punctuation, grammar, spelling, word or letter form on the Los Lunas stone, or at least at the same time we examine these details, we also need to think about the archaeological context of such an artifact—or, actually, the complete lack of any archaeological context.

Unless ancient Hebrews parachuted into central New Mexico or were beamed there in some alternative reality, they must have traveled there by land. Look at a map. You can't exactly get to Albuquerque by boat. If they traveled there by land, they must have stopped along the way, encamped, eaten food, broken things, disposed of trash, performed rituals, and so on. And those actions should have left a trail of physical archaeological evidence across the greater American Southwest, discovery of which would undeniably prove the existence of foreigners in New Mexico in antiquity with a demonstrably ancient Hebrew material culture (see the entry **Discovery of America** for a general discussion of the issue of confirming archaeologically the presence of a band of interlopers, migrants, or colonists in someone else's territory).

But there is no such evidence in greater Albuquerque, nor in New Mexico, in the greater Southwest, or anywhere in North America—or, for that matter, in the New World. There are no pre-Columbian ancient Hebrew settlements, no sites containing the everyday detritus of a band of ancient Hebrews, nothing that even a cursory knowledge of how the archaeological record forms would demand there would be. From an archaeological standpoint, that's plainly impossible.

For the stone to be genuine, we are left with a scenario in which at some point in antiquity, a group of obsessive-compulsive neat-freak Hebrews snuck into New Mexico, quickly left a version of the Ten Commandments, and then quickly left, cleaning up after themselves so completely that, other than the inscription, there's not a single shred of physical evidence that they were any-where in New Mexico. Of course, applying **Occam's Razor**, the other explana-tion, the simpler and more likely one, is that the Los Lunas Decalogue Stone is a fake. Until sufficient archaeological evidence surfaces that ancient Hebrews journeyed through the Southwest, that's the explanation I'm going with, and I'll let the linguists and epigraphers sort out the details of the bogus inscription.

Lost Civilizations

A popular undercurrent in fringe archaeology concerns the ostensible presence of a "lost civilization" hidden somewhere in the proverbial "dim mists of time." This lost civilization is usually portrayed as having been amazingly and precociously advanced, possessing technological skills as yet still not developed even by our modern civilization and paranormal capacities of which we are not even aware. This lost civilization (or civilizations) is usually presented as the "mother culture" of all subsequent, historically known civilizations, having passed down their knowledge to them. The lost civilization was, tragically, destroyed, through either a natural cataclysm or some catastrophic technologi-cal mishap, and has been somehow hidden from us.

The fundamental assumption of supporters of the lost civilization myth is that known human groups—including the ancient Egyptians, the Mesopotamians (in Iraq), the Shang (in China), the Indus Valley civilization in Pakistan, and the Olmec, **Maya**, and Teotihuacanos of Mesoamerica—were all incapable of developing the kinds of sophisticated cultures with advanced technologies abun-dantly reflected in the archaeological record. Unable to believe that pyramid-building, metallurgy, a written language, astronomical knowledge, mathematics, calendars, and all of the other trappings of ancient civilizations were within their own capabilities, a powerful and extremely ancient lost civilization is proposed as the source for all of these things.

Underpinning the lost civilization paradigm is the old **diffusionist** libel that most human groups are essentially pretty dull and uninventive, but that somewhere, some-place, at least one or, if more than one, very few human groups were otherwise. These exceptional "genius" cultures were intelligent, vibrant, and highly advanced, and it is to these people that all ancient civilizations owe their inspiration.

Several of these anciently lost civilizations are discussed in this encyclopedia, including those of **Atlantis**, **Lemuria**, and the **Grand Canyon**; the builders of the **Bosnian pyramids**; and the highly advanced civilization of 10,500 BCE discussed by **Graham Hancock**. There isn't a lick of archaeological evidence for the existence of any of them, however, nor any geological evidence for some global catastrophe striking them down; there simply isn't any evidence for a great civilization that self-destructed 12,000 or 100,000 or a million or more years ago. Most importantly, there isn't any *need* for a lost civilization. The known cultures listed above were all fully capable of developing the sophisticated technologies reflected in their archaeological records. Like the evolution of the **Egyptian pyramids**, the development of ancient technologies and skills such as metallurgy, writing, agriculture, and all the rest is reflected in the archaeological record as a process of trial and error, dead ends, sharp turns, inspiration, and hard work. Lost civilizations simply don't fit into the scenarios exhibited in the archaeological record and are little more than mythic versions of human antiquity.

Lost Tribes and Sunken Continents

Lost Tribes and Sunken Continents: *Myth and Method in the Study of American Indians* was a popular book in which its author, Robert Wauchope (1974), debunked a series of widespread pseudoscientific claims about human antiquity, focusing on the New World. Wauchope, an American archaeologist who specialized in Mesoamerica and the American Southwest, included chapters on lost continents such as **Atlantis** and **Lemuria** (Mu); **diffusionism**, in which technological developments in the New World were ascribed to visitors from Europe or Asia; claims made by explorer **Thor Heyerdahl** that Rapa Nui in the Pacific, where the remarkable **Easter Island moai** statues are found, was settled by seafaring South Americans; and claims that Native Americans are remnants of one of the biblical Lost Tribes of Israel.

Robert Wauchope was born in 1909, got a bachelor's degree in English from the University of South Carolina in 1931, and then went on to receive a Ph.D. in anthropology at Harvard University. He taught at Tulane University from 1942 to 1975, where he served as director of the Middle American Research Institute (MARI). He died in 1979.

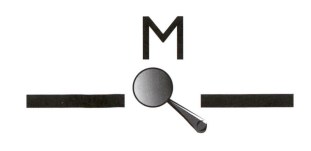

Madoc, Prince

Prince Madoc is a mythical figure, a Welsh prince whose existence is not supported by any historical data. Madoc's purported father, Owain of Gwynedd, was real enough, however, a prince who ruled in the twelfth century. The historical Owain was prolific, fathering at least 13 children, and a great warrior, but wasn't very good at establishing a firm line of succession to his throne. Madoc is supposed to have been one of those children, or perhaps another, born out of wedlock. Whatever the case, the legend tells us that upon Owain's death in 1170, and while his sons battled for his throne, Madoc and a brother, Rhirid, organized a flotilla and sailed west from Wales, into the Atlantic, eventually reaching the shores of the North American continent more than 320 years before the first voyage of Christopher Columbus. The story continues that Madoc, or at least some of his Welsh compatriots, returned to Wales to report the existence of a new land and recruited others to migrate there. These additional migrants made the voyage across the Atlantic and settled permanently, mixing in with the aboriginal people already living there.

As is the case of the preponderance of—though clearly not all—claims of European, **African**, or Asian pre-Columbian visitors to the New World, there is absolutely no physical archaeological evidence of Madoc and his twelfth-century band of Welshmen in the New World. For a time, ridgetop stone forts found in Kentucky and Tennessee were suggested by some to represent defensive structures built by Madoc's band, but archaeological excavations of one of the best known of the sites showed it to be little more than a stone wall enclosing a hilltop. No artifacts traceable to Wales or to the twelfth century were found in the excavation (Faulkner 1971). Archaeologist Charles Faulkner reports the discovery of stone tools, including stone spear points, and cutting and scraping tools typical of those found at other prehistoric Native American sites in the region. Furthermore, charcoal recovered at the site and associated with its construction has been carbon dated to between 30 and 430 CE.

Other than this, the only evidence presented to support the claim of a twelfth-century Welsh presence in America is seventeenth-century reports by explorers or settlers of light-skinned Indians in the area, Indians with light eyes, or Indians speaking a language that sounded like Welsh (although some versions of these reports maintain that the language spoken by the Native people was actually Irish or Portuguese). No competent linguist of Native American languages has ever found any similarity to Welsh or any other European language. For some eyewitnesses, the mere fact that some of the Native villages in the region were neat, well-made, and well-maintained was an indication that the people living there must actually be Welsh (or some other non-Natives) rather than Indian.

There is a possibility that the story of Madoc's discovery and settlement of the New World was, at its heart, an attempt by the English, about 1580, to assert their primacy in the New World; in other words, the claim of Madoc making it to North America may have been a fiction appended onto the original story in an attempt to strengthen the English claim to the lands of the New World.

In the mid-1960s, the Daughters of the American Revolution (DAR) erected a historical marker on the shore of Mobile Bay in Alabama that reads, in part: "In Memory of Prince Madoc, a world explorer who landed on the shores of Mobile Bay in 1170 and left behind, with the Indians, the Welsh language." That there is no historical or archaeological evidence supporting the discovery or settlement of the New World by Madoc's Welsh followers—much less that, if he did make it here, he landed in or near Mobile Bay—seems not to have bothered the DAR.

Man Tracks

Tracks representing the preserved footprints of dinosaurs have been found along the Paluxy River in Glen Rose, southwest of Fort Worth in east-central Texas, at least as far back as 1908. Between 1908 and 1938, a broad and diverse array of tracks were found by locals, and some of those locals, hoping to generate extra income during the tough economic times of the Great Depression, began quarrying some of the best tracks out of their bedrock matrix in order to sell them to tourists who were flocking to Glen Rose for the purportedly salutary qualities of its mineral water. Among the footprints of sauropods (four-footed dinosaurs like *Apatosaurus*) and theropods (upright-walking dinosaurs) was another group of long, clawless prints that local people began referring to as "man tracks" (Kuban 2009). The so-called man tracks were not terribly convincing-looking—they were simply elongated depressions—and the term likely was applied playfully, not on the basis of any real belief that the footprints were human. Inspired by the notion of giant human footprints alongside dinosaur prints, at least one local resident began carving fake footprints that looked like comically large human footprints. It almost certainly was all done in good fun; the fakes look more like the prints left by big clown feet than genuine footprints.

Working for the American Museum of Natural History in New York City in 1938, paleontologist Roland Bird was in New Mexico when he saw a couple of the fake giant human fake footprints in the window of a trading post. When the owner told Bird the tracks came from Glen Rose, Texas, and that there were lots more to be seen there, Bird altered his itinerary and visited Glen Rose. While there, he encountered a wonderful array of prints of various sizes and forms and examples of the footprints the locals referred to as man tracks. Bird recognized that the majority were genuine footprints, not made by giant human beings but by some sort of ancient animal. Bird worked on exposing, examining, and removing some of the footprint trails for transport back to the American Museum of Natural History for two years, using workers supplied through the Work Projects Administration (WPA), a federal program to provide jobs for unemployed laborers. He also clearly recognized the fake footprints for what they were

The giant "man tracks" of the Paluxy River bed in Glen Rose, Texas, aren't human tracks at all, but the footprints of large, bipedal dinosaurs. Arrows point to claw marks in two of the footprints. (K. Feder)

After Bird's work, interest in the Paluxy tracks subsided until the 1970s, when they became a cause célèbre of "scientific creationists" who believed the footprints—both the genuine dinosaur prints as well as the carved fakes—were proof of biblical stories of giants (similar to the **Cardiff Giant**) and, of equal importance, of the belief that the world is only about 6,000 years old, with dinosaurs and human beings living in that same 6,000-year time frame. In other words, some scientific creationists maintained that the Paluxy footprints provided direct, physical evidence that human beings and dinosaurs lived at the same time and side by side—in not-so-ancient Texas, anyway. A creationist film production company produced and distributed a film in 1973 titled *Footprints in Stone*, which presented the evidence, such as it was, for the presence of genuine giant human footprints in the same place and same geological strata as the genuine dinosaur footprints. Creationist literature, especially in the 1970s but reaching into the 1980s, commonly referred to the Paluxy footprints, touting them as precisely the kind of material, physical evidence that true science relies on to test and prove a hypothesis. In their view, the analysis of the Paluxy evidence rendered creationism more than simply a religiously based worldview, but into a viable, scientific alternative to the evolutionary perspective.

Unfortunately for their theory, however, the genuine tracks were not those of a giant human but of a variety of upright-walking dinosaurs. Recent examination of the tracks shows them to have been made by bipedal theropod dinosaurs that walked plantigrade (heel-down, instead of the digitigrade or heel-up, on-the-toes fashion of most theropods). The elongated depressions were produced by the long, narrow metatarsals of these dinosaurs (Kuban 2009). Primarily as a result of Glen Kuban's (2009) analysis, most creationists backed off, realizing that their interpretation had been incorrect. Today, very few creationists put much stock in the claim that the genuine Paluxy "man tracks" are anything more than those of upright-walking dinosaurs.

Further Reading

Glen Kuban has been a one-man wrecking crew concerning the man tracks, definitively debunking them again and again. The best place to read about his work is at his own Web site: http://paleo.cc/paluxy.htm. It's a great model of scientific analysis.

Mars Face

At least in a general sense, the ultimate source of the Mars Face controversy can be traced to the musings of Italian astronomer Giovanni Schiaparelli, who, in 1877, observed linear markings on the face of Mars. He called them *canali* (the Italian word for channels or canals), clearly recognizing them as natural features of the Martian landscape. American astronomer Percival Lowell became the chief proponent of the hypothesis that Schiaparelli's *canali* were, in fact, the result of intelligent activity, actual canals whose purpose was to distribute water to the agricultural fields and settlements of Martians. Speculation about the possibility of intelligent life on our planetary neighbor has burgeoned ever since.

The proximate source of the Mars Face controversy was a grainy photograph (exposure 35A72) taken on July 25, 1976, by a camera mounted on the *Viking 1* orbiter spacecraft. Searching for potential landing areas on the Martian surface while flying some 1,162 miles (1,860 kilometers) above a region of the Red Planet called Cydonia, the orbiter camera caught a surface feature that appeared to bear a striking resemblance to a human face (Malin Space Science Systems 1995).

Though conspiracy theories abound surrounding this feature of the Martian landscape, it cannot be said that the National Aeronautics and Space Administration (NASA) made any attempt to hide or cover it up. In fact, on July 31, just six days after the photograph was radioed back to Earth and processed, NASA released the image to the public and included the caption: "The huge rock formation in the center, which resembles a human head, is formed by shadows giving the illusion of eyes, a nose and a mouth" (NASA press release P-17384; see

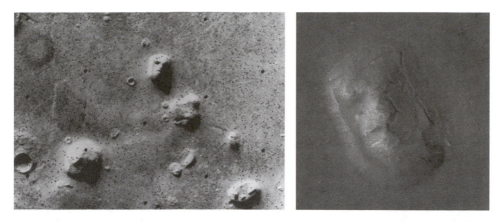

The Mars Face (left), supposedly proving the existence of an ancient civilization on Mars, is nothing more than an interesting play of light and shadow in a low resolution image. When better cameras were aimed at the Martian landscape, the face disappears, leaving behind an entirely natural mesa. (NASA)

http://www.msss.com/education/facepage/pio.html for the complete text of the press release). Ultimately, nine images of the so-called face were captured by the orbiter, but none was as evocative as the original (to view a selection of these images, see Malin Space Science Systems 1995).

Soon thereafter, some were suggesting that the nearly 2-mile-long (3-kilometer), 800-foot-high (240-meter), face-like feature on Mars was no "illusion" of light and shadow nor a fortuitously shaped natural feature, but an actual artistic depiction of a face, a monumentally scaled archaeological artifact of an ancient and now most likely extinct Martian civilization (DiPietro and Molenaar 1982). Some went beyond the face, seeing in its proximity the archaeological ruins of a great city replete with a five-sided pyramid, a fortress, transportation arteries, and an artificial mound or "tholus" surrounded by a moat (Hoagland 1987). Richard Hoagland, who has been a lightning rod in this debate, has argued that the Cydonia images show the remains of a complex settlement not of indigenous Martians but of aliens who colonized Mars as much as half a million years ago. In Hoagland's speculation, these extraterrestrials next colonized Earth; we are their descendants, explaining the fact that the Mars Face is recognized as a face, precisely because it looks human.

Much of the Mars Face argument seems to be based on an iteration of the kind of "Rorschach archaeology" applied by **Erich von Däniken**. In other words, those who support the hypothesis that the face and associated features are artificial have come to their conclusions subjectively, by eyeballing low-resolution photographs taken of the Martian surface. They argue that the Cydonia feature must actually be a carved human face because it seems to resemble one.

A fundamental problem in this line of reasoning is the fact that it is not at all uncommon for natural features of the landscape here on Earth to suggest artificial images, in the way Rorschach inkblots suggest specific pictures. For example, the late and lamented "Old Man in the Mountain," so emblematic of New Hampshire that its profile is on that state's license plates, indeed looked like an old man (until the rock outcrop forming the face collapsed in 2003) but was an entirely natural feature. Wisconsin has its remarkable, and entirely natural, profile of the Indian leader Black Hawk. Virtually all solution caverns have rock formations suggesting the Statue of Liberty, the U.S. Capitol dome, Abraham Lincoln, two eggs sunny-side up, and so on.

NASA image researchers have found other remarkable elements of the Martian landscape that bear a striking resemblance to seemingly nonnatural features. For example, even a cursory glance at a five-mile-wide (eight-kilometer) Martian meteor impact crater indicates that it deserves its designation as the "largest happy face" in the known universe (http://www.msss.com/education/happy_face/happy_face.html). Another feature produced by two intersecting craters is readily recognizable as a Valentine's Day heart. And one Martian lava flow bears an uncanny resemblance to the Muppet character Kermit the Frog.

More detailed—and, ostensibly, more objective—claims concerning the possible artificial source of the Cydonia features rely on mathematical arguments concerning their alignments and locations. It is maintained that these alignments are not random, as would be expected if the features were natural, but, instead, reflect precise mathematical relationships that only a highly sophisticated society could incorporate into their design (Hoagland 1987).

NASA scientists are quite skeptical of any such conclusions based on measurements taken from the *Viking* orbiter photographs of Mars. These photographs are extremely low resolution—each pixel in the original Mars Face photograph corresponds to 141 feet (43 meters) on the ground—and are quite imprecise and, therefore, highly inaccurate. For example, the so-called pyramid's location on the face photograph varies by as much as 10.5 miles (17 kilometers), depending on which positioning system is employed when analyzing the photograph (Malin Space Science Systems 1995).

New photographs of the Cydonia region have been taken by the Mars Global Surveyor (MGS) satellite, which has been in orbit around Mars since September 1997. The MGS camera is able to take photographs of far higher resolution than the *Viking* orbiter, and in April 1998 it snapped an image of the Mars Face feature (http://www.msss.com/mars_images/moc/4_6_98_face_release/compare.gif). Each pixel in this photograph represents only 14.1 feet (4.3 meters) of the Martian surface, 10 times higher than the best images of the face taken by the *Viking* orbiter. One would be hard pressed to coax any kind of a facelike image from the 1998 photograph, though there was apparently enough ambiguity left (the photograph was taken at a substantial angle—45°—and there was significant cloud cover) that supporters of the face hypothesis held out hope that subsequent images might provide clearer evidence.

In one sense, they were correct. On April 8, 2001, the MGS was rolled to an angle of 24.8° to its left and photographed the face from a distance of only about 280 miles (450 kilometers). The Martian atmosphere was quite clear when this photograph was taken, and the image has an even higher resolution than the April 1998 image (each pixel represents only about 5 feet/1.6 meters, the maximum resolution possible with this camera). According to NASA (2001), an object the size of a small building would be discernable in this image; genuine cultural features, especially monumental features like pyramids or temples, would be easily recognized. No such features are present in the new photograph and the fabled Mars Face has disappeared completely; all that is left is an eroded mesa with a rather nondescript depression where the "eye" was located and a linear valley where people saw a mouth (http://www.msss.com/mars_images/moc/extended _may2001/face/face_E03-00824_proc.gif).

The "Face" mesa is only one of many on the Cydonia plain. The geological processes that produced these landforms are uncertain; the mesas may have been eroded by wind, water, or even glacial activity sometime in Mars's past. Measurements taken with the Mars Orbiter Laser Altimeter (MOLA) provide precise measurements of the heights, proportions, and volumes of these mesas. The Face mesa is in no way unique or unlike the other mesas that dot the plain, except for the fact that with a low-resolution camera and the right lighting conditions, it looks like a human face. The measurements are so precise—the MOLA has a remarkably accurate vertical precision of between 20 and 30 cm (8–12 inches)—that NASA scientist Jim Garvin has even produced a trail map leading to the top of the mesa, should astronauts ever reach the Cydonia region of Mars. He estimates it will be a two-hour hike.

With the application of high-resolution photography and instrumentation like the MOLA, the face on Mars has disappeared, feature by feature, like the Cheshire cat in *Alice in Wonderland*. The Cydonia mesas provide no proof that intelligent life once existed on Mars.

Further Reading

About the best places to find the details behind the Mars Face are on Web sites provided by NASA, including:

- http://www.msss.com/education/facepage/face.html
- http://www.msss.com/education/facepage/face_discussion.html
- http://science.nasa.gov/headlines/y2001/ast24may_1.htm?list540155
- http://www.msss.com/mars_images/moc/extended_may2001/face/face_E03-00 824_proc_50perc.gif

There are fantastic photographs on these sites, and you can plainly see that, as the technology improved and the resolution of the images was heightened, the "faceness" of the hill greatly diminished.

Maya

With a homeland centered in the tropical and subtropical lowlands of Mesoamerica, including the modern nations of Guatemala, Belize, Honduras, and Mexico (in the east of that country, in Chiapas and the Yucatan Peninsula), the Maya were one of the ancient world's remarkable civilizations. Their society was characterized by powerful city-states lorded over by hereditary rulers who controlled vast territories surrounding their capital cities. The cities were carved out of the jungle and featured beautiful temples, impressive and monumental pyramids, palaces of the nobility, and workshops of the craftspeople and artists whose work, in jade, obsidian, ceramics, and fabric, ended up in the homes and tombs of the elites of Maya society. With their extremely complex and accurate calendar systems, intensely detailed hieroglyphic writing, and a sophisticated system of mathematics, the Maya represent, in cultural evolutionary terms, an American iteration of the ancient Sumerian city-states of Mesopotamia and the Egypt of the pharaohs.

Europeans became aware of the Maya civilization only relatively recently, in the sixteenth century. By the time European visitors entered into Maya territory to explore their ancient culture, their cities had largely been swallowed by the jungle. Their books (accordion-folded bark books called *codices*), festooned with a hieroglyphic language, had—with just three exceptions—been destroyed by an early Spanish bishop who decided that these works represented a form of devil worship. Their architecture appeared alien and their sculptures phantasmagorical to European artistic sensibilities. At least partially as a result of this, the Maya were, and continue to be, the subject of all manner of speculation concerning their origins, their abilities, and, ultimately, the demise of their civilization.

The Maya are the focus of a number of the entries in this encyclopedia. Reading these entries, you will hopefully be convinced that, indeed, the Maya were not inspired to become civilized by **ancient astronauts** (the Maya are a favorite subject of **Erich von Däniken**) nor was one of their great leaders—Pacal, ruler of the Maya city-state of Palenque—one of those astronauts (see **Palenque sarcophagus**). The evidence is abundantly clear, as well, that the Maya were not descendants of survivors of the catastrophe that supposedly decimated the Lost Continent of **Atlantis**, that no **Hall of Records** exists at an undiscovered Maya site (the equivalent of a similarly nonexistent Hall of Records under the **Great Sphinx** in Egypt) containing records saved by those escapees of Atlantis's destruction, and that the Maya calendar does not prove that the world will end on December 21, **2012**.

The Maya produced a spectacular ancient civilization replete with vast cities, powerful armies, and magnificent monuments. Depicted here are the Pyramid of the Feathered Serpent at Chichen Itza (left) and the Pyramid of the Magician at Uxmal. (K. Feder)

Though there is quite a bit of debate concerning the precise origins of the Maya, much of that uncertainty stems from the fact that their civilization evolved in a tropical habitat. The presence of a civilization in such a setting long surprised nineteenth-century cultural geographers, historians, and archaeologists, who thought that "complex cultures" could develop only in drier, presumably more productive environments, especially large, broad river valleys like that of the combined Tigris and Euphrates rivers in Mesopotamia (modern-day Iraq), the Nile in Egypt, the Yellow in China, or the Indus in Pakistan. It was commonly believed that only this kind of habitat was productive, predictable, and controllable enough to support an economic system that allowed for the production of a vast food surplus. Such a food surplus was necessary to free large segments of the populace from subsistence pursuits, thus providing the material basis for the evolution of socially stratified hierarchies, including the evolution of classes of specialists like artisans, architects, and engineers; the ability to marshal the communal labors of large populations to produce great monuments; the need for power to be concentrated in the hands of leaders who could organize these large, dense populations; and the development of mathematics and methods of keeping records (e.g., for taxes or military conscription) as part of a system of social control.

Unfortunately for Maya researchers, there has been no equivalent of the Rosetta Stone found in Maya territory. The Rosetta Stone, discovered in Egypt in 1799, was a rather mundane written text from 196 BCE about a tax amnesty awarded to priests. Though the content wasn't terribly important (well, except to the priests getting the tax break), the fact that the same content was inscribed on the stone in three different languages—Greek, demotic (a late form of Egyptian), and hieroglyphics—was vitally important. In 1799, the vast body of Egyptian hieroglyphic writing—on papyrus, on temple walls, inside tombs—was incomprehensible, a dead language without any way in which to translate it. But the Rosetta Stone afforded scholars a crucial language key, since the Greek on the tablet was readable. With a known version of the text right next to an unknown version of exactly the same message, the unknown language became decipherable. Without a similar lucky find in Mesoamerica, translating Maya hieroglyphs has been far more difficult and only slowly cumulative, without any epiphanies provided by breakthrough artifacts. Slowly but surely, however, scholars have been unlocking the secrets of their language, and increasingly the Maya have been able to tell us their story in their own words.

Here's what we do know. Beginning more than 2,500 years ago, the Maya people developed a highly productive agricultural economy based on maize (corn) and beans. As their individual communities grew, some settlements developed into small cities. With cities came the need to organize and coordinate the labors and social lives of an increasingly dense population, and classes evolved in whose hands power became concentrated. The need to increase the land base to produce more food for a growing population led to increasing competition among the developing city-states and, eventually, the institutionalization of warfare as a way of dealing with this competition. With warfare came prisoners and booty and the further concentration of wealth, power, and control in the hands of an elite class topped by a king.

We even know the names of many of these rulers. In their book *Chronicle of the Maya Kings and Queens*, Simon Martin and Nikolai Grube (2008) enumerate the names, kingdoms, time periods, and recorded accomplishments of many Maya rulers. We know further that one military ruler in particular—a foreigner from another Mesoamerican civilization, Teotihuacán, a vast urban complex located near modern-day Mexico City—played a pivotal role in forming alliances, fighting wars, and controlling the vast economic and social wealth (in the form of people) of the Maya territory. This leader, known as "Fire Is Born," arrived in Maya territory on January 8, 378 CE, and within a year had installed new rulers in Maya city-states. These new rulers weren't Maya; they were from Teotihuacán, in an apparent attempt by Fire Is Born to personally control the Maya citizenry.

I guess you could say that Fire Is Born was an alien, but he was not of the extraterrestrial variety, nor was he an Atlantean. His story, like the entire story of the Maya, is one of complex economies and social systems exploiting the labors of the many to accomplish communal tasks and, in so doing, concentrating wealth and power in the hands of an elite or noble class, who were ever desirous of more wealth and power. It is an all-too-human story and, in that, shows that the speculations about extraterrestrials of **lost civilizations** are not only unsupported by evidence—they are wholly unnecessary.

Further Reading

There's no dearth of excellent books that focus on the factual archaeology and history of the Maya civilization. Among the best are Arthur Demarest's *Ancient Maya: The*

Rise and Fall of a Rainforest Civilization (2007) and Martin and Grube's *Chronicle of the Maya Kings and Queens* (2008). Though it's getting a little old, one of the most beautifully written of the books about the Maya is Linda Schele and David Freidel's *A Forest of Kings* (1990). I also like David Webster's *The Fall of the Ancient Maya: Solving the Mystery of the Maya Collapse* (2002), which, despite its title, covers not just the end but the entire range of Maya history. *National Geographic* published a lengthy article about the rise of the Maya, "The Maya Glory and Ruin," in 2007; written by Guy Gugliotta, it's a great read, and the photographs are mind-blowing.

McCrone, Walter

Walter McCrone (1916–2002) was a world-renowned chemist and microscopist who, through his McCrone Research Institute, was much in demand for his forensic expertise. Among the most significant cases McCrone worked on involved the serial murders of African American children in the Atlanta area in the late 1970s and early 1980s. McCrone's analysis of forensic evidence in the case, including blood residues, human hairs, and fibers, contributed to a solution of the murders and the arrest of the killer.

Two of McCrone's best-known investigations were those he directed into the **Vinland Map** and the **Shroud of Turin**. In the case of the Vinland Map—ostensibly a **Norse** map evidencing their **discovery of America** before the voyages of Christopher Columbus—McCrone (1976, 1988) examined the parchment with a scanning electron microscope and ion microprobe. He found residue of titanium dioxide, the primary ingredient in a slightly yellow pigment called titanium white. If the map were a genuine Norse navigational guide recording their discovery of Newfoundland, in Canada, it should date to the tenth or eleventh century. Titanium white, however, was not manufactured until the twentieth century, indicating that it was, most likely, a recent forgery.

McCrone's work on and conclusions about the Vinland Map garnered him the acrimony of the parchment's supporters, but that was nothing compared to the response generated by his work on and conclusions regarding the Shroud of Turin, a cloth that was claimed to be the burial shroud of Jesus Christ, bearing a miraculously wrought image of Christ at the moment of his resurrection. McCrone was brought in to investigate the shroud by the **Shroud of Turin Research Project**, a group of what ended up being primarily believers in the authenticity of the shroud. McCrone (1982) and his associates examined thousands of shroud fibers and collected samples from the surface of the linen. They found clear evidence of pigment on the shroud—specifically, red ocher (commonly used to produce red paint) and mercuric sulfide, an ingredient used in the Middle Ages to make vermilion, a deep red pigment. When he tested the brown staining on the shroud, which many thought might be dried human blood, McCrone found no evidence of blood—all standard forensic tests for blood used in modern criminal investigations were negative. McCrone (1996) later worked with artist Walter Sanford to experiment with a number of methods by which the image on the shroud might have been produced. Their experimental replicas were convincing, at least to some researchers.

Further Reading

Walter McCrone died in 2002, but his research lives on in the McCrone Research Institute. You can read more about his refutation of the authenticity of the Vinland Map and the Shroud of Turin at the Institute's Web site at http://www.mcri.org/home/section/63/research.

Michigan Relics

More than 800 clay, copper, and slate artifacts constitute the Michigan Relics, certainly one of the more elaborate (and prolific) of the hoaxes surrounding alleged pre-Columbian visitors to the New World. The imagery and inscription on this object are meaningless. (Thom Bell)

The Michigan Relics reflect an elaborate archaeological hoax in which literally hundreds of artifacts were found, festooned with crude and bizarre inscriptions written in various Old World languages. All told, between 1890 and 1920, it is estimated that excavators (none of them professional or trained archaeologists) found upwards of 800 clay, copper, and slate artifacts (Halsey 2009). A literal interpretation of the artifacts seemed to prove that Michigan had been populated by groups of Jews, early Christians, and ancient Egyptians. None of the Michigan Relics were particularly convincing, however, and most looked like very crude attempts at archaeological humbugs.

The earliest examples aren't just crude, they're impossible. For example, some of the first of the Michigan Relics were made of unbaked clay. Unbaked or unfired clay—objects made of clay that has been allowed to air- or sun-dry but has not been fired in a kiln and, therefore, not made into ceramics—will simply either be reduced to clay dust when subjected to any kind of rough handling or regain moisture and revert to soft clay when placed in a wet environment. In either case, an unfired clay object is simply not going to survive in an intact state after being buried in the wet soils of Michigan, especially since it will experience seasonal freezing and thawing. It is impossible for an unfired clay object pulled out of the soils of a Michigan site to have been there for very long, certainly not thousands of years—in fact, not hundreds of years, not decades, and maybe not even days. Therefore, the initial discovery of unfired clay objects that were supposed to be authentic artifacts from thousands of years ago was a dead giveaway that the relics were **frauds**. The fact that later discoveries included *fired* clay objects is a good indication that the individual or individuals behind the hoax learned from the initial criticism and skepticism and improved on their fakery in subsequent rounds of the hoax.

Further Reading

There's a very informative virtual museum exhibit dedicated to the Michigan Relics, produced by the Michigan Historical Center available at http://www.hal.state.mi.us/mhc/michrelics/ (Anderson, Halsey, and Stamps 2004).

Moundbuilder Myth

The most vexing part of the moundbuilder myth is that it was inspired by a mystery that could easily have been dispensed with had eighteenth- and nineteenth-century scholars in northeastern North America and the American Midwest bothered to read the memoirs and accounts of Spanish explorers and travelers through the American Southeast in the sixteenth century and French traders who navigated the Mississippi River in the seventeenth century. Had they done so, those scholars would have read accounts of American Indian societies living in dense, citylike settlements, surrounded by enormous swaths of territory converted to agricultural fields. Those scholars who promulgated the myth of a mysterious civilization in North America whose identity was unknown—but which, they were certain, could not have been any of the known groups of local Indians—would have read about the construction of enormous pyramids of earth on which stood the chief's residence or temples of various kinds of worship. They would have been made aware of the existence of great rulers or kings and classes of nobility, much in the manner of ancient civilizations and, in the spirit of full disclosure, in many ways not all that different from the kingdoms of medieval Europe.

However, they either did not read Spanish or French or did not avail themselves of the works of people like Hernando de Soto's chronicler—who, in

Examples of some of the more impressive earthen mounds built, not by some mysterious Old World visitors to the New World in antiquity but by American Indians: (a) Miamisburg (Ohio); (b) Etowah (Georgia); (c) Cahokia (Illinois). (K. Feder)

keeping a journal of that four-year-long expedition across most of the southeastern United States, wrote about Indians living in vast walled towns with populations in the thousands. Otherwise, they might have read the French trapper and cartographer Louis Joliet's description of the Natchez Indians of the lower Mississippi River who lived in urbanlike settlements and had powerful kings who lived on artificial mounds of earth.

Because these historical accounts went unread, when Europeans from northeastern North America expanded their settlements to the west, into Ohio, West Virginia, Illinois, and Indiana, and encountered hundreds, even thousands, of large and elaborate artificial tumuli of earth, they had no historical context in which to view them.

These sometimes monumental conical mounds, within which complex burials were found, raised questions about who had built them and who the great rulers buried within were. When European settlers recognized the existence of vast swaths of land enclosed by geometrically precise circular or octagonal earthworks, or when they came upon vast plateaus entirely circumscribed with earthen mounds that conformed to the configuration of their edges, they wondered at the amount of labor it must have taken to make these enclosures and for what purpose were they made. And then there were the effigies: beautiful and alien sculptures of soil in the form of great birds, bears, and even a coiled snake (see **Serpent Mound**). What ancient artists—in Ohio or Wisconsin—had been able to command the labor of so many to produce such works of beauty that could only be appreciated from up in the air? Finally, what complex civilization had built the giant pyramids of earth at places like Cahokia in Illinois, and other, smaller, ancient settlements scattered across the American Midwest and Southeast—monuments that, at least in terms of their volumes, were the equal of many of the stone pyramids of Mesoamerica and Egypt? What great, ancient, but now extinct civilization, they wondered, had thrived along the banks of the Mississippi River and its tributaries, extracting resources from places located across the expanse of the American Midwest and Southeast, and had buried their rulers in sumptuous splendor?

Bringing with them a biased perspective about Native American abilities to labor cooperatively, to live in large social groups, and to organize their labor efficiently, many of those who attempted to put those mounds in context began with the assumption that Indians—at least the Indians of North America—could not have had anything to do with them. These thinkers came up with myriad possibilities for who had built the mounds, but most of them adhered religiously to the notion that it couldn't have been the Indians.

Perhaps the mounds had been built by members of the Lost Tribes of Israel. The Old Testament of the Bible enumerates 12 ancient tribes of the Jewish people, but only 2 can be traced to the present era. For some, the fate of the missing 10 tribes has long been a historical mystery. Most historians believed they simply disappeared by intermarriage with non-Hebrews, but some preferred to believe they up and went somewhere. Placing them in ancient North America where they could have built the mounds seemed like an interesting solution, but it raised the question, since when did ancient Jews build mounds? They hadn't done it in ancient Israel, so why did they start building them like crazy when they got to the New World?

Or perhaps it was globe-trotting Egyptians. Others suggested it had been "Hindoos" who built the mounds, or Phoenicians or Atlanteans. Or maybe it *was* Native Americans, but not of a local variety—possibly the ancient Toltec of Mexico, predecessors of the Aztec. Whoever might have built the mounds, for most the underlying assumption was: anybody but the Native Americans living in their shadows.

The manufactured moundbuilder mystery was a topic of dinner table conversation for many in the eighteenth and nineteenth centuries. Learned societies, museums, and research institutes, including the Peabody Museums at Harvard and Yale and the American Philosophical Association (founded by Benjamin Franklin), were dedicated to study of the mounds and the mysterious, unknown moundbuilder culture. Thomas Jefferson excavated a mound on his property, so fascinated was he about the origin of moundbuilder culture. By the way, Jefferson got it right: He concluded that there was no reason to believe people other than American Indians were responsible for the mounds.

Even the U.S. government became involved and set aside part of the funding allotted to the federal Bureau of American Ethnology for a solution of the moundbuilder mystery. **Cyrus Thomas** was hired to direct the project. Among his important accomplishments was debunking many of the **fraudulent** objects placed into or near mounds by those who had a particular ax to grind, cross to bear, hypothesis to uphold, or dollar to make. Thomas exposed fake inscriptions and determined that misidentified "iron swords" were, in reality, weapons made from local copper. Thomas sought out those historical eyewitness accounts of American Indians living in contexts that were very similar to those suggested by the ancient mound sites. And he supported the excavation of the mounds and the collection of artifacts. Together, the data Thomas collected and compiled broke the back of the moundbuilder myth.

The mounds represent the works of several different Indian groups living in different regions, bearing different cultures, and living in different time periods. There are the Adena (2,800 years ago) and Hopewell (2,200 years ago) burial-mound builders, centered in Ohio, and then later, 1,000 years ago, there are so-called temple-mound builders of the Southeast and the Mississippi Valley, who developed the equivalent of city-states centered within the drainages of major waterways. Cahokia in Illinois; Moundville in Alabama; Kolomoki, Ocmulgee, and Etowah in Georgia; Town Creek Mound in North Carolina; Crystal River in Florida, and many other sites scattered across the eastern United States are not mysterious at all. They are the well understood reflections of complex societies developed by Native Americans. Fascinating, incredible, spectacular—but not a mystery.

Further Reading

I devote a chapter to the myth of the moundbuilders in my book *Frauds, Myths, and Mysteries* (Feder 2010). The best historical account of the myth, filled with insights about why people so embrace the notion of a mysterious, non-Indian race of moundbuilders, can be found in Robert Silverberg's book *The Moundbuilders* (1989).

Mystery Hill

Mystery Hill is the name once attached to a site located on a hill in North Salem, New Hampshire, characterized by a complex array of stone walls, stone chambers, and an assortment of other kinds of stone features. The site was originally called Pattee's Caves, for the Pattee family, which owned the land on which the site is located and is credited by some with having built the complex. The site name was changed to **America's Stonehenge** when the owners decided to focus not on the supposed mysterious elements of the site but, instead, on what they believed to be the **astronomical alignments** of some of the stone structures at the site. At least for some, the name change reflects a belief that the site may be historically connected to the people who built **Stonehenge** or, at least, their **Celtic** descendants. (See the entry on America's Stonehenge for a more detailed discussion of the site and the controversies that surround it.)

Mystery Park

Mystery Park was a mercifully short-lived attempt by **Erich von Däniken**—of **ancient astronaut** fame—to cash in yet again on that bit of pseudoscience by taking a page from Walt Disney's book and building a theme park based on the ancient astronaut fantasy. With well-known financial backers, including major firms like Coca-Cola, Fujitsu, Sony, and Swatch, supplying more than $60 million in start-up money, von Däniken built his Mystery Park in Interlaken, Switzerland, where it opened in 2003.

The park consisted of a ring of seven buildings, each representing what, to von Däniken, anyway, were major mysteries of the ancient world:

1. Orient, where the focus was on **Egyptian pyramids**
2. **Maya**, where von Däniken explained that the fact that the ancient Maya developed an accurate calendar shows they must have had assistance from a superior intelligence
3. Megastones, like **Stonehenge** and other megalithic sites
4. **Nazca**, a look at the famous South American **geoglyphs**, well understood by archaeologists, not so well understood by von Däniken
5. Vimanas, about South Asia, including India, with a focus on legends of flying machines
6. Contact (with extraterrestrials)
7. Challenge, which focused on the challenges of spaceflight—by human beings, not extraterrestrials

In the middle of this circle of seven pavilions was a sort of home-base Earth, where von Däniken maintained an office and library.

Each themed pavilion presented a rehash of von Däniken's ancient astronaut hypothesis, with interactive exhibits, movies, and dioramas (and, in the Maya building, a mariachi band, although how Mexican folk music figured into the whole notion that human beings weren't smart enough to develop technology—agriculture, math, engineering, metallurgical, and the like—without the assistance of extraterrestrials wasn't made clear).

Much of the park appeared to be unintentionally offensive to our very intelligent, creative, artistic, and clever human ancestors. For example, the highlight of the Maya pavilion was a movie in which extraterrestrials visited the Earth in the ancient past and abducted a group of children, bringing them to ET's home planet. There, the children were schooled in the various technologies that von Däniken believes were too difficult for humans to develop on their own. Once civilized by the extraterrestrials, the children were returned to Earth to share their newfound knowledge with their ignorant compatriots. I assume (well, I hope) that the writers of the movie were unaware of the fact that in real Earth history, Europeans had the habit of kidnapping native people and bringing them back to their home countries where they were displayed, humiliated, and exploited, all in the name of civilizing them.

Attendance figures show that the park was a success, at least initially. The park experienced its highest level of attendance in its second year of operation (2004), when 440,000 people visited. Unfortunately for von Däniken and his backers—though fortunately for a rational and scientific perspective of the human past—public fascination with Mystery Park dropped precipitously, with a 50 percent drop in annual attendance in the following year (2005), and by November 2006, the doors were closed and the park declared bankruptcy.

Under new management and with a new name—Jungfrau Park (though Jungfrau literally means "young woman" and is usually translated as "virgin," the name relates to a nearby mountain)—von Däniken-land is open again in 2010. Apparently, the original pavilions are only a part of the draw as the new owners are aiming for a broader audience with go-karts, a mini-zoo (with llamas and goats!), and "bouncy castles." It is unclear how, exactly, any of the new attractions relate to the ancient astronaut hypothesis.

Further Reading

Alas, I didn't have an opportunity to visit Mystery Park before it closed the first time. But Eric Powell, a writer for *Archaeology* magazine, went and reviewed it. Although it's not as good as having been there, Powell (2004) does a very good job of describing the absolute weirdness of the place.

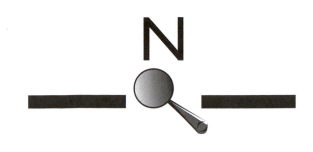

Navigatio

The *Navigatio*—more properly, the *Navigatio sancti Brendani abbatis*, or in English, *The Voyage of St. Brendan, the Abbot*—was a book first published sometime in the ninth century. It presented the story of navigational exploits of the Irish monk **Brendan** in what was described therein as a seven-year-long ocean voyage westward into the Atlantic Ocean.

Born in 484 in County Kerry, in the southwest of Ireland, Brendan—later to become Saint Brendan, not coincidentally, the patron saint of sailors and travelers—was one of a number of Christian monks called **anchorites** who left their homes in Ireland aboard ox-hide boats called *curragh*, seeking outposts where, isolated from other people and the vicissitudes of ordinary life, they could meditate and commune with God.

There is abundant archaeological evidence that anchorites actually successfully navigated deep-sea expanses in the northern Atlantic during the late fifth and early sixth centuries. The actual archaeological remains of their settlements and monasteries have been found on various islands north and west of their Irish homeland. Radiocarbon dating of organic remains indicates that there were anchorites living, meditating, and worshipping God—not to mention eating and throwing away refuse—on the Orkney Islands, north of the Scottish mainland, by 579; even farther north on the Shetland Islands by 620; and in the Faeroe Islands by 670. In fact, archaeological evidence shows quite clearly that anchorites made it at least as far as Iceland by no later than 795, beating the **Norse** there by more than 60 years; the Norse settled Iceland no earlier than 860.

Brendan ostensibly left on his sea voyage sometime after 510, with—depending on which version of the story you now read—anywhere between 14 and 60 voyagers. The *Navigatio* is quite descriptive and, beyond the clearly fantastic tales of sea monsters and such, some of the features encountered by Brendan seem to lend support for the historicity of his voyages. According to the *Navigatio*, Brendan saw floating columns of crystal in the far northern Atlantic—plausibly a reference to icebergs, the earliest written documentation of them by a European explorer. In another reference, Brendan records passing a smoking, foul-smelling mountain from which, according to the *Navigatio*, natives pelted them with flaming rocks, likely a description of a volcano. Iceland has 130 volcanoes, (the one that's currently erupting is wreaking havoc with air travel in 2010) and it seems likely that Brendan was describing a sixth-century eruption of one of them.

The *Navigatio* is representative of a genre of Irish literature of the time called *immram*, brave tales of sea voyages. The *immram* are legendary stories, but in the case of the *Navigatio*, it seems probable that at least certain elements of the story describe actual encounters of Irish monks, maybe Brendan himself, with natural features of the North Atlantic, encountered during an actual sea voyage. What is uncertain is what, precisely, the authors of the *Navigatio* were talking about when they discussed Brendan's journey far to the west, to the place called the "Land Promised to the Saints." The *Navigatio* relates fantastic stories of the exploration of this territory and Brendan's discovery of a great river.

Situated by the *Navigatio* to the west of Ireland, far away in the Atlantic, could the Land Promised to the Saints be America? Could the great river Brendan discovered be the Mississippi, or, at least, the Hudson? Adventurer Tim Severin attempted to replicate Brendan's ostensible voyage in 1976, overcoming a number of difficulties—including having the boat pierced by a piece of ice—but he eventually made it all the way to Newfoundland. It's questionable whether that proves that the anchorites could have accomplished the task, but regardless, it begs the question: Is there any physical archaeological evidence that sixth- (or seventh-, eighth-, ninth-, or later) century Irish monks were actually in the Americas? The answer to that question is an unequivocal no. No Christian crosses, Irish rings, or buttons have ever been found in archaeological contexts here reflecting a pre-Columbus or pre-Viking visit to the New World. That being the case, the story of St. Brendan and his journeys to the Land Promised to the Saints may be an interesting one, but its historical veracity is not supported by any archaeological data.

Further Reading

There's an informative article about the *Navigatio* and Brendan in the 1971 edited volume *Quest for America*. The book's editor and the article's author is Geoffrey Ashe.

Nazca Geoglyphs

Geoglyphs—literally, "earth-writing"—are artistic depictions, on a grand scale, often of animals or of people, made either by the patterned piling up of rocks or by the patterned removal of stones to reveal a lighter or darker underpavement. Among the most famous ancient geoglyphs are the Nazca lines and animal effigies in Peru. Here, beginning at least 2,200 years ago and continuing until about 1,300 years ago, native people swept away dark pebbles that covered the surface to reveal the lighter, sandy layer beneath, along straight, wide swaths of the Altiplano, some measuring miles in length. These lines sometimes parallel one another and, more

Large-scale artwork, visible in its entirety only from above, is common throughout the ancient world: the Uffington Horse in England, Serpent Mound in Ohio, and the Blythe Intaglios in California are just three examples. Perhaps the best known of this kind of ancient art are the Nazca figures, and among the best known of these is the monkey figure shown here. (AP Photo/Martin Mejia)

often, crisscross, creating what appears to be a fantastic jumble of linear features. **Erich von Däniken**'s assertion that the Nazca lines resemble the distribution of runways at a modern airport is interesting, but of little significance; the underlying soil is unconsolidated and far too soft to sustain the weight of an aircraft. It is also difficult to believe that extraterrestrial aliens landing on our planet would need runways in the first place.

Among the Nazca geoglyphs are a few hundred effigies, images on an enormous scale of animals like monkeys and llamas, birds (hummingbirds and condors), fish (possibly sharks), whales (or maybe dolphins), and spiders. The largest of the effigies measures more than 650 feet (200 meters) across.

Claims that the Nazca lines could have been made only if the native people of Peru could have lifted themselves up in some sort of aircraft for a literal bird's-eye view are pretty inane on their face, and ultimately unnecessary. Further assertions that seem to imply that the effigies were built at the behest of extraterrestrial visitors to our planet are bizarre in the extreme. Such a hypothesis begs the question: Why would extraterrestrials travel across the galaxy to induce South American natives to produce images of giant monkeys, spiders, and condors?

Researcher Joe Nickell produced a perfectly reasonable Nazca spider effigy replica to scale using little more than a drawing and a tape measure. Nickell used an aircraft only to take photographs after the fact, showing, if not his great artistic abilities, at least how relatively easy it is to make a Nazca geoglyph.

A question more intriguing than how were the lines made is why they were made at all. Hypotheses revolving around possible **astronomical alignments** have not been supported by data; the lines do not point consistently to important points on the horizon (for example, the summer or winter solstice). Some of the effigies repeat similar, much smaller-scaled images on pottery and may reflect simply symbols of spirits or gods worshipped by the Nazca people. Whatever their meaning, their construction certainly was well within the capability of ancient human beings.

Nazi Archaeology

One of the most pernicious applications of archaeology rests in the attempt by the Nazis to use the archaeological record to support claims of Aryan superiority and non-Aryan inferiority or to support assertions of previous Aryan sovereignty over land in other people's nations. In some cases, this misappropriation of the archaeological record was accomplished merely through a twisted misinterpretation of that record, and in some cases, it was based on outright **fraud**.

As archaeologist Bettina Arnold (1992) maintains, when officially sanctioned Nazi archaeologists claimed that an artifact found in an excavation anywhere in the world was "Germanic," it meant that wherever that artifact was found had once been German territory and, by implication, still should be. How, specifically, an artifact might be judged to be Germanic is, of course, an open question, but archaeology served the purpose of the National Socialist People's Party (the Nazi Party) when it claimed the presence of evidence of an ancient Germanic presence in countries surrounding Germany in the 1930s and 1940s that were occupied by Slavic people. By invading these sovereign nations, the argument went, Germans were merely reasserting sovereignty over territory that the archaeological record showed had been theirs in the past.

With a keen understanding that, by controlling the telling of history, the Nazis could recast that history to support their desire for domination, archaeology experienced enormous growth during Nazi rule. Archaeological excavations were supported by the state, and open-air museums were constructed at several of them. University archaeology programs saw a spike in funding, hundreds of books were published following a Nazi theme in the interpretation of prehistory (ancient Aryans were more intelligent and more advanced than other people in antiquity; Aryans were the developers of civilization and generously shared their advances with the rest of the world in antiquity), and there was even a popular film series presenting a Nazi view of the human past.

Arnold (1992) nailed it in the title of her article about Nazi archaeology in *Archaeology* magazine: "The Past as Propaganda." Many of the Nazis recognized this correlation. It made no difference that none of the claims were legitimately backed up with scientific data. Arnold quotes Heinrich Himmler, Hitler's minister of the interior, overseer of the concentration camps, orchestrator of the deaths of millions of people, right-hand man, and all-around evil incarnate, as saying:

> The one and only thing that matters to us, and the thing these people are paid for by the State, is to have ideas of history that strengthen our people in their necessary national pride. In all this troublesome business we are only interested in one thing—to project into the dim and distant past the picture of our nation as we envision for the future. (33)

Himmler may have been the closest thing our species has ever seen to the Devil with DNA, but in this he likely spoke the truth. He cared nothing about the actual archaeological record, only how it could be invented and/or manipulated to give the masses of German people a past that would instill in them the notion that they were superior to other groups and always had been.

Further Reading
The best source about the Nazi interest in appropriating the archaeological record to support their worldview is Arnold's 1992 article in *Archaeology*. The photograph of Hitler and his cronies visiting an archaeological site is beyond creepy.

New Age Archaeology

At the heart of New Age archaeology is the belief that the archaeological record presents evidence of an ancient world filled with wisdom, psychic power, love, peace, and music. In this reconstruction of the past, ancient people were far more intelligent than we are today, and they applied that intelligence not to produce violent, hurtful, and crass technologies to subdue the Earth but to provide for their own physical needs through the paranormal application of thought and spirit. Reading the rantings of New Age archaeologists, one is led to believe that in antiquity people lived in peace and harmony; there was no conflict and no war; there was no disease—or, at least, diseases could be healed through the application of wisdom and the occasional herb poultice—there was no pollution, no racism or hate; sex was always awesome; and people lived in tune to the vibrations of Mother Earth and were at one with the cosmos. In other words, the ancient world was a lot like Woodstock—without the bad acid and before it started raining.

This cliff dwelling, located in Sedona, Arizona, is viewed by some New Agers as a place imbued with mystical power. Archaeologists perceive its power, not as emanating from anything mystical or occult, but from its ability as an archaeological site to convey to us in the present the story of the lives of the ancient people who lived there and viewed it, simply, as their home. (K. Feder)

At the heart of New Age archaeology is the desperate hope that the past was a lot better than the present, that in deep time, there was a golden age when people had figured out how to be happy, to fulfill their potential without conflict, without competition, and without death.

As our modern world is nothing like this mythical utopia, the New Agers are forced to propose that something awful happened in antiquity that resulted in our current state of decay. Perhaps there was a natural cataclysm like the one that befell **Atlantis** (in this view Atlantis represents the ancient utopia, which reflects a woeful ignorance of **Plato**'s description of the island nation). In another scenario, some folks turned to the dark side, usurped control from the elders, and ended up blowing everything up. In most of the scenarios, whatever the ultimate cause, the destruction of the perfection of antiquity occurred sometime between 10,000 and 12,000 years ago.

There isn't a scintilla of physical evidence that anything of the kind occurred. There is no archaeological evidence of a supersophisticated civilization 10,000 years ago—no gleaming cities, no factories powered by Earth energies harnessed by human thought, no crystal palaces. Similarly, there is no evidence of a vast and terrible catastrophe that would have destroyed this ancient perfection, though some New Agers, rather conveniently, assert that the catastrophe, whether natural or the result of human foibles, was so great that it erased every last bit of evidence of the existence of this ancient civilization. You will admit, this would make the claim impossible to actually investigate. After all, would the lack of evidence be viewed as proof of the existence or nonexistence of the vast catastrophe?

The fact that New Age archaeology is tripe has not prevented enterprising entrepreneurs from trying to cash in on the desire on the part of some people to believe in a past when everything was better than it is today. For instance, you can take any one of a number of jeep tours to archaeological sites and **vortexes** in Sedona, Arizona. Visits to genuine archaeological sites often are included in such tours, where the fascinating remains of the homes of ancient people and their accumulated trash middens are elevated to the level of the sacred. It likely would have amused the ancient residents of these places that, more than 1,000 years after the fact, baby boomers would be desperately searching for answers to the riddles of existence by visiting the ruins of their abandoned homes.

New England Antiquities Research Association (NEARA)

The New England Antiquities Research Association (NEARA) is an organization dedicated, in its own words, "to a better understanding of our historic and prehistoric past through the study and preservation of New England's stone sites in their cultural context" (www.neara.org). Among the sites and features NEARA is dedicated to understanding are "lithic sites," including stone chambers, rock piles, stone cairns, **astronomically aligned** stone walls, upright stones, and balanced rocks, scattered across the New England landscape. For a very interesting "picture glossary" representing most of the categories of stone features or lithic sites that the organization focuses on, go to www.boudillion.com/glossary/glossary.htm.

For many in NEARA, these lithic sites represent a wealth of remarkable evidence of the ancient occupation of New England by ancient **Celts** and other western Europeans long before the arrival of the Pilgrims in Massachusetts or even Christopher Columbus in the Caribbean. Orthodox archaeology and history reject this claim, ascribing most of the lithic sites to more recent migrants to New England, namely, seventeenth-, eighteenth-, and nineteenth-century settlers and farmers. Archaeological skepticism about claims of much earlier dates for the chambers is based on the complete lack of any artifactual evidence found in any of the chambers that would allow us to confidently trace these features to an earlier time period (see **Discovery of America**).

NEARA publishes a paper journal, provides a free online journal, publishes books, and holds conferences. In its dedication to the preservation, study, and understanding of these lithic sites, NEARA deserves great praise and gratitude from the historic preservation community. Most professional historians and archaeologists might disagree with the ascription of these lithic sites to pre-Columbian settlers to the New World but are in full agreement with NEARA that these sites and features are significant historical resources that deserve protection and study.

Newark Holy Stones

Among the motives for perpetrating a historical or archaeological **fraud**, there are instances in which individuals of a particular religious persuasion feel justified in doing so if they think that a fraud is likely to bring people to their faith, to cause people to accept a tenet of their religion, or perhaps to save their souls. Such a deception is justifiable, they would say, because it serves a greater good. It's a small lie, in the greater scheme of things, that serves a greater purpose. As revealed by Brad Lepper and Jeff Gill (2000), the Newark Holy Stones are an example of just such a fraud.

Though several artifacts were involved, there were two primary Newark Holy Stones. The first was discovered, if that is the correct word, in June 1860, in Newark, Ohio, by David Wyrick. Wyrick was a land surveyor and a doctor with an active mind. Outside of the professions in which he was trained, Wyrick had a lifelong fascination with the seemingly ancient earthworks that were abundant in his home state of Ohio, and none of these earthworks commanded his attention more than those located in Newark. There, and to this day, can be seen elaborate and monumentally scaled patterns sculpted in soil. There are enormous circular enclosures, tens of acres (hectares) circumscribed by mounds of earth, as well as beautifully symmetrical, great octagonal landscapes measuring, again, in the tens of acres and again demarcated by long barrows of thick, dark soil. Two elongated parallel walls of earth, as much as 10 feet (3 meters) high and 200 feet (60 meters) apart, stretch for as much as a cumulative 60 miles (100 kilometers) linking some of the larger earthworks.

The origins of the earthworks of Ohio, Illinois, Indiana, Mississippi, Georgia, and Alabama and, in fact, across the Midwest, mid-South, and Southeast was a long-standing mystery among historians, archaeologists, and intellectuals of all specialties, along with a fascinated general public, in eighteenth- and nineteenth-century America. It was during this time that the myth developed of a mysterious group of non-Indian **moundbuilders** who were responsible for monuments like the Newark earthworks. Wyrick's discovery of artifacts in the Newark mounds with Hebrew writing on them and the ensuing scientific and public reaction must

The "decalogue" stone, front and back, presenting a copy of the Ten Commandments in an archaic form of Hebrew. The decalogue was one of the Newark Holy Stones, infamous archaeological hoaxes perpetrated to show a linkage between the builders of America's Midwestern mounds and the Lost Tribes of Israel. (The Johnson-Humrickhouse Museum)

be viewed within this historical context; there was much confusion about the source of the American earthworks, and any artifact that appeared to contribute to a solution for this mystery garnered the rapt attention of just about every thinking person.

At the same time, the discovery—or, as it actually turns out, the fabrication and planting—of the Newark Holy Stones must be viewed within the context of an ongoing debate about the origins of American Indians. For some, the biblical story of Adam and Eve in the Garden of Eden referred only to the history of white people of European descent. As Lepper and Gill (2000) point out, there were those who suggested that the different, accepted races of humanity were entirely separate (and unequal). Those who supported this view of "polygenesis" were opposed by those who interpreted the Old Testament of the Bible as the story of the creation of all people as part of a single human race. As Lepper and Gill show, the Newark Holy Stones seem to have been tailor-made, at the right place and the right time, to support "monogenesis," the perspective that all human beings were of the same race and all were descended from Adam and Eve.

When David Wyrick made his initial discovery in Newark, he was already a believer that the Newark earthworks had been constructed by descendants of the so-called Lost Tribes of Israel, remnants of some of the original Israelites mentioned in the Old Testament of the Bible. His hypothesis seemed to be verified by his discovery of what became known as the Keystone, a four-sided stone, looking for all the world like a plumb bob, with Hebrew writing on all four of its faces. Not fluent in Hebrew, Wyrick brought the artifact to Israel Dille, a friend also interested in antiquity. Coincidently (or not so coincidently), Charles Whittlesey, a well-known archaeologist, was staying in Dille's home. Dille and Whittlesey brought the Keystone to the Reverend John Winspeare McCarty, a local Episcopal minister, who translated the writing on the stone: "The Laws of God"; "The Word of God"; "The Holy of Holies;" and "The King of the Earth."

As much as Wyrick wished to believe the artifact was genuine, proving that Jews lived in Ohio in antiquity and had constructed the Newark earthworks, McCarty remained unconvinced. His skepticism originated in the fact that the Hebrew on the Keystone was an anachronism; it was a modern variety of Hebrew on a stone that was, ostensibly, quite ancient. McCarty concluded that the Keystone had been produced only very recently and bore no connection to the ancient mound in which it had been found by Wyrick.

In what was either a coincidence of epic proportion or the result of a hoaxer learning a lesson and doing a better job in his second effort, within five weeks of the skeptical assessment of the Keystone, none other than Wyrick discovered another stone with Hebrew writing on it, one that seemed almost supernaturally to negate McCarty's criticism of the earlier discovery. This second Holy Stone was a far more elaborate artifact, a piece of black limestone bearing the image of what appeared to be Moses of the Old Testament encircled by the Ten Commandments written, unlike the messages on the Keystone, in an appropriately archaic version of Hebrew.

It was quite remarkable, at least in retrospect, that with all the archaeological research being conducted in the mid-nineteenth century in the American Midwest, the only two artifacts that seemed to support a Jewish connection were found by the same individual just five weeks apart and a few miles from one another. It also seemed like another astonishing coincidence that, after the first Holy Stone was determined to be a modern artifact because the Hebrew on it was of a recent vintage, five weeks later in the same region, an artifact was discovered with a much more ancient variety of Hebrew. It was as if someone had discovered a new Shakespeare play that had been written in modern English and was interpreted to be a recent forgery and immediately thereafter, the same researcher discovered another new, this time possibly authentic, Shakespeare play, now replete with Old English *thee*'s and *thou*'s. What are the odds of that? It would seem vastly more likely that an ignorant forger, learning from his mistake the first time, and with the unintentional assistance of the critics of the first discovery, went back to the drawing board and did a more convincing job on the second try. This seems precisely to be the case with the Newark Holy Stones. The Decalogue, while written in a more appropriate variety of Hebrew, was still a mess; a Harvard University professor of Near Eastern languages has labeled the Decalogue a "grotesque" forgery.

The intent of the forger—Lepper and Gill (2000) assert that it may have been McCarty in an attempt to get the attention of higher-ups in the Church in his connection to evidence proving a Jewish presence in ancient Ohio—cannot be known for sure. What *is* sure, however, is that the Newark Holy Stones were fakes, part of a host of similar fakes concocted to show that the moundbuilders were Europeans, lost Israelites, Egyptians, or Atlanteans, in an effort to rob Native Americans of their true history.

Further Reading

There is no better summary of the Newark Holy Stones—and no better solution to the mystery behind this whodunit—than Brad Lepper and Jeff Gill's 2000 article in *Time-lines*, a publication of the Ohio Historical Society. Lepper and Gill placed the final nail in the coffin of this fake.

Newport Tower

The Newport Tower is located in Newport, Rhode Island. Its construction history is incomplete, and some have argued that the tower is pre-Columbian, constructed by Norse settlers of the northeast coast of North America. In an attempt to ascertain the origins of the tower, an archaeological investigation was conducted in its vicinity and a report was published in 1951 (Godfrey 1951). Thousands of artifacts were recovered, including clay tobacco pipes, iron nails, pieces of crockery, buttons, and buckles. All were all traceable to England and Scotland and evidenced a seventeenth-century date of construction. The preserved impression of a boot print from footwear datable to the colonial period found under one of the tower's columns seemed to cinch the date for construction as no earlier than the seventeenth century (Newport was first settled by Europeans in 1639).

More recently, organic material incorporated into the mortar used to bond the stones during construction has been dated with the radiocarbon technique. The date derived from this method, most likely sometime between 1635 and 1698, matches with the general time period suggested by the artifact assemblage recovered during the archaeological investigation of the tower (Hertz 1997).

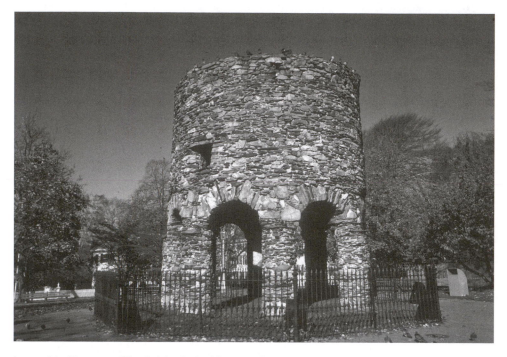

Located in Newport, Rhode Island, the Newport Tower was built by Benedict Arnold, the great-grandfather of the infamous traitor to the American cause in the Revolutionary War. It is not a Norse structure. (K. Feder)

We also have information that Benedict Arnold (not the infamous traitor to the American fight for independence, but his great-grandfather), then the governor of Rhode Island, had the structure built after his arrival in Newport in 1661; a very similar structure, actually a windmill, was located in Chesterton, England (it still exists there), where Arnold was born and raised. Arnold even refers to it as "my stone built windmill" in a document dated to 1677.

Additional excavations were conducted at the tower in 2006–2008. Once again, lots of artifacts were found in the vicinity of the tower and the oldest date to the seventeenth century. There is no archaeological or documentary evidence that supports a Norse connection to the Newport Tower. The Newport Tower almost certainly represents the remains of Governor Arnold's seventeenth-century windmill.

Further Reading

Take a look at the article written by J. Hertz in *Newport History* in 1997 for a discussion of the Newport Tower, including a radiocarbon-dating program of organic material in the mortar that indicates a relatively recent age for the structure. A short discussion of the results of the most recent dig at the tower (Flynn 2006) can be found online at http://www.newportdailynews.com/ee/newportdailynews/default.php?pSetup=newport dailynews_archive.

Noah's Ark

Noah's ark is the purported great boat built by the biblical character Noah, as instructed by God, to save representatives of every species from divine retribution. Though most people have heard that God commanded the 600-year-old Noah to save two individuals, one male and one female, of every animal species, the Bible actually specifies that Noah was to save on board the ark seven of every "clean beast" and two of every "unclean beast" (Genesis 7:2). Noah and his family—his wife, their three sons, and his sons' wives—were the only human beings on board the ark. God tells Noah that once the great boat is filled, he will cause it to rain for 40 days and 40 nights, declaring that "every living substance that I made will I destroy from off the face of the earth" (Genesis 7:4).

The flood story as told in the Bible was likely inspired by even older stories, very similar in their specifics, told in Mesopotamia. The flood story in the Bible was first written down sometime between 550 and 450 BCE. The Mesopotamian version was first recorded as early as 1800 BCE, and possibly before that. Just for the sake of comparison, in the Akkadian version, the god Enki warns the pious Atrahasis of an impending great flood and instructs Atrahasis to build a huge boat and coat it with pitch. Atrahasis fills the boat with possessions, animals, and plants and survives and so, therefore, does humanity.

There are a number of published works that deconstruct the flood story. For example, there is no geological evidence for a worldwide flood. And it simply would not have been possible to collect and then care for representatives of thousands upon thousands of animal species. How would koala bears from Australia, llamas from South America, and penguins from Antarctica have managed the trip to the ark's location in the Middle East? And how would their human caretakers have looked after this vast menagerie of animals? Noah, his wife, and his three sons and their wives (that's a total of only eight people) providing water and food to the animals would have been an impossible task. What (or who) would the carnivores, living in close quarters with all of those delicious herbivores, have eaten? And, I hesitate to ask, when would those eight people find the time to clean out the poop-filled stalls of all those thousands of animals (Isaak 1998)?

More to the point in terms of the focus of this encyclopedia, consider the enormity of the ark's dimensions: 300 cubits long by 50 cubits wide. Using the standard conversion figure for a cubit (18 inches or 45 centimeters), that makes the ark a stunning 450 feet (137 meters) long and 75 feet (23 meters) wide. Archaeological evidence shows that the largest boats that date to the approximate period of the supposed flood (5,000 years ago), found in Egypt, are no more than about 75 feet (23 meters) long and 7 feet (2 meters) wide.

If a universal deluge obliterated all of humanity save for a handful of people on a single boat, cultures all over the world would have been destroyed. One would certainly expect there to be archaeological evidence of this kind of devastation. The archaeological record of 5,000 years ago would be replete with Pompeii-style ruins—the remains of thousands of towns, villages, and cities, all wiped out by flood waters, all simultaneously. In the sequence of cultural evolution, including the development of technologies like agriculture and metallurgy, the sciences and mathematics, architecture and writing, we would see progress up to a certain point in time and then obliteration, followed by a new beginning as the descendants of Noah necessarily picked up the pieces to start again. We see no such break in the archaeological record. It would appear that the near annihilation of the human race, if it happened, left no imprint on the archaeological record anywhere.

Nevertheless, all of the problems inherent in viewing Noah's Flood as veritable history, instead of a cautionary tale about disobeying God's will, have not prevented people from looking for and even claiming to have found Noah's ark, in whole or in part. Interestingly, whenever photographs have been taken of the ark resting on Mount Ararat in Turkey or Mount Suleiman in Iran—entirely intact, in some versions of the story—the images have disappeared or are too blurry to make out (autofocus mechanisms on cameras seem never to work when taking photographs of the Loch Ness Monster, Bigfoot, or Noah's ark). Eyewitnesses disappear or have died mysteriously. And, in those few cases where evidence has been presented of purported boatlike formations on mountaintops, geologists and archaeologists have shown the features to be entirely natural. As the flood story itself is unsupported by any archaeological evidence, it is not surprising that there is no archaeological evidence for the existence of an impossibly large boat dating to 5,000 years ago.

Further Reading

There are at least two excellent deconstructions of the Noah story. Robert Moore wrote a point-by-point refutation of the historical accuracy of the Bible story that appeared in *Creation/Evolution* in 1983. Mark Isaak wrote an online article in 1998 that provided another perspective. If you are interested in the context of the Noah story in a broad perspective, take a look at the book *Noah's Flood: The Genesis Story in Western Thought* by Norman Cohn (1996).

Norse in America

The claim that the Norse discovered, explored, and settled the New World before the voyages of exploration of Christopher Columbus is an excellent test case for how claims of the **discovery of America** in antiquity originate, how they generate controversy and skepticism, and how, ultimately, they can be tested with archaeological data—and, in this instance, are supported by such data.

The primary source for the claim that the Norse were in the New World long before Columbus are the Viking sagas. The sagas began as Norse oral traditions extolling the bravery, ferocity, and accomplishments of their "Vikings." Most of the sagas were eventually written down, some centuries after the events described were supposed to have transpired.

Two of the sagas, the *Greenlander's Saga* and *Eric the Red's Saga*, tell a similar story of the accidental discovery of new lands at the western margin of the Atlantic Ocean. According to these stories, in 986, a young Norse farmer, Bjarni Herjolfsson, got lost on a sea voyage from his home in Norway to his father's farm on Greenland. The Norse had discovered, explored, and established a couple of colonies on the southern tip of Greenland in 985–986. Herjolfsson missed Greenland and continued sailing west where, by the account presented in the sagas, he spied three territories he called Helluland (Flat Slab Land), Markland (Forest Land), and Vinland (Wine Land). Herjolfsson did not make landfall, however. He turned back to the east, made it safely to Greenland, and told all the Norse he encountered about the lands to the west.

Seeing this as a great opportunity, another Norseman living on Greenland, Leif Ericsson, sailed west with a contingent of 35 men, attempting to retrace Herjolfsson's steps. According to the sagas, they made landfall on Vinland, built some houses, and stayed for a while before returning to Greenland. Another attempt was reportedly made to settle the newly found land to the west, this time by Thorfinn Karlsefni and 65 colonists. This colony lasted about a year, but the native people, the "Skraelings," weren't particularly inviting, and the Norse left.

These written versions of the *Greenlander* and *Eric the Red* sagas were interpreted by some historians as evidence that the Norse had, indeed, made contact with and even attempted to settle in the New World almost 500 years before Columbus's voyages. For others, however intriguing the stories contained in the sagas may have been, the legends did not provide definitive proof that the Norse had done so. Many scholars were understandably skeptical about the sagas and the motives that fueled them. For archaeologists, the ultimate proof for a Norse presence in the New World is physical evidence, and until such archaeological evidence was forthcoming to support the tales told in the sagas, there was quite a bit of skepticism about the historical validity of the stories told therein.

That skepticism was answered fully in 1960 when explorer and writer Helge Ingstad and his wife, archaeologist Anne Stine Ingstad, discovered the physical remnants of a Norse settlement at the end of a peninsula on the northwest coast of the Canadian island of Newfoundland, at a place called L'Anse aux Meadows. Anne Stine Ingstad's work at the site revealed the presence of the footprints of typically Norse houses called "booths"; a ring-headed bronze pin (bronze was unknown in pre-Columbian North America); iron boat rivets, nails, and the smithy where the iron had been produced (though the Inuit people of North America used iron from meteorites to fashion tools, the smelting of iron was unknown in the aboriginal New World); a soapstone spindle whorl used in wool spinning; and ember boxes where fires were kept. The site looked much like similar Norse outposts in Greenland. When the charcoal from the ember boxes was radiocarbon-dated, the deal was sealed: the mean age of 21 samples was 920, a little early for the saga story of Leif Ericsson, but close enough.

Since the discovery and excavation of L'Anse aux Meadows, a thin scattering of artifacts has been found in the northeastern margins of North America that are alien and intrusive, looking nothing like the material culture of the native people of the region and often made of raw materials whose sources are Greenland, Iceland, or mainland Europe. Smelted iron, a cast bronze pot, nonnative copper artifacts, spun yarn (on Baffin Island), and part of a bronze balance (on Ellesmere Island) add to a picture of a Norse presence in the New World in the centuries before Columbus (Sutherland 2000). No longer speculative, the interpretation of the sagas as reflecting a Norse presence in the New World has been borne out by archaeological evidence.

Further Reading

You can find the Norse sagas online. Eric the Red's can be found at www.gutenberg .org/files/17946/17946-h/17946-h.htm. The Smithsonian Institution has a spectacular Web site devoted to the Viking discovery, exploration, and colonization of North America: www.mnh.si.edu/vikings/voyage/. And the Ingstads' own book, *The Viking Discovery of America: The Excavation of a Norse Settlement in L'Anse aux Meadows, Newfoundland* (2000), is another great source of information, while at the same time conveying the excitement of a breathtaking scientific discovery.

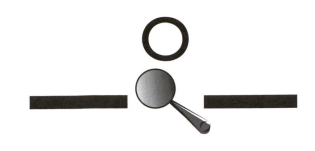

Occam's Razor

Occam's Razor (a *razor*, in this context, means a rule), states that, in scientific reasoning, "entities are not to be multiplied beyond necessity." What this means, essentially, is that when faced with multiple possible explanations for a given phenomenon, it is best at least initially to go with the explanation or explanations that require the fewest other "entities"—other unverified facts, assumptions, or logical leaps. This rule of logic is credited to a fourteenth-century English friar, William of Ockham, and so it bears (a variation of) his name.

For example, if you see a light in the sky and you think it might be a meteor, a satellite, an airplane, or an extraterrestrial spacecraft, you really ought to investigate one of the first three possibilities before jumping to number four. I mean, you *might* have seen an actual alien spacecraft, that's true. But for that to have been the case, so many other as yet unproven "facts" need to be verified—that there *are* extraterrestrial aliens, that they have spacecraft, that they are capable of interstellar flight, that they have found Earth, and that they came here to visit. We cannot deny the fact that these are all possibilities (though we have no real idea of the probability of any of them), but they are all as yet unconfirmed by any evidence. These, in fact, are examples of those "entities" we need to multiply and that William warned us about.

To turn to an archaeological example, when we suggest methods by which ancient Egyptians may have quarried, transported, and then erected 2.5 million blocks of stone into a nearly 500-foot-high pyramid, Egyptologists, architects, engineers, and masons focus on the likelihood that their ancient counterparts relied on tried-and-true methods we all know work on smaller-scale projects. These researchers (unlike **Erich von Däniken**) don't seriously consider the possibility that extraterrestrial aliens built the pyramids with lasers, tractor beams, and antigravity devices, at least until they have some direct evidence that those things actually existed in ancient Egypt. If you think that means these researchers are being closed-minded, you are partially correct. The doors to their minds aren't fully closed, but they're only slightly ajar. They won't open those doors widely until there's a good reason to.

A popular version of Occam's Razor states that "the simplest explanation is probably the best," but that's a bit oversimplified. It's better to phrase it like this: Unless and until there's evidence that leads you away from a simple or mundane explanation for an observation or phenomenon to one that requires a bunch of other stuff that you can't verify, stick with the simple and the mundane. In that way, you avoid being pulled down a lot of blind alleys that lead nowhere.

On the basis of (sometimes, admittedly, limited) physical data, archaeologists attempt to come up with an explanation for events that happened in antiquity. That's not easy. Following Occam's Razor, careful—and, okay, conservative— archaeologists will initially embrace those explanations that seem to fit what we already know and that don't demand the existence of a bunch of facts that we don't know. It makes sense, and it's a rule followed by all scientists.

Ogham

Ogham is a 25-letter alphabet developed in Ireland in the third century CE and used there into the sixth century. Between the third and sixth centuries, its use spread into Scotland and Wales.

Ogham letters consist mostly of one or more parallel and angled marks carved, scratched, or notched onto stones along a centerline. Most of the roughly 400 extant inscriptions in Ireland, Scotland, and Wales have been read as personal names.

Because the individual letters in the Ogham alphabet consist of little more than parallel lines, some people have been fooled into thinking they have found Ogham inscriptions in what are, in fact, little more than tally marks, plow blade scratches, or natural striations on rock. In fact, marine biologist **Barry Fell** interpreted a series of such tally marks, striations, and hoaxes found in the New World as Ogham inscriptions, proving to his satisfaction—and the satisfaction of his followers— that ancient **Celtic** people had been to the New World long before either Columbus (in the late fifteenth century) or the **Norse** (in the late tenth century), leaving inscribed messages in Ogham as they made their way through the New World, especially but not exclusively in the American Northeast. Interestingly, Fell dates many of the inscriptions in the New World that he examined to well before the third century, leading to the remarkable conclusion that Celts entering into the New World were leaving inscriptions in a language they had not yet developed.

Experts in Ogham have examined at least some of the New World artifacts that Fell has claimed as genuine inscriptions and concluded that none were authentic. Ives Goddard and William Fitzhugh of the Smithsonian Institution examined a number of Fell's inscriptions and determined that "all of the alleged ancient New World inscriptions examined by specialists to date have been found to contain linguistic or epigraphic errors or anomalies consistent with modern manufacture but inconsistent with genuine ancient origin" (1979, 167). Two British experts in ancient Celtic culture, archaeologist Anne Ross and historian Peter Reynolds, have characterized Fell's translations of scratch marks as a "semantic phantasy of the wildest nature" (1978, 106). Finally, Brendan O Hehir, founder of the Department of Celtic Studies at the University of California, Berkeley, after performing a detailed analysis of one of Fell's Ogham translations, described it as "a stupid and ignorant **fraud**" (1990, 1).

Ogham is a genuine, alphabetic, written language dating to between the third and sixth centuries in Great Britain. No genuine Ogham inscriptions have been found beyond Great Britain, and certainly none have been found in the New World.

Olmec Colossal Heads

The Olmec Colossal Heads are, exactly as their name describes, colossal sculptures made of basalt, a volcanic rock, carved into the form of human heads and faces. The heads were made between 3,200 and 2,900 years ago by the Olmec, the earliest civilization in Mesoamerica. The Olmec built a series of large ritual centers, each covering a few square miles and marked by large earthen pyramids and platforms.

The heads are the most impressive of the Olmec artworks. To date, 17 have been recovered at 4 ritual centers: 10 at San Lorenzo, 4 at La Venta, 2 at Tres Zapotes, and what appears to be an unfinished one at La Cobata. The heads are all large and reflect an enormous amount of cooperative labor in quarrying, transporting the stone (at least 37 miles/60 kilometers from their geological source in the Tuxtla Mountains to the sites where they were found), and sculpting them into the shape of a human head with a very realistic and detailed face. The smallest of the sculptures is 4.8 feet (1.5 meters) tall, and the largest is more than 11 feet (3.4 meters) from top to bottom. They range in weight from 6 tons (5,440 kilograms) to a truly monumental 50 tons (45,000 kilograms). Because the heads have all been found at major Olmec ceremonial centers and as each one has a unique and realistic face capped with a distinctive headdress, researchers suggest that the heads are depictions of actual rulers (Diehl 2004; Pool 2007). In other words, the Olmec Colossal Heads are the equivalent of our much more recent sculpted depictions of kings and presidents.

Though there is no controversy among Mesoamericanists about the heads, **Ivan van Sertima** maintains that the faces depicted in the sculptures are all **African**. He bases this claim on three facts:

1. The stone used to sculpt the heads is black.
2. The noses of the heads are broad and flat.
3. The lips of the sculpted faces are broad and thick.

To date, 17 monumental sculpted human heads have been found in Mesoamerica and credited to the Olmec culture. Though some suggest that the faces have an African appearance, there is no evidence to suggest an African inspiration for the Olmec civilization, or an African presence in Mesoamerica in antiquity. (AP Photo/Denis Paquin)

In other words, on the basis of little more than eyeballing the sculptures, van Sertima concludes that the Olmec rulers were migrants from Africa and takes this to mean that the earliest civilization in Mesoamerica was inspired by pre-Columbian African visitors and settlers of the New World.

To be fair, van Sertima is not the first scholar to note a similarity between the faces depicted on the Olmec heads (and in other Olmec representations of human faces) and those of people of African origin. For example, when the first of the Olmec heads was discovered and discussed in 1869, José Melgar stated, "That which most impressed me was the Ethiopic type which it represents; I reflected that indubitably there had been negroes in this land" (as translated by archaeologist Christopher Pool [2007, 35]).

Melgar's assertion and van Sertima's conclusion are based on little of evidentiary value. The black color of the sculptures is meaningless; black is the color of the readily available, durable volcanic stone that abounds in Olmec territory, and it bears little resemblance to the actual skin color of people of African descent. Further, not all of the raw material actually was black; at least one of the heads is made from a white raw material. Beyond this, if we are going to rely on morphological features to determine the continent of origin of the models for the sculptures, it must be pointed out that the heads show flat facial profiles, similar to the profiles of Native Americans and quite different from the commonly prognathous profile (the lower face thrust out from the upper) of people of African descent. Finally, a close examination of the sculptures shows what appears to be a skin fold in the eyelids, seeming to depict the epicanthic fold typical of Asian and New World native people.

There is no evidence for the presence of African migrants to the New World before Columbus. No artifacts have been found whose raw material source can be traced to Africa; no artifacts whose style could only come from a pre-Columbian African source have been found in the New World; and finally, no skeletal remains have been found, dating to a pre-Columbian context, with DNA proving an African source. The civilizations of the New World, including those in Mesoamerica and South America, exhibit archaeological evidence for a long sequence of indigenous development and no evidence for inspiration outside of the New World. The Olmec heads were the product of indigenous skills in quarrying, transportation, and sculpting, as well as the ability to conscript and organize labor for monumental undertakings. The Olmec heads provide no support for hypotheses of the presence of Africans—or Europeans, or recent Asian migrants—to the New World.

Further Reading

There are some terrific books about the Olmec, all of which discuss the monumental Olmec heads. Christopher Pool's *Olmec Archaeology and Early Mesoamerica* (2007) and Richard Diehl's *The Olmecs: America's First Civilization* (2004) are great places to explore the Olmec in general and the colossal stone head sculptures in particular.

Ossowiecki, Stefan

Stefan Ossowiecki (1877–1944) was a Polish spiritualist in the 1930s and 1940s. Between 1937 and 1941, Ossowiecki was tested for his psychic abilities by ethnologist Stanislaw Poniatowski. He was provided a series of stone artifacts from the Paleolithic and asked, essentially, to make up stories about them. Such stories or **psychic archaeology** are, unfortunately, notoriously difficult to test in terms of their accuracy for the simple reason that the psychics tend to provide details that we don't, and likely can never, actually know. As pointed out by archaeologist Marshall McKusick (1982), when confronted with stone tools, Ossowiecki tended to provide descriptions of their makers that sounded suspiciously like stereotypical Neanderthals, replete with sloping foreheads and large brow ridges. The problem here is that he was often provided with artifacts that had been made not by Neanderthals but by ancient, anatomically modern-looking human beings (often called Cro Magnons for the cave site in France where the type specimens were first defined). In other words, whereas the accuracy or legitimacy of most of Ossowiecki's pronouncements cannot possibly be assessed, where they *can* be, he was pretty consistently wrong.

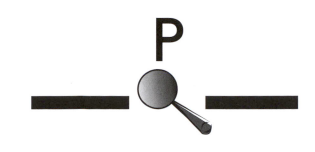

Palenque Sarcophagus

The **Maya** city of Palenque is located in eastern Mexico, in the lowlands of the state of Chiapas. Palenque was a major Maya ceremonial center, replete with beautiful and imposing monuments in a city carved out of the tropical jungle. Arguably the most imposing of the monuments constructed by the Maya at Palenque is the Temple of the Inscriptions, a four-sided truncated pyramid topped with a stone temple. (Technically, none of the Maya pyramidal structures are true pyramids by the standard geometric definition of a three-dimensional shape with triangular faces that meet at a common apex.) Like most Maya pyramids, the Temple of the Inscriptions has the standard form of a pyramid at its base, but the top is incomplete, looking like it has been sliced off ("truncated"), which produces the flat platform where sits the temple.

The Temple of the Inscriptions differs from the other Maya pyramids in a number of ways, not the least of which was that archaeologists found an entryway in the floor of the pyramid's platform leading down into the pyramid itself. When this doorway was discovered in 1949 by Mexican archaeologist Alberto Ruz Lhuillier, researchers had no idea what to expect; this was a unique feature in Maya architecture. Certainly there was enormous excitement as archaeologists commenced what turned out to be a nearly three-year project to remove the rubble filling the steep passageway with stairs leading to the base of the pyramid. At the end of the passageway, archaeologists discovered a corridor, and at the end of the corridor was a stone box in which they found the disarticulated skeletons of a half dozen people. To the side of the corridor was another door. The door was removed on June 13, 1952, revealing a small room with a tall, sharply angled corbeled ceiling above and a floor entirely taken up by a covered sarcophagus, a large burial box carved from a solid block of limestone. The thick and heavy limestone cover was lifted, revealing the richly adorned burial of an aged man, almost certainly in his eighties when he died. The old man's body had been covered with cinnabar, a bright red, mercury-based pigment, and the sarcophagus was filled with jade jewelry, including a beaded collar, wristlets, rings on every finger, and a cube of jade in one hand, a sphere in the other. Topping it off, literally, the man's face was covered by a mask made from a mosaic of jade tiles.

The bas-relief on the sarcophagus lid of the Maya ruler K'inich Janaab Pakal I (usually referred to just as Pacal) shows the great king in his period of transition from the living to the afterlife. It does not depict Pacal as an extraterrestrial astronaut. (Jennifer Davis)

The Maya left detailed written information about the man in the tomb and his place in the genealogy of Palenque. His name was K'inich Janaab Pakal I; he is usually referred to as Pacal and was a ruler of the city of Palenque. The hieroglyphs left behind by the Maya on the walls of the palace on top of the pyramid and on the sides of the sarcophagus tell his story.

Pacal ascended to the throne of Palenque nearly 1,400 years ago on July 29, 615. He was just a child, barely 12 years old when he became king, but his mother, Lady Sak K'uk', likely held the reins of power—or at least played a major role in running Palenque—until her death in 640 when Pacal was 37 years old.

Pacal's rule was long and eventful; he commissioned or oversaw the construction of several impressive structures in the city. And when he died, the citizens of Palenque buried him in splendor in this sarcophagus topped with a splendidly carved lid. It is that lid, more than any other element of Pacal's tomb and perhaps more than any other single element of the Maya culture, that has inspired so much speculation.

The carving on the lid is perhaps one of the finest examples of Maya sculptural art. The artist depicted in bas-relief the dead king himself, seated atop a platform, gazing upward. For those not knowledgeable about Maya religion, beliefs, or ceremonies, the image may seem chaotic, with an incomprehensible jumble of faces, animals, and shapes.

Hoping, I suppose, to impose order on the scene depicted on Pacal's sarcophagus lid, **Erich von Däniken** decided that the image is that of an astronaut seated in the pilot's seat of a spacecraft. I am not making that up. Read for yourself how he interprets the image:

> There sits a human being with the upper part of his body bent forward like a racing motorcyclist; today any child would identify his vehicle as a rocket. It is pointed at the front, then changes to strangely grooved indentations like inlet ports, widens out, and terminates at the tail in a darting flame. The crouching being himself is manipulating a number of unidentifiable controls and has the heel of his left foot on a kind of pedal . . . With our knowledge of similar pictures, we should be surprised if the complicated headgear were missing. And there it is with the usual indentations and tubes, and something like antennae on top. Our space traveler—and his is clearly depicted as one—is not only bent forward tensely; he is also looking intently at an apparatus hanging in front of his face." (von Däniken 1970, 100–101)

In all honesty, I cannot imagine anyone coming up with anything quite that "out there"; it certainly isn't the first thing that pops up into my mind when I look at Pacal's sarcophagus lid.

Mayanists—people who have spent their professional careers examining, studying, translating, interpreting, and understanding Maya iconography, art, and writing—recoil at a suggestion quite that bizarre. Instead, looking at each of the individual elements, Mayanists see Pacal depicted in a state in between life and death. The configuration of Pacal's body suggests that the sculptor depicted him falling, which would make sense; beneath Pacal's body are symbols of Xibalba, the Maya underworld, destination of the souls of the dead. Next to the image of the falling king is a carving of a monster's head. The monster is carrying a bowl marked with the Maya glyph for the sun. Just as the sun dies each evening and is then reborn in the dawn, the dead Pacal is shown falling into the pit of death, but like the sun, he is certain to be reborn. Around the sides of the coffin, the sculptors carved the names of Pacal's relatives, including his mother, father, and children, depicted with tree roots, as if growing from the earth.

Despite von Däniken's positively hallucinatory interpretation, beneath the image of the dead king are not the flames of a rocket in midlaunch but the face of a Maya water god, guardian of the underworld. Surrounding the base of the lid are the stylized jaws of two gape-mouthed dragons, representing the gates of the underworld. Behind and looming above Pacal is a cross, commonly seen in Maya artwork. The Maya themselves, in their own voice through their written language, call it the Tree of Life that holds up the sky. Perched on the top of the cross/tree very clearly is a bird, almost certainly the Maya quetzal, again a common image in Maya art and iconography. What any of these images—the large crosslike tree, dragon jaws, water monsters, skulls, or quetzal birds—are doing inside or nearby to the nose cone of a rocket, von Däniken makes no effort to explain.

Ultimately, it is important to point out that the body of the dead king, the earthly remains of Pacal himself, is right there in the sarcophagus for anyone to see. Are they the skeletal remains of an extraterrestrial alien? Is the skull that of a bulb-headed Grey, as shown in so many artistic representations of ETs? Are there lasers or faster-than-light communicators in the tomb? How about superadvanced BlackBerries or iPads? Nope. Just the artistically splendid, but otherwise technologically mundane, jade objects already enumerated.

Pacal was a great ruler, a successful king of an impressive Maya city-state that held sway in eastern Mexico 1,400 years ago. He was rich and powerful but, ultimately, all too human, and he succumbed, like the rich and poor alike, the powerful and the powerless, to the final, most powerful force of all: mortality. Pacal's coffin lid was the product of human beings attempting, through the ritual of art, to memorialize the death of a human being.

Further Reading

You can read the real history of Pacal and the iconographic context of his burial, including the Maya meaning of the images on his sarcophagus lid, in *Chronicle of the Maya Kings and Queens* by Simon Martin and Nicolai Grube (2008).

Palos Verdes Stones

In 1973, a vessel dredging a shipping channel off the coast of Southern California recovered a doughnut-shaped stone that resembled the stone anchors used by Chinese fishermen for more than 1,500 years. Two years later, divers off the Palos Verdes Peninsula southwest of Los Angeles recovered more than 20 additional similar objects, which became known as the Palos Verdes Stones. One interpretation of the anchors was that ancient Chinese fishermen or Buddhist monks had traversed the Pacific and made landfall—a **Chinese discovery of America**—1,500 years ago.

By his own word, in 499, just a little less than 1,000 years before Columbus, a Buddhist missionary by the name of Hui Shen sailed east of China and encountered a place he called **Fusang**. Based on the distances provided by Hui Shen in his narrative, there is long-standing speculation that Fusang was located in the New World. By those who embrace this scenario, the specific location of Fusang is usually believed to have been in California.

None of Hui Shen's descriptions of Fusang match the actual archaeological record of California for the fifth century or, for that matter, any point in California history. Hui Shen's description of the peoples and cultures he encountered in Fusang bear little in common with the native cultures of California and seem to be a much closer—though, to be sure, imperfect—match with the ancient people of the Korean Peninsula. Nevertheless, supporters of the supposed connection between Fusang and California were intrigued by the Palos Verdes Stones.

The stones were examined by the Geology Department of the University of California at Santa Barbara in 1980. Had the stones been geologically traceable to a rock source in China, and had there been any dating possible of the stones or associated artifacts placing them in a fifth- or sixth-century context, the Fusang–California connection would have been supported. A reasonable interpretation might have been that, indeed, Chinese mariners had traveled to the New World a 1,000 years before Columbus made landfall in the Caribbean and had, accidently or intentionally, left behind archaeological evidence of their presence here—their calling card, if you will—in the form of their stone anchors.

Unfortunately for that interpretation, the geologists identified the stone from which the anchors were produced as being good old Monterey shale, a common rock type in Southern California (Frost 1982). In other words, whoever left behind the Palos Verdes Stones had made them in California, not China or anywhere else.

That still leaves open the question, who *did* make and then lose or abandon anchors in an ancient Chinese style? It almost certainly was Chinese settlers of California who commonly fished off of the coast in the nineteenth century. These Chinese-Americans used traditional watercraft with traditional stone anchors. The

Palos Verdes anchors are important artifacts after all, but they don't provide any support for the hypothesis that ancient Chinese mariners traveled to California in oceangoing vessels in the fifth or sixth century and called it Fusang. Instead, the anchors reflect the persistence of a traditional seafaring technology among nineteenth-century Chinese settlers of the western United States.

Further Reading

Take a look at Frank Frost's article "The Palos Verdes Chinese Anchor Mystery" in *Archaeology* (1982) for a detailed examination of the Palos Verdes Stones.

Petroglyphs and Pictographs

Petroglyphs are a category of rock art that includes designs, drawings, images, or messages usually produced by scraping away at a stone's surface. When that surface is darker—primarily as a result of weathering—than the interior of the rock, the petroglyph maker, by scraping or engraving or etching away at that dark surface, produces a lighter, even bright, image that dramatically seems to pop out of its darker background.

Pictographs are painted images, usually on rock surfaces. The oldest rock art in the American Southwest may be as much as 8,000 years old, but Native people continue to produce images on rock as part of a continuing tradition of the ritual production of rock art.

Petroglyphs and pictographs are very common in the Southwest, where a large number of specific styles have been recognized (Schaafsma 1980). Petroglyph and pictograph images include naturalistic depictions of the local environment, such as local fauna like mountain sheep, deer, or snakes; geometric designs, including circles and especially spirals; clan symbols; shields; mountains; human hand- and footprints; people, including images of women giving birth; masks; and spirit beings (some of whom appear to share features of people and animals or may be human beings wearing masks or costumes).

As in any art tradition, ancient or modern, rock art styles vary geographically and temporally. Interestingly, the arrival of the Spanish in the American Southwest in the seventeenth century is marked in local rock art in the form of images of human beings riding on horses; the horse had become extinct in the Americas at the end of the Pleistocene (or Ice Age) and was reintroduced by Spanish explorers in the sixteenth century.

To be sure, petroglyphs and pictographs can be difficult to interpret. Many of them appear to be abstract, and all of them are part of traditions of ritual and religion worship that may be difficult to understand by those who are not part of those traditions. Nevertheless, there is no support for any claims that petroglyph images

Boulders, cliff faces, cave walls, and bedrock outcrops are ubiquitous and served as the canvases for artists in antiquity as well as the present. Here find two kinds of this rock art: (top) a petroglyph etched into a wall face in Chaco Canyon, New Mexico, and (bottom) a pictograph painted onto a rock face in Sedona, Arizona (K. Feder)

of what appear to be unearthly beasts, chimeras (combinations of different animals), and especially bipeds with what appear to be horns or antennae are actual, realistic depictions of paranormal creatures or extraterrestrial aliens; such claims are actually rather silly. Even a cursory examination of the artistic expression of the descendants of those who produced the rock art—many of whom continue to produce rock art—reveals the religious and ritualistic contexts of the images.

From the perspective of a twenty-first-century non-Native, I suppose a figure walking on two feet with lines emanating from its head might conceivably, at least superficially, conjure up a spaceman wearing a helmet with antennae. However, if you are aware, in this example, that the culture that produced the image practices a ritual in which a dancer wears a mask and headdress with antlers to portray a hunted deer, then perhaps a simpler explanation for the rock art would be that it depicts one of these dancers. Following **Occam's razor** and **Carl Sagan**'s suggestion that extraordinary claims require extraordinary levels of proof, we really ought to examine the deer dancer explanation before we start resorting to explanations based on unsupported assertions about the presence of extraterrestrial aliens among us.

Further Reading

Not only can you read about petroglyphs but, depending on where you live, you might have some nearby, on public land, that you can see for yourself. Take a look at Dennis Slifer's *Guide to Rock Art of the Utah Region* (2000) for some incredible ancient art.

Piltdown Man

Piltdown Man is almost certainly the most significant **fraud** in the history of paleoanthropology. It was successful, in the dual sense of generating so much support and being so long lived, because it precisely fulfilled a preferred vision of human evolution.

When the initial cranial fragment was found (apparently in 1908) by workers in a gravel pit at Barcombe Mills Manor in Sussex, in the south of England; was presented to **Charles Dawson**, a local lawyer, artifact collector, author, and amateur scientist who opened up an excavation there and found four more fragments of a skull (in 1911); and was then announced in the British science journal *Nature* in the December 5, 1912, issue, the concept of evolution in general and human evolution in particular was no longer considered heretical. Scientists and educated nonscientists had embraced Charles Darwin's concept of natural selection as he presented it in his seminal work, *On the Origin of Species*, first published in 1859. By the time of the discovery of the Piltdown remains, they no longer viewed the general concept of evolution, even as it applied to the human species, as anathema or even terribly controversial. Instead, the focus had shifted from "if" to "how"— how did the process of natural selection produce human beings?

Following Darwin's approach, the ape species appeared to be the closest living relatives to the human species, and thus they and we must share a common

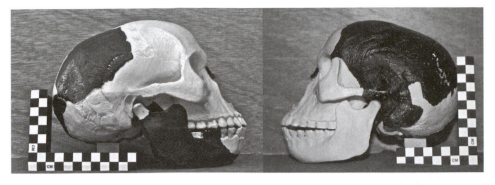

The Piltdown Man skull is probably the best known—and likely the most damaging—archaeological and paleoanthropological fraud. In this model (the left and right sides are shown in this double image), the cranial elements found at Piltdown are shown in black. The rest of the model reflects how paleoanthropologists reconstructed the skull. (K. Feder)

evolutionary ancestor. In other words, a past line of creatures must have bifurcated, with one branch leading to the apes and one to us. But what had it been that marked that break? What physical change led to modern humanity?

The assumption was that, to figure that out, one needed only to consider in which feature human beings and apes most significantly diverge. In the Darwinian view, evolution was slow and cumulative, with tiny changes building up over a long period of time, so it was thought that the characteristic most significantly different between the apes and people must have been evolving the longest and, therefore, happened first.

It should come as no surprise that, following this line of reasoning, it was decided that human beings most significantly differ from the apes not because of hairiness or thumb configuration or the appearance of our big toes (all of which do mark differences between the apes and human beings) but by our intelligence. Certainly, most human beings find our intelligence to be our most defining, salient characteristic—the thing that most definitively marks us as different from (and superior to) all other animal species. That intelligence was made possible by our large brains, which are between three and four times larger than those of even the largest ape brains (the mean volume of a modern human brain is about 1,450 cubic centimeters; a chimp's brain is only about 400 or 450 cubic centimeters). Since it appeared to be our most evolved characteristic, the human brain, housed in a commensurately large skull, must have been evolving the longest. Using this reasoning, scientists in the late nineteenth century expected the first human ancestor to be, essentially, an ape with an oversized head. This preferred interpretation was called the "brain-centered paradigm."

The problem with that nice, neat scenario was that the late nineteenth- and early twentieth-century database of ancestral human fossils did not support it. The reconstructed head of "Java Man," based on an ancient fossil calvarium (just the top of the cranium, without the face or base) found in 1891 on the island of Java in the western Pacific, looked decidedly apelike, but the calvarium had been recovered close by a femur (thigh bone) that looked entirely human. This implied that, contrary to the preferred evolutionary scenario, human ancestors looked like upright apes—creatures with apelike brains but humanlike bodies and modes of locomotion. Similarly, the famous group of specimens labeled "Neanderthals," though their brains were large, had craniums that seemed quite apelike, with large bony ridges about their eyes and a lower face that jutted out, looking like a snout. Below those large but simian heads, the Neanderthals looked more human and were fully bipedal, and, as a result, they served as further proof that the remains of human ancestral forms did not support the brain-centered paradigm.

This all explains why the Piltdown Man discovery so ignited the passions of paleoanthropologists. The Piltdown remains included several cranial fragments and about half of a mandible, the lower jaw. The reconstructed Piltdown cranium resembled that of a modern human, but the mandible was very apelike. So, the argument went, Piltdown Man showed that ancient human beings possessed heads—and, by implication, brains—that appeared to be fairly modern, but from the lower jaw down, they were very apelike.

Though there is no definitive proof as to the identity of the perpetrator of the Piltdown fraud, there are several suspects, including Dawson, who was at the heart of the discovery; Sir Arthur Conan Doyle, who lived near Piltdown and had it in for scientists who belittled his interest in the paranormal; and Arthur Smith Woodward, a well-respected scientist who coauthored articles with Dawson and participated in digs at the site. But the identity of the perpetrator is not all that important.

What we do know is this: After a careful reanalysis of the material was conducted and after the bones were dated beginning in the late 1940s and early 1950s, it became clear that the whole thing had been a fake. The cranial fragments had come from the cranium of a human being, but the mandible was that of an orangutan! The teeth in the mandible had been ground down with a metal file, the point on the mandible where it attaches to the base of the cranium had been intentionally snapped off (otherwise it would have been clear that the skeletal elements didn't belong to the same creature), the animal teeth and bones found with the human remains were from Italy and Africa, and at least one of the artifacts, a bone blade that looked for all the world like a prehistoric cricket bat, showed evidence of having been carved with a metal knife.

Ultimately, Piltdown is instructive in a number of ways. If you provide people, even scientists, with ostensible proof for a preferred hypothesis, they may not apply a sufficiently skeptical approach and can embrace evidence that is poor, at best. Science is self-corrective, but not always quickly. Though Piltdown Man seemed to be the most significant paleoanthropological find of the twentieth century, when no other similar finds were made confirming the legitimacy and significance of the Piltdown discovery, it lost its luster in the minds of most scientists and was relegated to a footnote in textbooks about evolution—an outlier, an exception that could not be explained. By reexamining and dating the Piltdown remains, scientists could explain them not as a significant step in human evolution but as yet another example of the human need to fool other people and our unfortunate ability to let ourselves be fooled.

Further Reading

Maybe because no one has come up with definitive evidence of who the perpetrator or perpetrators were, it still makes for a terrific mystery. I devote a chapter to Piltdown Man in my book *Frauds, Myths, and Mysteries* (Feder 2010), and there are several entire books devoted to the Piltdown fraud. One good one is J. E. Walsh's *Unraveling Piltdown: The Science Fraud of the Century and Its Solution* (1996). Another is *Piltdown: A Scientific Forgery* by Frank Spencer (1990).

Piri Reis Map

In 1513, an Ottoman admiral, Piri Reis, produced a map of the world. The Piri Reis map presents an amalgam of information provided by several Old World explorers, including Columbus. Though some have made a big issue of the map, it is simply a fascinating but not terribly surprising example of sixteenth-century cartography.

After a careful and exhaustive examination of the Piri Reis map, cartographer Gregory McIntosh (2000) has concluded that the map is extremely accurate in those parts of the world that European explorers had visited and thoroughly investigated, less accurate for those segments of the world where those same explorers had made only brief visits, and not at all accurate—in fact, entirely inaccurate—for those parts of the world where they had never been. One point about the Piri Reis map that appears to confuse some thinkers who don't know much about the context of sixteenth-century cartographers is that they hated blank spots in geographic knowledge, were loathe to leave empty spots on maps, and therefore were more than willing to use rumor, unsubstantiated claims, and their own imaginations to fill in the picture. Assertions that the parts of the Piri Reis map that depict the New World are more accurate than should have been possible based only on the information provided by Columbus and the other, recognized explorers of the New World—and therefore must have been based on the work of earlier navigators unknown to or ignored by modern historians, for example, the **Chinese**—simply don't hold up. Claims by the likes of **Erich von Däniken** that the map's rendering of South America and Antarctica is so precise that it could have been produced only from data provided by an observer flying over those regions simply have no basis in fact. McIntosh's (2000) detailed, mathematical assessment of the Piri Reis map shows that it is a valuable historical resource, but not one that would cause us to rewrite the textbooks.

Further Reading

The best, most thorough source on the Piri Reis map is Gregory McIntosh's book *The Piri Reis Map of 1513* (2000). McIntosh places the map in cartographic and historical context, rendering it not nearly as mysterious as some suggest.

Plato

Plato (428–347 BCE) is one of the most famous of the philosophers of ancient Greece. He was a student of Socrates, and Aristotle was Plato's student.

Plato presented his philosophical arguments in the form of dialogues, fictionalized accounts of discussions between Socrates and his students. Altogether, Plato produced 35 of

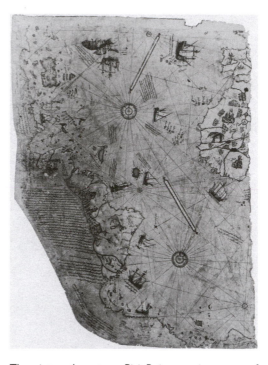

The sixteenth-century Piri Reis map is a sort of Rorschach test for would-be historians who see in it, variously, evidence of pre-Columbian Chinese circumnavigation of the world, seafaring Atlanteans, or even the existence of flying-saucered extraterrestrial aliens. In fact, it's just a map of the world as sixteenth-century cartographers understood it. (K. Feder)

these dialogues. In all likelihood, these conversations did not actually take place; in some cases, the individuals involved in the dialogues are unlikely to have ever met or did not even live at the same time. Plato's strategy was to engage interesting, well-known people in fictional conversations, putting words in their mouths that reflected their beliefs and perspectives, as Plato knew them. It has been suggested that Plato used this little bit of subterfuge to convey his own perspectives and beliefs, while creating a safe distance between him and any beliefs the authorities might find disturbing or dangerous. Remember that his own teacher, Socrates, was induced to commit suicide as a result of expounding ideas the authorities found threatening; perhaps the dialogue technique was a way Plato insured that this would not happen to him. Regardless of Plato's underlying rationale for sharing his ideas through the agency of philosophical discourses by other people, it characterized much of his work and was the method he used to introduce the story of the Lost Continent of **Atlantis**.

Pre-Clovis Sites

The story of the earliest settlement of the New World is fascinating and is still being written. In the early decades of the twentieth century, archaeologists and biological anthropologists believed that the New World had been settled fairly late in human history. It was commonly assumed that the ancestors of the American Indians had arrived in the New World only a few thousand years before the arrival of Europeans.

It has long been thought that the earliest Americans were transplanted Asians who had entered into the New World where Asia and North America are located most closely to each other. The farthest east terminus of northeast Asia, the Chukchi Peninsula, juts out to the east. On the opposite side of the narrow Bering Strait, the Seward Peninsula of Alaska pokes out toward the west. Barely 50 miles (80 kilometers) separates the two peninsulas. Sarah Palin was right: you really can see Russia from Alaska. Thus, it makes sense that the Bering Strait would be the most logical place for people in the Old World to become aware of and to travel to this new land.

It wasn't until 1926, when chipped stone spear points were found in New Mexico, alongside and in the same stratigraphic layer as the bones of a bison of an extinct species that had disappeared from North America 10,000 years ago, that archaeologists gained sufficient evidence to push back the age of the first Americans to that level of antiquity. The nearby town of Folsom loaned its name to the stone spear points found with the bison, and for a time, Folsom points were thought to be the diagnostic artifacts of the earliest settlers of the New World. Soon thereafter, though, even older stone tools were found, not in association with the remains of an extinct bison, but instead with the remains of woolly mammoths and mastodons. These spear points were larger than the Folsom points, though they shared with them a feature not seen in spear points found anywhere else in the world: a channel or "flute" on each face, likely to make it easier to haft the stone tip onto a wooden spear shaft. Just as was the case with the Folsom points, the town nearest to the find-spot of these larger points gave them their name: Clovis.

The Clovis variety of the "fluted point" became accepted as the oldest tool type in the New World. Upon the development and application of radiocarbon dating, archaeologists were able to provide more precise dates to these ancient tools. The dates for Clovis points found with preserved organic remains (that's what radiocarbon dating is performed on) like bone or charcoal, fell within a very narrow range from about 11,000 to 11,500 years ago. (Technically, these are "radiocarbon years," which need to be calibrated for a calendar year range. In fact, in calendar years, the oldest Clovis points date to 13,340 years ago.) The date makes even more sense when you consider the fact that this marks the end of the Pleistocene or Ice Age, during which a substantial amount of the ocean's waters was bound up in glaciers on dry land. Sea level was depressed by more than 330 feet (100 meters) and at times closer to 500 feet (150 meters). The world's coasts looked entirely different, and land bridges were formed between bodies of land currently separated by seawater of a depth less than a few hundred feet. Sea level is relatively shallow in the Bering Strait, and, in fact, during the height of the Pleistocene, not just a bridge but a broad shelf of land as much as 1,000 miles (1,600 kilometers) from north to south connected the Old World to the New. This would have provided a broad avenue for animals to cross, followed by the humans who hunted them, expanding their territory toward the east, into a new continent. It also would have provided a continuous coast characterized by a rich diversity of habitats for coastal-dwelling Asians to follow, first to the east and then south, along the shores of what today is Alaska, Canada, Washington, Oregon, California, and points south.

Though a "Clovis-first" view of American prehistory long prevailed, there has been a persistent undercurrent in the field suggesting that, while Clovis may have been the first broadly successful adaptation to the New World—Clovis and Clovis-like fluted points have been found across the entire breadth of North America, and similar points have been found in Mesoamerica and even South America—the bearers of the Clovis culture were not the first people to enter into and settle the New World. In one alternate scenario, Clovis doesn't represent a first movement of people into the New World, but merely a new technology that spread rapidly across an already existing, thinly dispersed population.

Though many archaeologists were slow to accept it, there now is a growing consensus that Clovis was not the first, and that there are a number of sites that predate Clovis in the New World. Perhaps the best known of these include the Meadowcroft Rockshelter in western Pennsylvania, where there is a detailed stratigraphic record of human occupation of the site. The lowest levels of the site with indisputable artifacts have produced radiocarbon dates of 12,800 years ago. That's not much earlier than Clovis, but the location of the site is significant. Unless folks sprinted from the entry point to western Pennsylvania (or were beamed directly there by **ancient astronauts**), rather than undergoing a slow expansion of the population of migrants, they must have arrived in North America hundreds and perhaps thousands of years before the 12,800-year date.

The same argument holds true for the Monte Verde site, another site whose pre-Clovis date is well supported. Monte Verde is at least 12,500 years old, and it is located in Chile, some 10,000 miles (16,000 kilometers) from the most likely entry point across the Bering Strait. Again, this implies a far more ancient initial entry into the New World, perhaps in this case by coastal dwellers who slowly expanded their territory southward along the western coast of North and South America.

A handful of additional similar sites in North America include Paisley Cave in Oregon (dating to 12,000 years ago), Cactus Hill in Virginia (perhaps as old as 18,000 years), and the Topper Site in South Carolina (an estimated 15,000 years old). Completed reports on these sites have yet to be published, so the strength of the supporting data has yet to be assessed. Nevertheless, the data released so far suggest to many that the so-called Clovis barrier has been broken, and we can now conclude with some degree of certainty that the first Americans predate the Clovis culture.

Now to the discussion of the dubious. There are a number of ostensible sites in the New World with suggested dates far older than both Clovis and any of the likely pre-Clovis sites just mentioned. For example, the Calico Hills site in Southern California has been dated by its excavators to more than 200,000 years ago. Skeptical archaeologists and geologists who have examined the Calico Hill "artifacts" (use of scare quotes is a dead giveaway here) say they aren't cultural or human made, but are instead what geologist C. Vance Haynes labels "geofacts," stones fortuitously fractured by nature (Haynes and Agogino 1986). Calico Hills is located on an alluvial fan, a place where water once flowed, constantly banging millions upon millions of rocks into one another for more than 200,000 years. It should come as no surprise that, if you pick through enough of these rocks, as researchers at the site have, you are bound to come up with a few that look like they could have been the product of human toolmaking. But the very crude, simple appearance of the Calico Hills specimens betrays the fact that they aren't tools at all, just rocks broken up by natural processes.

The Hueyatlaco site in Mexico has been controversial ever since supposed artifacts were found there with a geological date of 250,000 to 600,000 years, while another test, this one based on radiocarbon dating of shell in that same deposit, suggested a date of between 9,000 and 22,000 years (Meltzer 2009). To confuse things further, some of the original artifacts from the site have disappeared. With wildly divergent dates and disappearing artifacts, you can understand why Hueyatlaco isn't on everyone's top ten list of credible pre-Clovis sites.

Nearby the Hueyatlaco site at Toluquilla is a fascinating footprint trail preserved in a volcanic deposit. The site's excavators have identified the footprints as human and have dated the solidified ash deposit in which the footprints were found to 40,000 years ago. Unfortunately, the date of the ash bed is highly problematic, and another procedure derived a date of 1.3 million years for the same ash. Furthermore, some have questioned the identification of the footprints as human, suggesting that researchers have confused the tracks with those of an animal, much in the way the Paluxy River **man tracks** turned out to be misidentified dinosaur tracks. One geologist who visited the site, Paul Renne of the University of California Berkeley's Geochronology Center, said that the "footprints" he saw weren't even "moderately convincing" (Archaeological Institute of America 2005).

At least as it now stands, the Clovis-first view has been toppled and replaced with the "a little before Clovis but not too much before" view. The most widely accepted of the pre-Clovis sites predate Clovis by only a millennium or two. However, given the locations of these sites—thousands of miles from the most likely point of entry by human groups migrating into the New World, the Bering Strait—archaeologist David Meltzer suggests an initial foray across the Land Bridge or along its coast about 20,000 years ago. Further research is needed to confirm this and to come to a definitive understanding of sites like Topper, Paisley Cave, Cactus Hill, and Toluquilla.

Further Reading

The most up-to-date work on the earliest peopling of the Americas, including discussion of pre-Clovis sites, is *First Peoples in a New World: Colonizing Ice Age America* by David Meltzer (2009). Another good book on the same topic is *The Settlement of the Americas: A New Prehistory* by Tom Dillehay (2000).

Pseudoarchaeology

Pseudoarchaeology, short for "pseudoscientific archaeology," is one of a number of all-encompassing terms used, usually by professional archaeologists, to label a broad panoply of claims about what happened in the human past and about the ways in which that past can be studied that do not adhere to the scientific method. Scientific archaeology is predicated on the careful collection of archaeological data, objective examination of that data, the recognition of patterns in the data, the deduction of cause-and-effect relationships, the suggestion of ways of explaining the collected data, and then the testing of those hypotheses. Assertions made about the past that are based on anything else—revelation, religious belief, intentionally ignoring data that are contrary to your thesis—is, by definition, pseudoarchaeology.

Assertions made about the human past that are outside of the mainstream, that appear to contradict the accumulated wisdom of academically trained archaeologists, or that would cause archaeologists to drastically reassess what we think we know about the human past (even stuff about the human past that we are pretty sure about) should not, merely on that basis, be labeled pseudoarchaeology. In fact, a fundamental tenet of science and the scientific method is the notion that even our most cherished views about the universe are challengeable and may need tweaking, major revision, or complete overhaul. Claims about a pre-Columbian invasion of New England by ancient **Celts**, assertions that extraterrestrial **ancient astronauts** helped build the **Egyptian pyramids**, the suggestion that **psychics** can find archaeological sites, hypotheses about lost continents and **lost civilizations** hidden in the deep mists of time—none of these are inherently pseudoscientific or categorically pseudoarchaeological. These *become* pseudoarchaeology when adhered to in the face of a dearth of evidence in their support (or even in the face of evidence that refutes them). These claims float away into the ether of pseudoarchaeology and **cult archaeology** when adherents claim, for example, that:

- psychic archaeologists can't be scientifically tested because of the "shyness effect" (an actual claim made that psychic power cannot be tested by scientists because the power, though real, disappears in the face of skeptical analysis)
- direct evidence of an ancient lost civilization cannot be found because it's hidden too far below the ocean or the Antarctic ice cap, or because it was completely obliterated in an ancient nuclear war
- a vast conspiracy among archaeologists and the government is effectively hiding the (presumably awful) truth about the human past that, for reasons not made clear, they don't want you to know.

Granted, extraordinary claims made about the human past, or any other sphere or knowledge—claims that might cause us to reassess patterns and processes we think are well supported in the archaeological record—won't necessarily win you any popularity contests among scientists. You may be called names, and your work may be belittled. There may be hard feelings. But science isn't for sissies. Your fellow scientists (as **Carl Sagan** notes) will require extraordinary levels of proof before accepting such claims. But demanding definitive proof for an assertion is intrinsic to the scientific method. Anyone claiming that they don't need to adhere to that requirement—because the requirement itself is unfair, or because his or her explanation of the past is based on divine revelation and therefore needs no evidence, or because professional scientists are part of a conspiracy—is conducting pseudoscience. With regard to archaeology, anyone making claims of immunity from proof about their explanations or scenarios of the human past is conducting pseudoarchaeology. Many of the specific claims made in the entries of this encyclopedia fall under that heading.

Psychic Archaeology

As social scientists, archaeologists are faced with multiple challenges, not the least of which is that the people whose lives they hope to reconstruct are, by the very definition of the discipline, dead and gone. Unlike other social scientists such as cultural anthropologists or sociologists, we can't interview people or watch them as they conduct their lives. Without a time machine, archaeologists are always removed from the objects of their study and, it must be admitted, are necessarily limited in how much we can ever know about an ancient way of life.

Though we can't interact with them, archaeologists who investigate the lives of past literate peoples—that is, societies who left behind a written record, such as ancient Egypt, the **Maya**, Mesopotamia, or colonial America—can, at least, read documents left behind by the people they study, statements written in their own voices. This still puts limits on how much we can truly know, because we can learn about only those things that past peoples cared to write about (and even here, we have to consider the possibility that what they wrote down on any given subject was incomplete, wrong, or intentionally misleading).

Things get even more difficult when dealing with nonliterate people. Prehistoric archaeologists study people who left behind no written record. By the nature— and even the name—of their discipline, prehistorians must rely on "reading" not documents but *things*, the material remains left behind by past peoples, their arti- facts and structures, food remains, and their own skeletons, in order to reconstruct their lives. It is in fact an enormous challenge to attempt to reconstruct and illumi- nate an ancient lifeway when the only data left to do so is, effectively, ancient trash, the stuff that people made and used and then lost or discarded.

As a result, prehistorians are always on the lookout for clever strategies to reveal, understand, and explain ancient societies. Some—computer simulations, DNA analysis, and trace-element chemistry, for example—have proven extremely useful. Others have turned out not to be of any use; psychic archaeology turns out to be one of those useless exercises.

The proposition that so-called psychic power—ways of knowing things that transcend the accepted five senses of sight, sound, touch, taste, and smell—might be applicable to archaeology depends, absolutely, on psychic power being genuine and not just based on wishful thinking. That controversy is far beyond the scope of this encyclopedia. Genuine or not, however, it is abundantly clear that when it comes to its attempted application to archaeology, psychic power fails entirely.

Ordinarily, psychic archaeology has been applied in two ways: to discover archaeological sites in the first place, and to gather information about the peo- ple behind the artifacts. In the first application, psychics point to locations on maps or actually walk through areas to indicate places where, they assert, their psychic sense tells them ancient people once lived and archaeologists will find evidence of those ancient people.

It might seem that this would be a claim easy enough to test simply by dig- ging in those specific places where the psychic instructs you to. If, indeed, an ancient site is discovered, then psychic power is confirmed; if no sites are found in this way, then it can be concluded that there is no such thing as psy- chic power or, at least, if psychic power does exist, it doesn't work in locating ancient sites and cannot contribute to archaeological research.

Unfortunately, this simple construct does not work, at least not definitively. Archaeological sites are not as rare as many might believe, and they are not distributed randomly across the landscape. Archaeological site survey—the procedures by which archaeologists search for sites—is not the equivalent of an Easter egg hunt where the treasures are sprinkled randomly across the landscape. Sites are places where people in the past elected to settle, hunt, gather plant food, cultivate, quarry, or bury their dead, and they made decisions about where to place their villages, hunting or gathering camps, farms, quarries, and cemeteries on the basis of a rational thought process. Just about anyone, with the application of a little common sense and a little experience, can find archaeological sites, not through any paranormal, supernatural, or psychic modality but merely by thinking rationally about where it would have made sense for people to settle or exploit resources. For instance, anyone who points to a location on a map where a swiftly moving, spring-fed freshwater stream flows into a large, navigable waterway along a flat plain with good, clean, fertile soil and says an archaeological site will be found isn't applying psychic power any more than a meteorologist is when he or she predicts snow in New England in January.

One example of this was the **Alexandria Project**. When Stephan Schwartz (1983) used a team of 10 self-proclaimed psychics in his search for artifacts dating to the time of the pharaohs in the harbor of the Egyptian city of Alexandria, there was little possibility for failure. The harbor was a busy place in antiquity, the city a major hub of trade and transportation; over the years, underwater archaeologists, without the benefit of any psychic assist, have found lots of artifacts, including the remains of sunken ships and their cargo, mixed up in the underwater muck at the bottom of the harbor. It takes little more than luck and statistical probability to point to a place on a map of the harbor and then find artifacts. It does not take psychic power, so such an exercise means little and does not serve as an adequate test of the efficacy of psychic archaeology.

I actually conduct the following exercise in my introductory archaeology course. I display a blowup of a Google Earth aerial image of the Farmington River Valley in central Connecticut, the area where I have conducted the majority of my archaeological fieldwork. The photo shows natural features of the landscape in great detail and the river, streams, hills, mountains, rock outcrops, and so forth can be seen clearly. After a brief discussion of what resources and landscape features would be beneficial and attractive to a hunting and gathering people, I ask students to identify spots on the image where they predict ancient people may have lived and, therefore, archaeological sites might be found. Students invariably point out numerous places where, unbeknownst to them, sites have already been located. Are those students psychic? Of course not. Are they being clever? Yes. With a little more experience, it gets even easier. I have frequently marked a location on a map with an X, predicting that a site will be found in the general vicinity. I am often right, but it has nothing to do with psychic vibrations and everything to do with common sense.

The second claim made by psychic archaeologists is that they can "psychomotrize" artifacts and provide details about the people who made and used them. Proof of this assertion is even more problematic. After all, for a hypothesis to be scientific, it must be testable—there must be some way to either validate it or disprove it. How exactly can the ordinarily vague, banal, and often meaningless descriptions offered by psychics when they examine artifacts be tested? They usually can't, and this makes these pronouncements not only untestable but useless.

For example, in the 1930s and 1940s, spiritualist **Stefan Ossowiecki** claimed to be able to "read" artifacts and describe the people who made them. His re-creations provided dramatic pictures of ancient life—his detailed description of the sex lives of Neanderthals are, put bluntly, incredibly funny—all ostensibly based on the vibrations he picked up from artifacts. But there is nothing there to test or gauge, no way of knowing if anything that he said was accurate, and nothing specific has ever panned out with subsequent data.

On one occasion, I performed an informal test of a psychic who claimed that his abilities could help me in my archaeological interpretations. He challenged me to provide him with a handful of artifacts, which he would then read. He was quite sincere, as far as I could determine, and felt that he might be able to provide me with specific information that would prove useful in my research.

I prepared several specimens, wrapping them in tissue and placing them in sealed boxes. I presumed that if he really had psychic abilities, he wouldn't need any of his other senses to provide clues about the specimens. It would be too easy and obvious, for example, to hand him a spear point and for him to then make up a vague story about a successful hunt and subsequent feast. Unfortunately, this *was*, apparently, asking too much; my psychic claimed that he needed to handle the pieces directly in order to get the vibrations left behind by the people who made and used them.

I accepted this rationalization and allowed him to open the boxes. Each box contained a stone tool. There was a black obsidian (natural volcanic glass) spear point, a couple of flint knives, and a small shard of broken pottery. In each case, the psychic handled the specimen and seemed to be intensely focused in what I assume to be a near-trance state. He then told a tale about the ancient person who had made and used each tool. For example, he described the person whose vibrations he was picking up on the spear point: He was a man with long, dark lustrous hair. The man was a hunter. He was youthful but likely in his thirties or forties. He hunted large mammals with the spear. He had an injured leg; the injury had healed, but he still walked with a limp. It went on like that for some time.

Now, ordinarily, you might expect me to maintain that there is no way to test any of these psychic visions. How would we know? How could we possibly test their accuracy? The hair color and shininess, the man's age, the injury; all of these would be, under ordinary circumstances, entirely untestable. But not this time. I made sure that I would be able to test the accuracy of the visions, placing some true scientific controls on this experiment. I know for a fact that each and every one of the psychic visions provided by this person was absolutely, completely, and resolutely wrong. The spear point had not been made and used by a man with long dark hair who walked with a limp (and neither were his descriptions of the other individuals he read in the artifacts accurate). I knew this, not because I am psychic, but because I knew who made the artifacts—*I* did. The objects I handed the psychic had not been found at any archaeological site, but were things I had made in a course where I teach stone tool and ceramic artifact technologies. If this gentleman had had any psychic ability whatsoever, he should have been able immediately to make the connection between the objects he was holding and the person standing next to him. The fact that he couldn't speaks volumes, and the fact that no one claiming to be psychic has ever been able to accomplish this task shows rather convincingly that such an ability simply does not exist.

Pyramid Air Shafts

Unlike all of the other **Egyptian pyramids**, the largest, **Khufu**'s at Giza, has four long channels or small tunnels called "air shafts," two of which originate in the King's Chamber (the burial compartment of the pharaoh, a room located approximately in the center of the monument) and continue out into the outside of opposite faces of the pyramid. The north King's Chamber air shaft is rectangular in cross-section, about 7 inches by 5 inches (18 by 13 centimeters) and is about 235 feet (72 meters) long. The south air shaft varies in size and extends for about 175 feet (53 meters). The other two air shafts originate in the Queen's Chamber (the final resting place of the pharaoh's queen, located below the King's Chamber); they are both about 250 feet (76 meters) long, and neither reaches the respective face of the pyramid, falling about 20 feet (6 meters) short of the outside.

The purpose of these shafts is a mystery. They may have functioned as a way of ventilating the interior of the pyramid, in particular the two chambers, during construction, but that begs the question of why, if ventilation was so important, there are no air shafts in any of the other pyramids. The shafts make no great sense as astronomical markers, affording the dead pharaoh and his queen a view of some important point in the sky because the shafts are not linear. They take turns and angles, making any such alignment irrelevant. Another possibility suggested by Egyptologists is that the shafts were ritually intended, avenues by which the pharaoh's soul or "ka" could leave the pyramid.

In a fascinating project, on a number of occasions, researchers have placed small vehicles outfitted with cameras into the shafts and attempted to run them

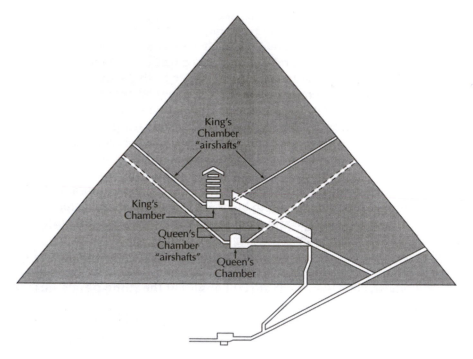

Was the purpose of the pyramid airshafts strictly practical, to improve circulation in the pyramid for workers during construction? Were they spiritual pathways for the pharaoh's soul to communicate with the heavens? The function of the pyramid airshafts ultimately is unknown. (From *Frauds, Myths, and Mysteries: Science and Pseudoscience in Archaeology,* 6th edition, by K. Feder, 2008. Reproduced with permission of McGraw-Hill.)

along the south shaft that originates in the Queen's Chamber. The little vehicle was first able to make it up the nondescript shaft for about 194 feet (59 meters), when it encountered a precisely sculpted stone slab filling the shaft and blocking its way. Researchers next outfitted the vehicle with a power tool with which they were able to drill through the stone block. Inserting a mini-video camera through the drillhole revealed what was on the other side: another block of stone. The purpose and significance of the pyramid air shafts remains a mystery.

Further Reading

There are some terrific Web sites devoted to the pyramids that provide the vital statistics for the air shafts, display useful diagrams of them, and discuss the pros and cons of some of the explanations commonly provided for their existence. I think the best of those might be Ancient Egypt Online: www.ancientegyptonline.co.uk/pyramid-air-shafts.html.

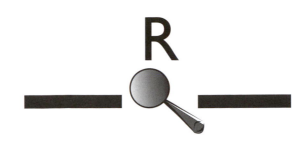

Rafinesque, Constantine Samuel

Constantine Samuel Rafinesque (1783–1840) is one of those historical characters who are terribly difficult to pin down. On the one hand, he possessed a brilliant mind and made several significant contributions in different fields of scientific study. He was knowledgeable in anthropology, archaeology, botany, geology, linguistics, meteorology, and zoology, writing well-received treatises in these various fields of knowledge. On the other hand, put bluntly, he was more than a little eccentric.

Rafinesque's contributions in archaeology included careful measurement and recording of ancient **moundbuilder** sites in the Ohio River Valley and in Tennessee. He was also an early investigator of the written language of the **Maya** of Mesoamerica and was precociously correct in recognizing that, in the Maya mathematical system of recording, dots represented ones and bars were fives. He was, however, incorrect in his insistence that Maya symbols were letters in an alphabetic system of writing. They are, instead, hieroglyphs in a kind of picture writing.

His purported discovery and translation of the **Walam Olum**, though, taints his other contributions to the archaeology, history, and anthropology of the Americas. By Rafinesque's testimony, the Walam Olum story was written on wooden tablets in a previously unknown script, which he was able to translate as the creation story of the Delaware Indians, but it is now believed to have been a **fraud**. The wooden tablets tragically were lost, according to Rafinesque, which is a very convenient fact for anyone responsible for their fabrication.

Though a brilliant scholar and today recognized for important contributions to science, Rafinesque was generally not well respected or honored during his lifetime. If he fabricated the Walam Olum to more firmly ensconce his memory in the annals of science, he succeeded—but not in a good way.

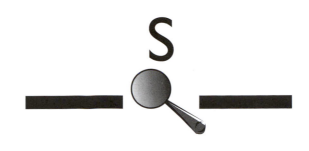

Sagan, Carl

You might not expect astronomer Carl Sagan (1934–1996) to merit inclusion in an encyclopedia dedicated to dubious archaeology—and you are not going to get a Wikipedia-like treatment of his life on these pages—but Sagan is here for one reason. In an article he wrote in 1963, "Direct Contact among Galactic Civilizations by Relativistic Interstellar Spaceflight," published in a relatively obscure journal titled *Planetary Space Science*, he suggested that archaeologists and especially geologists were the scientists most likely to encounter evidence of the existence of extraterrestrial civilizations.

Sagan's argument was based on his calculation, which was little more than a guess, really, that life was abundant in the universe. Though the precise prerequisites for the evolution of life, intelligence, and technological sophistication might occur breathtakingly infrequently, the number of stars even in just our own galaxy was so high that it seemed a statistical likelihood that civilization had developed elsewhere.

Continuing this line of reasoning, Sagan next suggested that in a galaxy, if not teeming with life, at least having a relative abundance—and assuming an inherent curiosity among these extraterrestrial intelligences about the existence of other civilizations—given sufficient time, some of them would have figured out a way to travel among the stars and done so. That meant, Sagan argued, that there was at least some incalculable level of probability that extraterrestrial travelers had visited Earth in the past (or, if they hadn't been here yet, might do so at some point in the future). Sagan went on to conclude that, in a planetary history that spanned some 4.5 billion years, such a visit was far more likely in one of those 4.5 billion past years than in the present year. In other words, looking at the big temporal picture, if extraterrestrials had visited Earth, it had most likely happened at some point in our planet's long history rather than in the present.

This is the argument that led Sagan to the conclusion that, if anyone was going to encounter evidence of an extraterrestrial intelligence, it would be scientists who focused on Earth's ancient history—geologists and, to a lesser extent, archaeologists. Sagan actually went so far as to suggest in the *Planetary Space Science* article what *kinds* of evidence might be found: essentially, some aspect of an advanced technology secreted in an ancient geological stratum or within the soil matrix of an ancient archaeological deposit. Not to appear too flip about it, Sagan was suggesting (and, to be entirely honest, hoping) that something like a lost or abandoned *Star Trek*–style communicator or "phaser" would be found by a geologist or archaeologist in a seemingly impossibly ancient soil layer, proving the visit of a highly advanced extraterrestrial space ship at some time in antiquity.

It is unclear whether Sagan's musings played any role in inspiring **Erich von Däniken** and his books about **ancient astronauts**. It is unlikely—after all, *Planetary Space Science* wasn't exactly the kind of popular magazine one is likely to encounter in a dentist or doctor's waiting room. Von Däniken has never mentioned the article in any of his publications, so it seems unlikely that he was aware of it, at least at the time he was authoring ***Chariots of the Gods***. What is interesting here is that the scenario at the heart of what became one of the most egregious, ignorant, and just plain preposterous of the archaeological pseudosciences was actually suggested by one of science's most brilliant and articulate spokesmen.

Sagan's scenario never panned out, and no geologists or archaeologists have ever found anything even vaguely approximating what Sagan suggested. Though it does not appear that Sagan ever explicitly abandoned the possibility of such a discovery, the fact that he did not revisit this scenario after the 1963 article seems to indicate that he understood that, though it merited consideration, it simply did not bear up under scientific scrutiny. It is uncertain what future geological or archaeological research may expose—never say never—but for now, the scientific records provide no support whatsoever for the ancient astronaut hypothesis.

Sagan is also credited with an aphorism that has become accepted as axiomatic in the sciences and certainly applies to archaeology: *Extraordinary claims require extraordinary levels of proof*. Of course, *all* claims in science require evidence to support them, proof sufficient to convince other scientists of the validity of a claim or assertion. In practice, if a new claim—a previously unknown chemical reaction, a newly discovered plant or animal species, a new archaeological site, or a new interpretation of a familiar fact or event—doesn't upset the apple cart *too* much, if it can be explained within the accepted paradigm or overall perspective, scientists may be willing to accept it without looking too closely or demanding a high level of evidence in support of it. That might not seem fair, but science isn't based on fairness—it's based on evidence and proof. If a claim seems to contradict everything we thought had already been "proven" about some aspect of the world, if it overturns our carefully constructed view of the world, it makes sense that we look much more closely at this claim, that we demand a much higher level of proof, before we accept it as correct.

For example, we all know that $2 + 2 = 4$. That is a well accepted fact. Now suppose that a mathematician claims that a new proof shows that, while $2 + 2$ is *usually* 4, sometimes it's 5. Such a claim is going to generate skepticism and a far more careful examination. Of course, for such a revolutionary proposition, you're going to have to come up with overwhelming evidence before anyone accepts it.

That was Sagan's point. A claimant who proposes to produce nuclear fusion in a teacup at room temperature; a researcher who asserts that she lived a past life as an Egyptian princess; a writer who claims that the archaeological record is replete with evidence that extraterrestrial aliens visited the Earth, mated with our ancestors, and provided them with advanced technology; or a physicist who declares that time slows down for an object as it approaches the speed of light is going to have to come up with very convincing evidence to back up his or her claim. That last one was a ringer; that's the extraordinary claim made by Albert Einstein about which scientists were extremely skeptical, but which they came to accept because, in fact, extraordinary levels of proof *were* provided.

Further Reading

If you read just one book about science and how it helps us understand our material world better than anything else, read Carl Sagan's great book, *The Demon Haunted World: Science as a Candle in the Dark* (1996). It really is terrific; in a life filled with major contributions to a public awareness of an appreciation for science, *The Demon Haunted World* may be Sagan's most important.

Sandia Cave

Sandia Cave, located near Albuquerque, New Mexico, was excavated by a team of archaeologists and archaeology students beginning in 1935. Excavators found the bones of extinct animals in the cave, including those of woolly mammoths, along with thick stone blades, called Sandia points by the excavators—the tools and weapons used by ancient people, ostensibly to hunt and kill animals like the mammoth.

Beginning in the 1930s and continuing into the 1950s, a series of articles about the results of excavations in Sandia Cave, a series of notes criticizing the articles, and a host of rejoinders to those critical evaluations were published. Claims and counterclaims were made, much heat was generated—and not enough light—and it is difficult in the extreme to assess the apparent contradictions in the stratigraphy of the cave, the associations of the cultural materials, and the sources of the reported radiocarbon dates.

The most severe of the issues raised about Sandia Cave has been the assertion that some of the Sandia points were recovered in an intact deposit stratigraphically underneath a layer of cave deposit called travertine that has been dated to more than 220,000 years ago. That would seem to prove that the human beings who made and then lost or deposited for safekeeping the Sandia points had done so at some point prior to when the travertine deposit had formed—in other words, more than 220,000 years ago. As the oldest indisputable evidence of a human presence in the New World among **pre-Clovis sites** is less than one-tenth that age—far less, in fact, than 20,000 years—the Sandia Cave site is a very distant outlier along the curve of oldest dates for archaeological sites in the New World.

There are at least four competing explanations for the Sandia Cave site and stratigraphy:

1. The Sandia points were excavated from a soil layer under a genuinely ancient, 220,000-year-old travertine deposit, but were buried there, perhaps by the inhabitants of the cave, far more recently.
2. The date derived for the travertine deposit is spuriously old, exaggerating by a large factor the actual date of the deposit.
3. The excavators incorrectly interpreted the integrity of the cave stratigraphy and, while the travertine actually is quite ancient, the artifacts were not deposited beneath the layer before it was formed.
4. The artifacts and the travertine are, in fact, located "in situ"—the term archaeologists use to mean in their original place of deposition—the date determined for the travertine is correct, and the artifacts truly date to before the deposition of the travertine layer.

The Sandia artifacts and stratigraphy were reexamined in the 1960s by a very well-respected geologist, C. Vance Haynes, and an equally well-respected archaeologist, George Agogino. They determined that what some previous researchers had interpreted as an intact layer of travertine that had been superimposed over the Sandia points as a single unit (which would imply that the artifacts were older than the cave deposit) was, instead, a mixed-up mess of virtually all of the strata in the cave, the result of "bioturbation"—soil movement or disturbance by biological activity. They attributed the bioturbation to rodents burrowing into the cave floor (Haynes and Agogino 1986). If that is the case, the stratigraphic positioning of the Sandia points cannot be used to prove that they are nearly a quarter of a million years old. They *might* be. Or they might be considerably younger. The disturbance identified by Haynes and Agogino makes stratigraphic dating simply impossible in this case.

Haynes and Agogino further note that, based on their analysis of deposits deeper in the cave, the interior probably wasn't available for occupation until about 14,000 years ago, making that the oldest possible age for the Sandia points. That's still plenty old, but even if the points really are that old, that's nothing that would make archaeologists rewrite the book of American prehistory.

Applying **Occam's Razor** to the Sandia Cave site, we would certainly need extraordinary levels of evidence before we accept the claim that the occupation dates to more than 220,000 years ago and undertake a major rewrite of American prehistory. To accept the authenticity of an interpretation that puts bifacially flaked spear points in a stratigraphic context that implies antiquity approaching a quarter of a million years in New Mexico—which, by the way, would make them older, by a factor of about five, than any bifacially flaked tools found anywhere else in the world—we would need absolutely firm stratigraphic evidence, and such evidence is lacking. As Haynes and Agogino show, the evidence indicates exactly the opposite is true.

Beyond this, no other indisputable sites have been found in the New World datable to the period suggested for the Sandia Cave site. Without extraordinary levels of proof for this extraordinary scenario, it makes the most sense—while keeping an open mind—to accept one of the other three explanations.

Further Reading

Though it is a technical report, "Geochronology of Sandia Cave" by C. Vance Haynes and George A. Agogino (1986) is the definitive work on the dating of the artifacts found in the cave. Their work in no way disputes the significance of the Sandia Cave site, but it does show that it cannot be of the extreme antiquity (220,000 years) that some claim it is.

Santorini

Santorini is the name given for an archipelago located in the southern Aegean Sea, about 120 miles (200 kilometers) southeast of the Greek mainland. The largest island in the Santorini island group is **Thera**. Because it is the largest in the ring of islands that constitute the archipelago, some use the names Thera and Santorini interchangeably.

The origin of the archipelago can be traced to the catastrophic eruption of a volcano; the steeply sloping side of that volcano's caldera today forms the cliffs of the island of Thera. The eruption of Santorini occurred sometime between 1639 and 1600 BCE (recent radiocarbon dating of an olive tree killed during the violent eruption indicates a date of somewhere between 1627 and 1600 BCE). And it was enormous; it has been estimated that the explosive force of the Santorini eruption was four times as powerful as that of Krakatoa, which erupted in 1883 and killed more than 36,000 people in the Dutch East Indies (Marinatos 1972).

Certainly the massively explosive eruption of the Santorini volcano utterly destroyed the village of Akrotiri, an outpost on Thera of the Minoan civilization, which was centered on the Mediterranean island of Crete, 68 miles (110 kilometers) to the south. The eruption had other, geographically far-reaching consequences;

Egyptian record keepers noted a spate of cold and rainy weather at about the right time that may have been the result of fallout from the eruption. Climatologists believe that seventeenth-century BCE records in China about weather disruptions, and evidence of frost damage in trees in Ireland and California, can be explained by the heavy concentration of ash spewed into the Earth's atmosphere when the Santorini volcano exploded (Friedrich et al. 2006).

It has been suggested that the eruption was so devastating that:

1. It destroyed the Minoan civilization utterly and virtually overnight.
2. The immensity of the eruption and the degree of disruption it wrought led to the catastrophe being immortalized in folk legend and still talked about more than a thousand years after it happened.
3. The story provided fodder for writers of history and philosophy, including a Greek writer named **Plato**, who devoted one of his dialogues to the destruction of a great, ancient civilization. In this scenario, the destruction of the Minoan civilization by the eruption of the Santorini volcano inspired Plato when writing the ***Critias*** dialogue, calling the island nation **Atlantis**.

It cannot be denied that Plato, like all authors, used in his stories things he had heard that fascinated and moved him, so, it cannot be denied in any absolute sense, the possibility that he had heard stories about a civilization ancient even for his time, that had ascended to a lofty level of sophistication, only to be destroyed virtually overnight, by a series of natural catastrophes, and incorporated those stories into a philosophical treatise about how a civilization ought to be configured. The problem with this apparently neat solution to the Atlantis mystery is that the culture and history of Minoan Crete is a very poor match for Atlantis. Plato places the Atlantis story in time some 11,000 years ago, far too old to relate to the Minoans and far too long ago to ascribe to the eruption of Thera. Plato places Atlantis out beyond the "Pillars of Hercules," that is, outside of the Mediterranean, beyond the Straits of Gibraltar, where Crete is located within the Mediterranean. Elephants are a major beast of burden used by the Atlanteans; elephants were unknown to the Minoans. The primary theme of Plato's telling of the Atlantis story relates to their military defeat by a much weaker, less wealthy, and less technologically sophisticated society, that of ancient Athens, and there is no evidence of any sort of a military defeat suffered by the ancient Minoans. Finally, though the eruption of Thera doubtlessly had a significant impact on agriculture and shipping on Crete, archaeological and geological evidence indicates that it was not a devastating impact—only a fraction of an inch of volcanic ash fell on Crete as the result of the Thera eruption.

Minoan civilization shows a robust rebound with a spate of construction following the eruption and only later, in slow decline, did the Minoan civilization fall, in more of a whimper than a bang. This stands in stark contrast to Plato's description of the utter destruction of Atlantis at the hands of the gods. Though it is not impossible that Plato had heard the story of the eruption of Thera as told through the lens of folk history and though it is not impossible that he likewise had heard the story of a great island civilization on Crete, and though it is not impossible that he used those tales in concocting the story of the Lost Continent of Atlantis, the extant evidence does not support those suppositions.

Scarith of Scornello

Curzio Inghirami was the scion of a wealthy, landed family in Tuscany, Italy. While wandering his family estate in 1634, Inghirami, then just 19 years of age, came upon a curious capsule made of bitumen, wax, pitch, and resin. Secreted within was a scroll written in the as-yet-undeciphered ancient Etruscan script and, as luck would have it, the same statement appeared in Latin, a language well known to the inhabitants of Tuscany, including the highly educated Inghirami. Like the Rosetta Stone found in 1799 with its side-by-side presentation of the same statement in Demotic, hieroglyphic, and Classical Greek, allowing for the first accurate translation of the ancient Egyptian written language, the scroll found in the capsule provided the keys necessary to translate the Etruscan written language.

Inghirami's find electrified the residents of Tuscany. As historian Ingrid Rowland (2004) maintains in her excellent monograph on what became known as the "scarith of Scornello," seventeenth-century Tuscans viewed themselves as the descendants of the ancient Etruscans who inhabited the same region. Even into the seventeenth century, the inhabitants of Tuscany had not gotten over the ascendance of Rome in the Mediterranean world and Rome's defeat of the Etruscans in 396 BCE. The writings found in the scarith, attributed to an Etruscan man named Prospero, provided seventeenth-century Tuscans with a validation of their glorious history. Prospero's pronouncements reflected great philosophical complexity, of a kind far more sophisticated than any the Romans had produced, as well as a religious precocity, including even resemblances to elements of Catholic doctrine.

Ultimately, even the strongest believers in the scarith became skeptical when Inghirami—and only Inghirami—found over 200 of them, each more detailed and remarkable than the last in providing modern Tuscans with an increasingly magnificent antiquity. The fact that Inghirami discovered the scarith in the correct historical order in which the events discussed on the scrolls occurred, was lost on few. Skepticism about the authenticity of the scarith abounded: Why was only Inghirami able to find them? Why was the handwriting on the parchment so similar to Inghirami's? Why had all previous Etruscan documents been on linen, while the scarith were all on paper? One final piece of evidence, not revealed until 1700, 45 years after Inghirami's death, was based on a forensic analysis of the paper on which Prospero ostensibly wrote his musings; it bore the watermark of a seventeenth-century paper factory in Colle di Val d'Elsa.

The scarith were, of course, fakes, and not all that well conceived. But like most archaeological fakery, degree of authenticity is secondary to the desire of people to believe them. Tuscans wanted to believe that an ancestor was, in a sense, speaking to them across a chasm of more than 2,000 years, and so, many suspended their skeptical sense and embraced a transparent archaeological **fraud**.

Further Reading

Ingrid Rowland's book *The Scarith of Scornello: A Tale of Renaissance Forgery* (2004) is a great read. She does a wonderful job of putting the hoax in historical context and showing how ethnic pride blinded some to the obvious fact that the entire thing had been a fake.

Serpent Mound

Serpent Mound is an effigy earthwork in the form of a giant snake. The snake form is located on a plateau overlooking Bush Creek near Peebles, Ohio. From the terminus of its coiled tail to the tip of its open mouth, the serpent is approximately 1,300 feet (400 meters) in sinuous length, marked by eight back-and-forth meanders, with the piled up earth averaging about three feet (a meter) in height. Recent radiocarbon dating of charcoal recovered from an excavation of Serpent Mound dates its construction to the period between 1000 and 1550 CE.

According to Ohio state archaeologist Brad Lepper, Serpent Mound has inspired a number of interesting speculations, including the claim that it represents the actual serpent that tempted Eve in the Garden of Eden, which would seem to imply that, rather than having been located somewhere in the Middle East, Eden could actually be traced to Adams County, Ohio. Others have claimed that a powerful energy **vortex** is located at the site and that people who climb the tower built by the state to allow for a bird's-eye view of the earthwork complain of dizziness and light-headedness (having climbed that tower on a number of occasions, I might suggest that feeling dizzy or faint at the top has more to do with a fear of heights or a need for aerobic exercise than any supernatural explanation based on power centers, vortexes, or ley lines). Most interestingly, Lepper reports that a

Serpent Mound in Ohio is one of the best known effigy mounds of the ancient world. It is a more than 1,300-foot-long sinuous snake with a coiled tail constructed sometime between CE 1000 and 1550. (K. Feder)

recent rumor that the effigy isn't of a snake at all but of a wriggling sperm cell has caused a spate of complaints about people sneaking onto the site at night for clandestine sexual escapades; the caretaker has complained loudly about having to clean up after these folks who commonly dispose of their condoms at the base of the plateau. Well, it's good that they are using protection, anyway.

Neither a sperm cell nor an energy vortex, Serpent Mound is a beautiful piece of art, a sculpture made of earth in the form of a creature that inspires fear and fascination in many cultures. That's interesting enough without the injection of fantasies.

Further Reading

The mounds of Ohio, including Serpent Mound, are discussed at great length in *Ohio Archaeology: An Illustrated Chronicle of Ohio's Ancient American Indian Cultures*, a wonderful book written by archaeologist Brad Lepper (2005).

Shroud of Turin

The Shroud of Turin is a burial linen that bears the image of a crucified man—purportedly the actual burial shroud of Jesus Christ with an image miraculously wrought at the moment of the Resurrection. For believers, the image on the shroud was a message, intentional or not, that can be read as announcing to the world the reality of the Resurrection and the divinity of Jesus Christ. For others, the shroud is a medieval artifact, a forgery, painted or in some other way applied to the linen in an attempt to fool the faithful or convert the doubters with the notion that it was the genuine article. In the most cynical scenario, the shroud was an attempt to exploit people's faith and extract money from them. And, in fact, the shroud is known to have been displayed in the fourteenth century, and individuals were paid to feign an illness or infirmity while making a pilgrimage to see the shroud and then to pretend to be healed—you know, walk into the church (in Lirey, Italy, where it was being shown) on crutches, at death's door, take one look at the shroud, throw away the crutches, dance a jig, suddenly appear to be in the best of health, make a big contribution (that's called "priming the pump"), and walk out. Others seeing or hearing about this, especially genuinely infirm, wounded, or mortally ill people hoping for a similar miraculous healing, would visit the church and make a financial contribution, as well.

A number of modern analyses of the shroud have been undertaken, including those by the **Shroud of Turin Research Project** (STURP). Of most relevance in an encyclopedia of dubious archaeology are the results of the archaeological dating technique applied to the shroud. One of three small snips of the shroud linen was supplied to three separate radiocarbon-dating laboratories. Each of the labs also received, at the same time, three additional swatches of cloth of known age, with clear historical proveniences: a thread from a medieval cloth cape, a piece of Egyptian mummy wrapping, and a piece of fabric from a Nubian tomb linen. The labs were not told which sample was which, so, in a sense, they analyzed them blind. This was done to minimize the possibility that anyone involved in the process, knowing which swatch was from the shroud, might attempt to alter the results, either to prove the shroud was legitimate or to prove that it was a fake. This kind of control is typical in scientific protocols in an attempt to prevent any funny business on the part of researchers.

Had the shroud been legitimate, radiocarbon dating would have produced an age of approximately 2,000 years for the linen. Of course, even had the linen dated to the right time period, scientists would not have concluded that the shroud was necessarily authentic. In the analogous application of the dating technique to the parchment on which the **Vinland Map** was drawn, for example, the parchment itself turned out to be the correct age, but ink was modern, proving that it was a fake map drawn on an old piece of parchment. So, if the shroud linen was 2,000 years old, the image of the resurrected man on the cloth could still have been applied far more recently in an effort to more convincingly hoax the world.

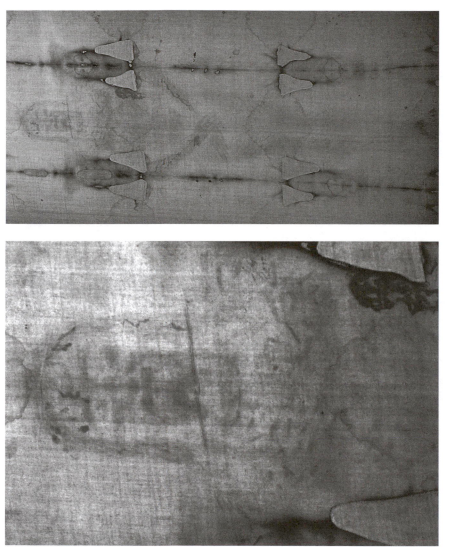

Ostensibly the burial shroud of Jesus Christ, the cloth itself has been dated to the thirteenth century CE. (AP Photo/Antonio Calanni, file)

The results of the radiocarbon dating of the four samples are shown in the table on page 241 (Damon et al. 1989). From the table, it is obvious that the radiocarbon dates for the samples of known age match very well the actual ages. This reflects both the utility and accuracy of radiocarbon dating. The results also show, unequivocally, that the linen tested from the shroud is of medieval age, dating to sometime in the thirteenth or very early fourteenth century. The shroud linen does not date to the time of Christ and, therefore, cannot be his burial shroud. The radiocarbon date for the shroud linen, however, is a remarkably good match for the first historical reference to its existence: CE 1389. This leads many to conclude that the shroud is an artifact that was crafted sometime during the fourteenth century, in other words, more than 1,300 years after the crucifixion is supposed to have occurred.

After publication of the radiocarbon-dating results in the February 16, 1989, issue of the venerable British science journal *Nature*, some members of STURP suggested that a fire in 1532 had somehow managed to contaminate the shroud sample, thus providing a spurious date. When that argument didn't hold up, some in STURP embraced the notion that all three labs that dated the shroud samples (three of the most highly regarded radiocarbon labs in the world, by the way) were all grossly and equally incompetent and hadn't noticed that the linen samples they dated were entirely contaminated with recent material. **Walter McCrone** (1996), however, showed that for there to be sufficient recent contamination on a piece of linen that actually was 2,000 years old to make it appear to date to the mid-thirteenth century, the samples would need to be two-thirds contaminant and only one-third linen. That's something the labs just might have noticed. Most recently, STURP has embraced the idea that the linen samples extracted for radiocarbon dating weren't actually from the shroud itself at all, but from more recent material used to patch the shroud when it was singed in the 1532 fire. STURP now calls for a second round of radiocarbon dating. The Catholic Church has, so far, ignored this suggestion.

Further Reading

There are a number of extremely detailed books that focus on the Shroud of Turin. For the best treatment of the historical context of the shroud, see Joe Nickell's *Inquest on the Shroud of Turin* (1983). For the most detailed account of the forensic analysis of the shroud, see *Judgment Day for the Turin Shroud* by microscopist and forensic scientist Walter McCrone (1996). For the most detailed treatment of the dating method applied to the shroud, see *Relic, Icon, or Hoax? Carbon Dating the Turin Shroud* by physicist and radiocarbon expert Harry Gove (1996). And for a fascinating attempt at solving the puzzle of who might have fabricated the shroud, read *The Turin Shroud* (Picknett and Prince 2007) in which the authors suggest that the Shroud of Turin was the work of none other than Leonardo da Vinci (who, it might be suggested, was the Imhotep of fifteenth-century Italy). By their reckoning, da Vinci produced the image on the shroud in an early and

	Sample	Known Age	Radiocarbon Date (Arizona)	Radiocarbon Date (Oxford)	Radiocarbon Date (Zurich)
1	Shroud of Turin	unknown	1304 CE	1200 CE	1274 CE
2	Burial Linen from Nubian Tomb	1000–1300 CE	1023 CE	1010 CE	1009 CE
3	Egyptian mummy linen	110 BCE–75 CE	45 BCE	30 BCE	10 CE
4	Threads from medieval garment	1290–1310 CE	1228 CE	1195 CE	1265 CE

primitive version of photography by projecting the image of a crucified man onto linen coated with a photo-sensitive compound, much in the manner of modern photo paper.

Shroud of Turin Research Project (STURP)

The Shroud of Turin Research Project (STURP) was constituted in 1977 by a group consisting of approximately 40 American scientists who had as their goal the investigation of the **Shroud of Turin**, a burial shroud whose existence had been known of only since the fourteenth century and which bore an unmistakable image of a crucified man. The goal of STURP, at least ostensibly, was to determine:

1. Whether the Shroud of Turin was a genuine burial shroud
2. Its age
3. The manner in which the image of the crucified man had been produced on the linen
4. The identity of the individual whose image appeared on the linen

Though STURP certainly paid lip service to the notion that it would conduct an entirely objective and scientific analysis of the shroud, several key members of the group went on record before they had conducted any of the planned scientific testing to say they believed the Shroud of Turin was the actual burial cloth of Jesus Christ and that the image had been produced miraculously (see Nickell 1987, 115, for a sampling of the a priori statements of support for the shroud's authenticity by members of STURP). In fact, two of the scientists most responsible for putting STURP together, John Jackson and Eric Jumper, were members of the Executive Council of the Holy Shroud Guild, a group which, by its very nature, fostered a belief in the authenticity of the Shroud of

Turin. By their own testimony, it would be fair to label most of the other STURP participants, too, as believers in one set of hypotheses about the shroud: that it was genuine, that it was about 2,000 years old, that the image could not be explained by science—that it was, in fact, miraculous—and that the image was that of none other than Jesus Christ.

During October 1978, the STURP team spent five days poring over the shroud, taking measurements, taking thousands of photographs (black-and-white, color, ultraviolet, infrared), looking at the linen under microscopic magnification, and collecting sticky-tape samples off the surface. In addition, the shroud was X-rayed, and assorted other forms of analysis—including X-ray fluorescence, spectrophotometry, thermography, UV-visible reflectance, and fluorescence—were performed.

Though STURP members had signed an agreement to remain silent on the results of the analysis until October 1980, word began leaking out as early as April 1979 that the official STURP conclusion would be that the shroud was the real thing or, at least, that it was a burial cloth with the image of a crucified man which, though it could not be identified definitively as Jesus Christ, bore the unmistakable marks of his crucifixion as enumerated in the Bible. In fact, the official STURP conclusion, published in 1981, was that the shroud was a genuine burial cloth that displayed the image of a real, crucified man. STURP's report went on to maintain that there was no evidence in the form of pigment, paint, or dyes that the image had been applied by an artist. On the contrary, STURP declared that the agency by which the image had been produced was a mystery, suggesting to some that the image was the result of a miracle.

Walter McCrone, a well-known chemist, microscopist, and forensic scientist, was in the original group that investigated the shroud, though his precise affiliation with STURP is a matter of some contention (having spoken to McCrone, I know that he considered himself to be a member of STURP until his conclusions contradicted those preferred by the other members of the team, but I am aware that at least some in STURP never considered McCrone to have been a full-fledged member of the team). In any case, it is fair to say that McCrone was the most highly regarded scientist to contribute to the shroud's investigation, certainly when it comes to the forensic analysis of historical fakery. Though it would be fair to label McCrone a skeptic, that word applies in the best sense of a hard-nosed scientist who demands high levels of proof for any conclusions drawn about a historical artifact, whether it be the shroud, the **Vinland Map**, or anything else.

McCrone appears to have been a lone voice among those who analyzed the shroud as part of STURP. In contrast to the group's findings, McCrone reports clear evidence of artist's pigments in the shroud image, in particular red ocher and the chemical components of vermillion, a deep red paint. Early on, STURP disassociated itself from McCrone's work, and one is left wondering if, to be blunt, they did so not because they could find any error in his work but because they didn't like the conclusions he reached. (McCrone's name does not appear on the current STURP Web site in the listing of 31 scientists who participated in the original analysis of the shroud [www.shroudstory.com/topic-sturp.htm]; whether he was officially a founding member is meaningless—it is absurd for his contribution to be ignored.)

STURP has long championed the authenticity of the Shroud of Turin, though always backing off, if ever so slightly, from certainty about who exactly is depicted on the shroud image. But its professed uncertainty is disingenuous in the extreme. STURP's party line—that the shroud bears an inexplicable image of a crucified man who just happens to display all of the marks of Christ's crucifixion as laid out in the Bible, but, okay, we can't prove it's Jesus—isn't a very convincing version of skepticism.

Sitchin, Zecharia

Zecharia Sitchin (1922–) is a fascinating character who has written 13 books spreading his hypothesis that the human species developed as the result of genetic engineering by extraterrestrial aliens called Anunnaki from the planet he calls Nibiru. Apparently, these aliens weren't here just for a quick visit, walkabout, or exploration. No, they had a very particular task in mind: they were looking for gold. In order to obtain this precious material, the aliens needed workers, and thus they engaged in a bit of biological tinkering that led to us.

Sitchin bases the vast majority of his work not on archaeological artifacts or even sites but on his own idiosyncratic translation of ancient written texts (Sumerian, Akkadian, Assyrian, and Hebrew, among others). Sitchin—in contradiction to all other translators of these ancient texts, who interpret them as mythological or religious discourses involving gods and spirits—views them as telling the true story of a powerful race of extraterrestrials (these would be the Anunnaki from Nibiru) visiting the Earth and mucking it up.

Sitchin's views are quite fantastic, of course, and the evidence he presents in support of them is, to put it mildly, lacking. Dr. Michael Heiser, who has a PhD in Hebrew, the Bible, and ancient Semitic languages and is fluent in a dozen ancient languages, has put up an extensive Web site (www.sitchiniswrong.com) debunking Sitchin's claims.

For example, Sitchin refers to Nibiru as the "Twelfth Planet," even using that as the name of one of his books (Sitchin 1976). Today, most astronomers acknowledge the existence of eight or nine planets, depending on whether or not they go along with the demotion of Pluto. Where Sitchin gets all these other planets—celestial bodies that scientists with far more powerful technologies to apply to the task have never been able to verify—is a great mystery. The physics implicit in the existence of a tenth, eleventh, and/or twelfth planet would certainly bring their existence to the attention of NASA, not just the ancient Sumerians, but the astrophysicists at NASA insist there are no such planets. It is also quite mysterious how life, and especially, intelligent life capable of cruising the solar system and visiting Earth, would be able to evolve on a planet usually so far removed from the source of heat and light (i.e., the sun).

Heiser points out that Sitchin's translations of Sumerian cuneiform and artwork are consistently wrong. Sitchin insists that when the Sumerians made reference to "nibaru," they were referring to a planet in our solar system beyond Pluto with a hugely elliptical orbit that passes by Earth only once in every 3,600 years. As Heiser suggests, I visited the online version of the *Assyrian Dictionary of the Oriental Institute of the University of Chicago* (http://oi.uchicago.edu/research/pubs/catalog/cad/), the fundamental reference—the "bible," if you will—for the ancient languages of Mesopotamia. Looking up the various meanings (and spellings) of *nibaru* or *neberu*, you find definitions that mostly center on concepts involving crossing water: ferry, ford, crossing, ferryboat, ferrying.

But *neberu* does have another meaning in Sumerian: it is a name given to one of the brightest lights in the nighttime sky, the planet we today call Jupiter. The Sumerians were avid observational astronomers and explicitly mention 5, not 12, planets. Heiser asserts that there isn't a single Sumerian, Akkadian, or other ancient Middle Eastern text that mentions any additional planets. The fact that scholars recognize that Neberu was a name applied to Jupiter clinches the argument against Sitchin's claim that it's some unknown twelfth planet.

And how about the Anunnaki? What do the Sumerians have to say about them? Well, according to Heiser, nowhere in any Sumerian (or Akkadian or Babylonian or Assyrian or Hebrew or other ancient) text does anyone say they arrived in spaceships or rockets or from another planet or that they wore spacesuits or had laptops, cell phones, iPods, or iPads. As scholar D. M. Murdock (2010) points out, the ancient Sumerians were quite clear in calling the Anunnaki gods or spirits, guardians of the gates through which the sun passes. To maintain that they are extraterrestrial aliens from a planet whose existence not only cannot be proven but cannot even be accounted for by the laws of physics (its gravity would have a measurable impact) is to apply twentieth- and twenty-first-century sensibilities to an ancient religion. It just doesn't work, no matter how many times Sitchin repeats it in his 13 books.

Further Reading

For a detailed debunking of Sitchin's claims, see Michael S. Heiser's Web site, www.sitchiniswrong.com. It's all laid out there by Dr. Heiser, a scholar in ancient languages of the Middle East.

Spence, Lewis

Lewis Spence (1874–1955) was a well-respected Scottish journalist and folklorist whose presence in this encyclopedia stems from the fact that in the 1920s he wandered away from topics in which he possessed some expertise and wrote a number of works about the lost continents of **Atlantis** and **Lemuria**, including *The Problem of Atlantis* (1924), *Atlantis in America* (1925), and *The History of Atlantis* (1926). As is so often the case, great intelligence and expertise in one field (here, Scottish folktales) does not confer any particular expertise in another (here, archaeology). Spence's musings on Atlantis and Lemuria are based on little more than a fevered imagination and certainly do not hold up to any sort of scientific scrutiny.

In *The History of Atlantis*, Spence admits to the reader that in his argument about the historicity of Atlantis, inspiration played a larger role than fact; he is dismissive of "mere scholarship," so much so that he avoids the use of scholarship entirely. Spence (1926, 3) explicitly eschews what he labels "the Tape Measure School" of archaeology, though one is hard-pressed to understand why any scientist would hope to avoid tape measures, both literal and metaphorical, in trying to prove a point or test a hypothesis.

True to his word, there are no references to tape measures in Spence's work, nor is there much in the way of data either. In Spence's construct, the archaeological record of Europe is best interpreted as coming from a series of waves of immigrants emanating from the Atlantean continent. It is the height or irony, however, coming from someone so intent on proving the literal veracity of **Plato**'s telling of the Atlantis tale, that the culture of migrants from Atlantis identified by Spence bear not even the slightest relationship to the Atlantean culture described by Plato. Where Plato relates the story of an economically powerful, militarily advanced, and technologically sophisticated civilization, Spence's proposed migrants from a slowly disintegrating Atlantis (the rate of its demise again contradicts Plato) are little more than Paleolithic hunter-gatherers.

For example, by Spence's reckonings, the first anatomically modern human beings in Europe, the Cro Magnons, were an initial population wave from Atlantis more than 20,000 years ago. Later, when the stone tool culture called Solutrean, with its finely chipped, beautifully crafted, wonderfully symmetrical blades, developed in Europe, Spence interprets it as another Atlantean wave, dated to 16,000 years ago.

Spence interprets the appearance of Upper Paleolithic art, including the cave paintings and figurines of Europe, as having resulted from yet another influx of Atlanteans escaping the slow-motion disintegration of their homeland. Spence claimed, in fact, that "Atlantis was the home of sculpture and painting" (93), thus making a connection between the paintings and sculptures of ancient Europe and Atlantis.

None of this made even the slightest bit of sense when Spence wrote it. Beyond this, of course, it seems rather absurd to assert that cave paintings of Late Pleistocene animals, sculptures of women, and symmetrically flaked stone tools needed to be introduced into Europe by bearers of an advanced civilization. Every bit of archaeological evidence available during Spence's time, and all evidence accumulated since, bears witness to the in-situ development of the tool technology and art of the Upper Paleolithic. Spence's work belongs in the fantasy category and does nothing to support a vision of the bearers of a lost culture bringing civilization to the world upon the destruction of their homeland.

Starchild

The story has a quintessentially *Weekly World News* air about it: a deformed skull, a secret cave, and extraterrestrial aliens in the mix. Who could ask for anything more?

As told by the purveyors of the tale (there is no way to verify any of the story), it all started more than 60 years ago when an American living in Mexico stumbled upon a double grave in a cave. The person removed the remains and held onto them until, near death, she gave them to another American, who then presented them to an American couple who retain ownership. (Of course, if the story is true that the remains were taken from a cave and then brought out of Mexico into the United States without permits, several laws were broken and treaties violated in the process.)

The remains were supposedly those of an adult female and a very young child, a boy probably about five years old at the time of death. The adult skeleton is, according to the account, completely normal. It is the cranium of the child that is extraordinary. While it appears to have the full complement of primate characteristics—two forward-facing eyes, two ears, an appropriately placed nose and mouth—and though it possesses each of the standard cranial bones of a human head (a frontal bone, two parietals, two temporal bones, two sphenoids, two zygomatic bones, and an occipital), the configuration of these bones is certainly out of whack for a normal human and the overall skull shape is completely wrong. It's far too wide across the top, and the front and top of the skull seem swollen, the face proportionally small and pinched.

Certainly the child who left behind the malformed skull ostensibly found in the Mexican cave was not normal—at least, not a normal human being. You can imagine how some have run with that fact, asserting that, in actuality, the skull is that of an extraterrestrial infant, or possibly a hybrid, the offspring of the human female and her extraterrestrial alien boyfriend. Supporters of this perspective—none of whom are archaeologists, forensic anthropologists, pathologists, or physicians—call the boy whose remains were found in the cave the "Starchild" and their attempt to ascertain the truth behind his origins the Starchild Project.

This conclusion is so absurd as to almost defy consideration. But I'll try. Steven Novella (2006), a medical doctor and professor of neurology at Yale University Medical School, has concluded that the cranium in question exhibits all of the characteristics of a child who died as the result of congenital hydrocephalus. Hydrocephalus results from a blockage in the normal drainage of cerebrospinal fluid in the brain; the fluid backs up and, in a newborn or young child, causes cranial deformations of the precise kind exhibited by the unfortunate five-year-old in the cave. As Novella indicates, because individual elements of the skulls of newborns and infants are not fused but are instead connected by flexible bands of cartilage, the cerebrospinal fluid accumulation in the skull causes the overall skull shape to shift to accommodate that buildup. A deformed skull exactly like the Starchild's is the result.

With the application of modern medical procedures, babies with hydrocephalus can be treated by draining the excess cerebrospinal fluid. But in the past, and certainly in third world nations where many citizens do not have access to modern medicine, hydrocephalus can be a deforming and, ultimately, deadly condition. This is what almost certainly was the case with the so-called Starchild.

In a clearly failed attempt to bolster their case, the individuals behind the Starchild Project had DNA analysis conducted on the remains of both the adult female and the Starchild, hoping to prove that the child possessed the genetic material of a creature that wasn't entirely human.

It turns out that the woman and the child possess mitochondrial DNA from different haplogroups—the adult female is haplogroup A, the child is C. Both of those haplogroups are typical of Native Americans (Trace Genetics 2003). However, the fact that the two reflect different haplogroups precludes the female from being the child's mother; we have no idea at this point how the two were related. So far, so good. The mother is human and an American Indian, and the child is also Native American. Mitochondrial DNA is passed down only in the female line, so it can't tell us anything about the child's father from this analysis.

An analysis of the child's nuclear DNA clinches the deal (Novella 2006). He possesses a Y-chromosome. This tells us not only that the Starchild was a male but also that his father was—alert the media—a human male. The Y-chromosome is passed along by the father of a child. Since the Starchild possesses a human Y-chromosome, his father must, of necessity, be human. Case closed. The Starchild was an unfortunate human baby, an American Indian with congenital hydrocephalus that went untreated and led to his sad death at about the age of five. Sadder still, 60 or 70 years after his death, his remains have been paraded around in support of a laughable hypothesis.

A diagnosis of hydrocephalus certainly isn't as romantic as the story of literally star-crossed lovers producing a baby, not quite human but not quite alien. The hydrocephalus diagnosis, however, does have the advantage of actually being supported by evidence.

Further Reading

For a definitive debunking of the Starchild myth, read the article "The Starchild Project," by physician Steven Novella, online at www.theness.com/the-starchild-project/.

Stonehenge

Stonehenge is one of the best known, most recognizable, and even iconic monuments of the ancient world. Stonehenge is, in fact, an astonishing testament to the surprising abilities of ancient people—people too often maligned as being "primitive" though the archaeological record repeatedly shows that they were anything but. Stonehenge's existence implies the presence of remarkable abilities among its ancient builders to conscript and organize a large labor force and to solve difficult challenges involving quarrying stone, transporting massive objects, and then engineering and designing massive structures from those quarried and transported stones. Even more remarkably, the builders of Stonehenge accomplished all this in a time before writing or before there is any evidence of an established mathematics in their region.

Though uniquely complex, southern England's Stonehenge is actually just one in a large number of stone monuments built between about 5,000 and 3,000 years ago in western Europe, primarily in England, Scotland, Ireland, Wales, and northern France. These monuments are called *megaliths* (meaning "very large stones") because they are composed of, obviously enough, very large stones. Some of these monuments consist of single, often large, upright stones called *menhirs*. Others have three or more upright stones with a ceiling or capstone balanced on top of the uprights. These are called *dolmens*, and, though most of them now have their component stones exposed, when initially constructed they were covered with soil and served as burial chambers. Most of the rest of the megalithic monuments are stone rings consisting of anywhere from a few to dozens of stones arranged in circles from just a few feet to a few hundred feet in diameter; there are hundreds of these stone circles scattered across western Europe.

Stonehenge is the best known of the stone circles or rings, though it does not have the largest diameter nor the greatest number of stones. The largest stone circle is located in nearby Avebury. The Avebury stone circle possesses a diameter about three times greater than that of Stonehenge and, upon its completion,

Though Stonehenge is iconic of the entire "mysteries of the ancient world" genre of speculation, it isn't a mystery at all. Stonehenge is a reflection of the spectacular capacities of human beings to produce monumental structures through collective labor. (K. Feder)

consisted of close to a hundred stones ranging in height from 7 to 18 feet (2.1 to 5.5 meters). Stonehenge, however, is certainly the most elaborate and complex of the megalithic stone circles and appears to have been a pilgrimage site, not just for the ancient farmers who lived in the south of England but perhaps for people across the breadth of western Europe.

Construction of Stonehenge began sometime around 5,000 years ago with the inscription of a circular ditch about 330 feet (100 meters) across in the chalky soil of the Salisbury Plain. At about the same time or soon thereafter, the builders erected a massive monolith called the "heelstone" outside the circular ditch. Then, about 700 years later (about 4,300 years ago), a new spurt of construction was commenced, and builders transported about 80 hard, dense stones to the site. These are the so-called *bluestones* from the Preseli Hills in southern Wales. The easiest way of transporting the stones, each weighing about 9,000 pounds (4,000 kilograms), involved a route that included land, river, and coastal segments for a total distance of about 250 miles (400 kilometers). The remaining bluestones, and the empty sockets left where bluestones had been erected but were then removed much later, show that the builders erected them in two concentric semicircles, which were, in turn, concentric with the monument's large original circle.

About 100 years later (4,200 years ago), the monument began taking its iconic form when the builders began erecting the 30 massive *sarsen* stones. The sarsens are from sandstone outcrops in the area of Avebury, about 18.5 miles (30 kilometers) distant. Each of the sarsens stands nearly 10 feet (about 3 meters) above the ground (with a couple of additional feet nestled belowground) and on average weighed an astonishing 22.5 tons (25,000 kilograms). Following the already established theme of the monument, the sarsens were erected in another circle, concentric with the original circle and the bluestones. The sarsen circle is about 100 feet (30 meters) in diameter.

Though Stonehenge's sarsens are taller than most of the component stones of other stone circles in western Europe, if its builders had stopped there, Stonehenge—though admittedly impressive—might have been, for the most part, just another stone circle. But they didn't stop there. The builders of Stonehenge carved two substantial bumps or, in the terminology of carpentry joinery, *tenons* on the top of each sarsen and then carved 30 curved crosspieces in stone called *lintels*. Smaller than the sarsens, the lintels are still substantial stones, each weighing more than 12,000 pounds (about 5,500 kilograms). On the bottom of each of the lintels, they carved *mortises* in the precise spots to match the tenons on adjoining sarsens. Then, in a brilliant and remarkably well-executed feat of engineering, likely using wooden platforms and levers, the builders raised each lintel up—remember, each weighed about six tons—and carefully placed it on top of a pair of adjoining upright sarsens, essentially connecting each sarsen to its adjacent neighbor. Because the lintels had to fit snugly with the sarsens and with the adjacent lintels on top of the great sarsen circle, each lintel had to be precisely curved on its interior and exterior faces with its ends angled properly to fit within a continuous circle on top of the sarsens. It was an amazing accomplishment that the entire thing hung together. Think giant Legos carved of and erected in solid rock, and you have a pretty good idea of the method employed by the Stonehenge builders to complete the circle of sarsens and to give it great stability and durability.

And (as they say in all of those annoying infomercials) that's not all! In the center of the sarsen circle, the builders erected 10 *more* sarsens—five sets of two—even taller and more massive than the stones used in the circle. The tallest of these are an astonishing 26 feet (8 meters) tall (with an additional 7 feet/ 2 meters set into the chalky ground) and weigh about 50 tons (45,000 kilograms). These large uprights break the pattern of concentric circles and were positioned in a horseshoe shape, with its opening toward the precise direction of the heelstone, the first upright stone erected at Stonehenge nearly 5,000 years ago. Each of the five sets of two massive uprights within the circle was, like the other sarsens, capped by a lintel (each weighing about 20,000 pounds/9,000 kilograms; and remember, these had to be raised by the builders to a height of at least 22 feet/7 meters to be placed on top of the uprights); an upright pair and its associated lintel is called a *trilithon*. These interior upright pairs stood separately; unlike the sarsens in the circle, each trilithon is separate from the other uprights.

It should not be surprising, given the sophisticated technology and social organization required for the construction of Stonehenge, that some thinkers, unaware of the remarkable abilities of ancient people, have long speculated about how ancient so-called primitives could have accomplished such a complicated and challenging project. In fact, one of the earliest speculations about the origins of Stonehenge was that it was built by Merlin, who magically levitated the stones into place. Latter-day Druids claim to be the descendants of the mystical builders of Stonehenge, though the religious cult they assert affiliation with didn't exist until at least a couple of thousand years after Stonehenge was built.

Predictably, **Erich von Däniken**, who takes a very dim view of human intelligence (which is deliciously ironic because his career is based on people being foolish enough to buy his absurd argument), asserts that "Stonehenge is an absolutely classic example of the need to take a visit by extraterrestrials into consideration" (1980, 80). He goes on to speak condescendingly about the claims of archaeologists that mere humans had been capable of building the monument by the slow, typically human process of trial and error: "Where are these climbing monkeys on the ladder of wisdom?" he asks (1980, 80). Von Däniken may be skeptical about human capabilities, but one is left to wonder how he explains all those stone pounding tools and antler picks found by archaeologists at the site that clearly were used by Stonehenge's builders to quarry and shape the stone and to dig sockets in the chalk for bluestone, sarsen, and trilithon placement. Were the extraterrestrials' lasers on the fritz the day they built Stonehenge?

There have been several attempts through experimental archaeology to replicate parts of the Stonehenge construction process. A concrete block the size, weight, and form of the largest trilithon upright has been moved and erected by a team of about 200 volunteers led by an archaeologist, a stonemason, and an engineer (Page and Cort 1997), and a lintel was successfully raised by the same crew. In another replicative experiment, another small crew was able to efficiently transport large blocks of stone by a method of sideways levering called "stonerowing." Even a retired American construction worker, Wally Wallington, has gotten into the act and shows how, with a little ingenuity, using a very simple set of techniques, even one person can move very large stones, erect them, and then raise capstones to their tops (www.youtube.com/watch?v=lRRDzFROMx0). It isn't certain which, if any, of the replicative experiments have hit upon the precise ways in which Stonehenge was built, but the point here is that with a little ingenuity and a lot of elbow grease and with a ready and willing crew of motivated workers, Stonehenge was completely doable without the assistance of extraterrestrial aliens.

A far less frivolous question than "Did extraterrestrial aliens build it?" is, Why did ancient Britons build it in the first place? No matter how Stonehenge was constructed, it certainly took an enormous amount of time and energy among a people who already spent most of their time providing the necessities of life. What purpose did Stonehenge serve that was important enough to warrant all of that work?

That question itself, however, is based on a misconception about ancient people: that they were trapped in a way of life that required their complete focus on utilitarian things, the mundane elements of subsistence, and therefore had little or no time for art or ideology. This simply is false. Time and again we see, in the archaeological record, evidence that even people who we might have thought were barely able to eke out an existence by hunting and gathering had, in fact, led rich lives filled with ritual, broad social networks, creativity, artistic expression, and monumentally scaled construction projects.

Recent work at the Gobeckli Tepe site in southern Turkey, for instance, shows clearly that, 11,000 years ago, people who subsisted on a diet of wild game and plants were fully capable of monumentally scaled projects related to their ritual life. The people at Gobeckli Tepe built a series of at least 20 rings of megaliths. The largest of the rings is about 65 feet (20 meters) across, and the most massive of the stones weighs about 10 tons (9,000 kilograms). The upright stones were carved into the shape of a *T* and are adorned with images of animals and birds, especially vultures. Gobeckli Tepe shows the capabilities of an ancient group of people, supposed primitives, to collectively produce an amazing monument—and to do this more than 6,000 years before Stonehenge.

Stonehenge's overall orientation in reference to the horizon as viewed from the center of the monument provides a possible specific meaning for its construction. Though we commonly refer to the sun rising in the east and setting in the west, this actually happens only on the vernal (spring) and autumnal equinoxes, those two days during the year (March 21 and September 21) when there are an equal number of hours of day and night. In actuality, the sun appears to rise (of course, we know the sun isn't doing any rising—the Earth is rotating on its axis) at a slightly different point on the horizon each day, a little farther to the north or south, than it did on the previous day. In the Northern Hemisphere, on December 21—the winter solstice and the day when the proportion of night to day is highest—the sun rises at the farthest yearly point to the south. On the day following the winter solstice, the sun rises a little farther to the north, and the next day a little farther, and so on until, on June 21, the summer solstice (the day when the proportion of daylight to night is the highest), the sun rises at its northernmost point. The next day, sunrise is back a little farther south.

The slow dance of sunrise from its most southerly to it most northerly and back again takes 365 days to complete, demarcating one year and providing a fixed, astronomical calendar by which people can gauge time and schedule significant events like holidays, feasts, and, more practically, planting and harvesting crops.

The precise extent of the north–south–north yearly migration of sunrise differs by latitude. At the latitude of Stonehenge, measured as a compass angle, the sun rises at its farthest south of east at 129° on December 21. It rises at its farthest north of east at 51° on June 21. The builders of Stonehenge aimed the horseshoe configuration of the trilithons toward the June 21 sunrise. In other words, an observer standing in the geometric center of Stonehenge on June 21 would see the summer solstice sun rise directly over the heelstone, one of the first stones erected in the monument. Because of the placement of the various upright stones there, most points on the horizon wouldn't have been visible to an observer 4,000 years ago; a bluestone or a sarsen or a trilithon upright would have blocked the view. But the sightline from the center out through the sarsens would have been unimpeded. The heelstone, acting in the manner of a gun sight, demarcates the target—the rising sun on the summer solstice—telling the people of Stonehenge that midsummer has arrived. It's a beautiful, elegant, monumental way of telling time, and it was constructed not by a pejoratively primitive people but by a creative culture several millennia ago.

Was Stonehenge a place of practicality, merely a utilitarian tool for telling time? Of course not. Stonehenge was a place of enormous ritual significance as well. There are upwards of 240 burials at the site, many of which were filled with remarkable grave goods (Schmid 2008). For example, consider the man called the "Amesbury Archer," located right outside the monument proper. His burial was filled with gold jewelry, copper knives, flint tools, and stone wrist guards.

The ratio of two strontium isotopes commonly found in teeth can be used to trace an individual's place of origin. The isotope ratio differs in various soils, and therefore in the foods found in different world regions, and it becomes fixed in the adult teeth of an individual even when those teeth are merely germs in a baby's jaws. Reference to that isotopic ratio in an adult's teeth can often pinpoint the region where a person was born and raised. The strontium isotope ratio in the mouth of the Amesbury Archer is entirely different from that found in the soils near Stonehenge and, in fact, from the soils anywhere in the British Isles. The isotope ratio in his teeth point instead to an origin in the foothills of the Alps, likely in today's Germany or Switzerland (Alexander 2008, 38). The Archer had been seriously wounded—one of his legs was badly damaged—and some researchers now suggest that Stonehenge may have been a pilgrimage spot where the sick and wounded came to be healed (Morgan 2008). So perhaps, for the builders of Stonehenge, the act of demarcating the summer solstice—though useful for a farming culture—was, by its very nature, an act of ritual sanctification of the movement of sunrise across the horizon, making the place where that point had been demarcated sacred. Stonehenge, therefore, was a very human achievement and had nothing to do with magicians or **ancient astronauts** visiting our planet.

Further Reading

There are uncounted books focusing on Stonehenge. Many of these are pretty loopy, but some are excellent. Among the latter are Christopher Chippindale's *Stonehenge Complete* (1983), the best place to go for the historical context of the monument; and Rodney Castleden's *The Stonehenge People* (1983), a terrific book about the culture of the people who built Stonehenge. For the best recent summary of new work at the site, read the *National Geographic* article by Caroline Alexander, "If the Stones Could Speak: Searching for the Meaning of Stonehenge," in the June 2008 issue.

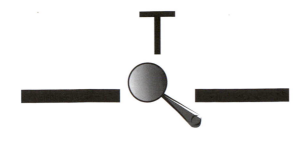

Thera (see Santorini)

Thomas, Cyrus

Cyrus Thomas (1825–1910) began his scientific career as a respected entomologist in Illinois. His career studying insects was set aside in 1882 when he was selected by John Wesley Powell to head the Bureau of American Ethnology's new Division of Mound Exploration. Powell wore two hats for the federal government of the United States; he was the director of the U.S. Geological Survey as well as the head of the Bureau of American Ethnology.

Thomas was charged with the task of solving the **moundbuilder** mystery. Earthworks—including conical mounds in which were found human burials, enormous flat-topped pyramids of earth, monumentally scaled effigy mounds in the shape of animals and birds, and linear or circular earthworks the purpose of which appeared to have been the creation of enclosures—had been found across the American Midwest, mid-South, and Southeast. The existence of these often monumental and elaborate mounds generated a tremendous amount of interest and speculation concerning the identity of the builders and the timing of their construction.

While many armchair archaeologists spent quite a bit of time—and spilled gallons of ink—speculating about the origins of the mounds, Thomas, with a budget of $5,000 per year, collected enormous quantities of data. His assistants investigated more than 2,000 mounds sites in 21 states, collecting more than 40,000 artifacts. Working primarily in Washington, D.C., Thomas compiled the collected data and produced a monumental report, published in 1894 as a book titled *Report on the Mound Explorations of the Bureau of Ethnology*. He concluded that there was no evidence that the mound had been built by Vikings or Egyptians or "Hindoos" or **Chinese** sailors or Lost Tribes of Israelites or Toltec or any of a bevy of other foreigners who, it had been asserted, populated North American in antiquity. At the end of his 700-plus-page magnum opus, Thomas concluded that American Indians had been the builders of all of the thousands of mounds found throughout North America, after all. His work, more than anyone else's, put the moundbuilder myth to rest, giving Native Americans the credit they truly deserved for being the producers of the impressive earthworks of North America.

Further Reading

Thomas's enormous *Report on the Mound Explorations of the Bureau of Ethnology* (1894), which significantly contributed to breaking the back of the moundbuilder myth, is still available in reprint. It's a classic piece of detective work and absolutely worth a read, or at least a skim.

Trenton Gravels

Trenton Gravels is the name given to a late glacial geological deposit located in New Jersey. In the late nineteenth century, C. C. Abbott, who lived on a farm nearby, brought the deposit to the attention of Frederick Ward Putnam, who had been named curator of the Peabody Museum at Harvard University in 1875, just nine years after the museum was established. Like many scholars of his time, Putnam was interested in the extent of human prehistory in the New World.

At least since the end of the eighteenth century, prehistorians in the Old World had been discovering stone tools, especially symmetrically chipped, finely made hand axes, in very deep soil layers alongside the preserved bones of extinct animal species. The stratigraphy and, especially, the association with extinct animals were interpreted as signifying great antiquity in these Old World tools. Even into the late nineteenth century, American prehistorians did not have a firm grasp of the extent of the time depth of a human presence in the New World. Though many thought it was fairly recent and certainly postglacial—meaning less than 10,000 years—there was an undercurrent of thought that suggested a far greater antiquity for the human arrival in the Americas.

Putnam, in his position at the Peabody Museum, was intrigued by the potential of a study of the Trenton Gravels. If human-made objects could be found ensconced with the gravels, it would provide proof that human beings had been in North America during the Pleistocene. To investigate that possibility, Putnam sponsored an excavation of the gravels by Abbott.

In the excavation, Abbott found what he interpreted to be primitive, chipped stone tools in stratigraphic layers that he believed were extremely ancient. Some were flint, a material commonly used throughout the ancient world for making sharp-edged weapons and cutting tools. Some of the specimens collected by Abbott were argillite, a metamorphic rock that was also commonly used by ancient people.

Newspaper articles published at the time (for example, in the *New York Times* on August 29, 1897) reflect a certain level of pride and nationalism tied up with the Trenton Gravels stone tools. The tools were labeled "Paleolithic," using the same term prehistorians used for specimens found in the Old World that dated to before the end of the Pleistocene (Ice Age). It was suggested, at least by some, that Abbott's discoveries in New Jersey proved that human antiquity in the New World was just as deep—and, therefore, just as important, just as significant—as it was in the Old World.

A closer examination of the stratigraphic context of the Trenton Gravels chipped-stone tools by European prehistorians intimately familiar with the Paleolithic tools of the Old World, especially Sir John Evans, revealed that the flint artifacts recovered by Abbott bore little in common with Paleolithic implements found in Europe and were likely of a far more recent vintage. The Trenton Gravels turned out not to support the notion of great time depth for the human presence in the New World.

Tucson Artifacts

The Tucson artifacts (also called the Tucson Roman artifacts, the Silverbell Road artifacts, or the Silverbell artifacts) consist of a series of 31 lead artifacts—extremely heavy crosses (one weighed 64 pounds/29 kilograms), swords, batons, and spear points—and a plaque made of caliche. The artifacts were found, beginning in 1924, in the remnant of an old lime kiln in the Picture Rocks area, just west of Tucson, Arizona. Lime kilns were abundant in the region and were used for extracting lime used in wall plaster in local adobe homes. The lime kiln in which the artifacts were found was no longer active, having been abandoned some 14 years previously, about 1910.

What made the artifacts of such interest among archaeologists and historians—and anyone interested in the archaeology and history of the United States—was the fact that they were inscribed with rather crude representations of human heads in profile. Various objects, including crowns, were found on the artifacts. Perhaps as a sign that the whole thing was an elaborate hoax, one sword has an image of what looks for all the world to be a dinosaur (specifically a *Diplodocus*, a long-necked, four-legged herbivore usually dated to about 150 million years ago). If that weren't bizarre enough, there was quite a bit of writing all over the artifacts. Great excitement resulted when a professor at the University of Arizona identified the writing as crude versions of Latin and Hebrew. And in that writing, he identified a date on one of the objects: 800 CE.

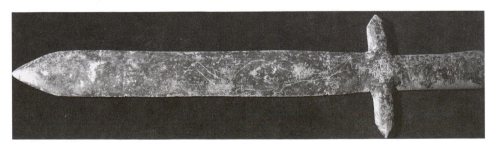

The Tucson artifacts were an elaborate hoax perpetrated to show that an ancient colony of Jews lived in Arizona in antiquity. Shown here is a rather ridiculous artifact: a lead sword with an inscribed image of a dinosaur (you can barely make it out right in the center of the sword blade), showing that the colony was older than most suspected. (Don Burgess)

It was difficult to explain how artifacts with a depiction of a dinosaur and Latin and Hebrew writing, perhaps dating to 800, came to be cached in an early twentieth-century lime kiln located just outside of Tucson. But this was clarified, sort of, once all of the writing had been translated. It appeared that the writing on the artifacts told the story of an ostensible Roman-Jewish colony in Arizona, dating from 775 to 900.

When experts in Latin, Roman history and archaeology, and Southwest prehistory examined the Tucson artifacts, they declared them to be complete nonsense—not just fakes, but bad ones at that. When a University of Arizona professor and highly respected Latin scholar, Dr. Frank Fowler, pored over the inscriptions, he discovered that, taken together, the writing made no sense. The inscriptions did not represent a comprehensive or comprehensible message, but were instead a jumble of largely nonsensical and disconnected, discontinuous phrases. But the argument for fakery seems to have been cinched when Fowler discovered that *all* of the individual Latin phrases inscribed on the artifacts had been lifted verbatim from three Latin textbooks—Harkness's *Latin Grammar*, the *Latin Grammar* of Allen and Greenough, and *Rouf's Standard Dictionary of Facts*. The earliest publication date for any of these works was 1864, which is rather more recent than the dates inscribed on them. Fowler went on to state that, when whoever inscribed the Latin on the Tucson artifacts attempted to in any way change the phrasing from what appeared in those publications—to change the tense, for example—he or she betrayed the lack of even a rudimentary knowledge of Latin. As a result of Fowler's analysis, it is clear that none of the artifacts can date to before 1864, and therefore none of them date to the purported period for the Roman-Jewish colony they mention.

Byron Cummings, director of the Arizona State Museum, was an eyewitness to the removal of at least one of the artifacts. He stated that the artifact in question was embedded in an already existing hole—that it had, in other words, been planted in a hole in the sand and gravel, which had then been only imperfectly tamped down around it. Cummings included his testimony in a report he presented to the University of Arizona, which at the time was considering purchasing the Tucson artifacts for a substantial sum of money. Geologist James Quinlan maintains that it would not have been difficult to have planted the artifacts in the gravel and suggests that the artifacts were placed there after the lime kiln was abandoned.

The Tucson artifacts are another example of attempts made to connect an ancient Old World culture to America long before the voyages of Christopher Columbus. Like so many of the others, the Tucson artifacts are **frauds**.

Further Reading

For a thorough and extremely well-written debunking of the Tucson artifacts, see the article published in 2009 in the *Journal of the Southwest* titled "Romans in Tucson?

The Story of an Archaeological Hoax," written by Don Burgess. The Burgess article is a model for good investigative journalism related to an archaeological fraud.

2012

Imagine finding a friend, neighbor, or relative, on December 31, cowering in the corner, giving away all worldly possessions, acting in a way that reflects abject terror, and babbling that the world was about to end in a cataclysm of unimaginable proportions. When you, naturally, inquire of them about the source of their fear, they thrust out a copy of the current calendar, excitedly pointing out to you that, oh my God, today is the last day on the last page of the calendar and, horrors, after that, nothing. No month following December, no day following the 31st. Finality. Ending. Omega.

How would you respond to that bit of insanity? Well, if you can answer that question, you can imagine how Mayanists respond to the idiocy currently revolving around the coming to the end of the current cycle in the **Maya** calendar—on December 21, 2012, in our calendar.

The Maya were a brilliant people centered in Mesoamerica. The Maya world was, essentially, contained within the borders of the modern nations of Guatemala, Honduras, Belize, Nicaragua, El Salvador, and Mexico (the eastern margins including the Yucatan Peninsula). Along with their many accomplishments in writing, agriculture, architecture, and mathematics, they possessed an extremely complex calendrical system.

Much of this complexity stems from the fact that the Maya didn't use a single, all-encompassing calendar but, instead, relied on a series of calendars, some interconnected, and each with a different purpose, some purely ceremonial. One, called the Tzolkin, consisted of a year with 260 days. Of equal importance was the calendar called the Haab, which was similar to our own and possessed a year of 360 days.

While the Tzolkin and the Haab were used to keep track of the days in the Maya year, the Maya also had a method for keeping track of longer periods of time. Just as we divide up time into various units (7 days in a week, 12 months in a year, 10 years in a decade, and so forth), the Maya calculated long stretches of time, based—with one exception—on periods of 20 units: Twenty days was a *uinal* (effectively, a Maya month). Eighteen *uinals* (not 20) made a *tun*, a 360-day year; the Maya chose 18 rather than 20 *uinals* to obtain a year length that came close to matching the actual length of a solar year—if they had kept counting in twenties, a Maya year would have been 400 days long. Twenty *tuns* was a *katun*, and 20 *katuns* made up a *baktun*. Counting up the days, a *baktun* is 144,000 days, or about 395 years.

Just as we identify each calendar day by the month name, number of the day, and the year, in their "long count" calendar, the Maya labeled each day in relation

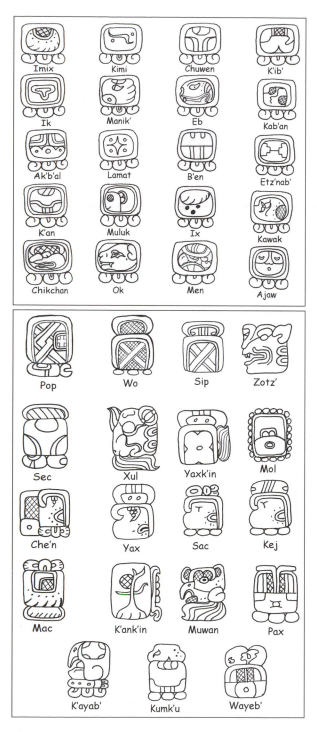

The Maya calendar consists of 20 days that repeat during each of their 18 months for a total of 360 days. The names and symbols of each of the days (top) and months (bottom) are shown here. A nineteenth month of just 5 days, bringing up the number of days in a year to 365, is also shown. (Jennifer Davis)

to its *uinal, tun,* and *katun* numbers as well as its *baktun* number. In our common calendar, the reference point from which years are numbered is an approximation of the year of the birth of Jesus Christ. For the Maya, the reference point was the beginning of the current cycle of time, which they believed to have occurred on August 11, 3114 BCE (just as, in 1650, Bishop Ussher of Ireland calculated that God had created the universe on September 21, 4004 BCE). For example, the Maya date 12.8.0.1.13 is 12 *baktuns,* 8 *katuns,* 0 *tuns,* 1 *uinal,* and 13 days since the beginning of the current cycle or, in our calendar, July 4, 1776.

In terms of its start date, the Maya calendar has more in common with the Jewish calendar than the standard calendar now in use. Just as is the case with the Maya calendar, the zero point in the Jewish calendar is supposed to be the year of the creation of the universe by God. As I write this in 2009, right after the celebration of the Jewish New Year, it is the year 5770—in other words, 5,770 years since the creation week described in Genesis. But the analogy between the Jewish calendar and the Maya ends there.

Okay, then what's the story with December 21, 2012? That day is auspicious in the Maya calendar because, while the Jewish and Maya calendars begin with their respective calculation of the creation of everything, the Jewish (and standard) calendar continues in what amounts to a straight line off to an unknown horizon. The Maya calendar, on the other hand, isn't a straight line but a circle—or, rather, a spiral—that inexorably returns to the same point, finishes, but then, and always, begins again. In other words, next year the Jewish calendar year will be 5771 and the year after 5772, and so on, ad infinitum. The Maya calendar simply adds another, grander cycle. On a date predetermined by the mathematics behind the Maya calculation of time, the long cycle ends after a stretch of 13 *baktuns* or about 5,125 solar years, and a new cycle begins. That appears to be the fundamental fact that the 2012 doomsayers are ignorant of. Time in the Maya calendar doesn't end. It merely completes a cycle and starts anew.

December 21, 2012—the Maya date is 12.19.19.17.19, or, the 19th day of the 17th *uinal* of the 19th *tun* of the 19th *katun* of the 12th *baktun*—is the date that marks the final day in the Maya *calendar,* not the entire history of time. It's the end of the current cycle of 13 *baktuns,* the current cycle of 5,125 years. That's it. On that day, the great Maya odometer of time turns over and returns to zero, but there's no indication whatsoever that the Maya thought this was something to fear or that the universe would end.

Certainly, the end of the 13th *baktun* likely had momentous implications for the Maya, not unlike the end of a millennium, like December 31, 2000 (yes, I know people were confused about that, but the year 2000 was still in the twentieth century; the first day of the twenty-first century was January 1, 2001). It likely would have been a time for renewal and reflection, or maybe some End-of-the-13th-*Baktun* parties, but on this the Maya were largely silent. Just as the end of our own millennium didn't mark the end of the universe, the Maya never said that the end of the current set of 13 *baktuns* marked the end of the universe, just the end of the current cycle of time. The Maya recognized this had happened before. Time didn't end then, and they didn't expect it to end this time either. In fact, at the Maya site of Palenque, part of the inscription found in Pacal's burial pyramid (see the entry **Palenque Sarcophagus**) mentions celebrations that would occur on a Maya date that translates on our calendar to October 15, 4772 (Schele and Freidel 1990). So the Maya certainly didn't believe that time would end in 2012.

By some calculations, the big date is actually December 23, 2012, so, when the world doesn't end on the 21st (it won't), some optimistic pessimists will still hold out hope that the end will occur a couple of days later (again, it won't). However, it will just be the beginning of a new cycle. Luckily, no computer systems are based on the Maya calendar, so at least we won't have to worry about all those Windows machines going kaflooey like they did on January 1, 2000 (if that was the Y2K scare, could this one be the Y13.0.0.0.0 scare?). I bet Steve Jobs had this all figured out already and Macs won't miss a beat, either.

For all of you who are really hoping that the Maya or the Mesopotamians or someone—anyone—had really predicted the end to the world and you were look- ing forward to that end with great and eager anticipation, don't despair. Though 13.0.0.0.0 just marks the end of one cycle and the beginning of the next, the Maya actually did predict a point in the future when the cycles *would* end and time itself would run out. According to Mayanists Linda Schele and Stuart Freidel (the late Linda Schele was such an accomplished Mayanist, I suspect she could think in Maya), a monument at the ancient Maya site of Coba actually had an inscribed date that might be interpreted as the truly final day according to Maya cosmology. That inscription added multiple levels above the *baktun* and can be expressed as: 13.13.13.13.13.13.13.13.13.13.13.13.13.13.13.13.13.13.13.0.0.0.0.

Schele and Freidel (1990) converted that Maya date, the time when the Maya believed the universe actually would come to an end, as residing 4.134105×10^{28} years in the future, which is a whole lot longer than the universe has existed (the most widely accepted estimate for the age of the universe is 1.3×10^{10}). So, though that wouldn't make a very interesting movie title, it would be a lot more accurate in terms of when the Maya actually predicted the end will be nigh. I will wait eagerly to find out if the Maya were right on this point.

Further Reading

For more about the ancient Maya civilization, see Simon Martin and Nikolai Grube's *Chronicle of the Maya Kings and Queens* (2008) and Arthur Demarest's *Ancient Maya: The Rise and Fall of a Rainforest Civilization* (2007).

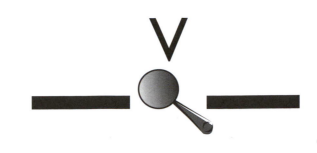

Van Sertima, Ivan

Ivan van Sertima (1935–2009) was a professor at Rutgers University in the Department of African Studies. While he was a respected scholar who investigated and celebrated the scientific achievements, literature, astronomy, mathematics, metallurgy, and more of native Africans, he is, perhaps, best known for his 1976 book, *They Came before Columbus*, in which he argued that the complex civilizations of Mesoamerica developed as the result of contact with representatives from the kingdoms of western Africa. As shown in the entry, van Sertima based his argument of an **African inspiration of the Olmec** on:

1. The claimed presence of the discovery of morphologically African skeletons in archaeological sites in the New World that long predated Columbus
2. The presence of *gua-nin*, which he maintains is a metal developed in Africa
3. His interpretation of the physiognomies of the enormous, stone-carved **Olmec heads**, which he believed were realistic depictions of African rulers who were migrants to the New World

Ultimately, though there is no reason to believe that West African travelers could not have visited the New World in antiquity, there is no evidence to support the claim that they did so. There are no morphologically African skeletons in pre-Columbian archaeological contexts in the New World. DNA analysis of bone, developed and applied to archaeological material long after van Sertima wrote *They Came before Columbus*, has shown that all pre-Columbian skeletons discovered and analyzed to date reflect one of the five mitochondrial haplogroups known among Native Americans. Nothing identifiable as *gua-nin* has ever been discovered in a pre-Columbian archaeological context in the New World. And any interpretation of the Olmec heads as being realistic depictions of Africans as opposed to Native Americans is entirely subjective and insufficient as evidence of an African presence in the New World.

Van Sertima's claims in *They Came before Columbus* about pre-Columbian Africans in the Americas and their role in inspiring the earliest development of complex civilization in Mesoamerica have been roundly criticized by experts in Mesoamerican archaeology. Richard Diehl summarizes the response of these

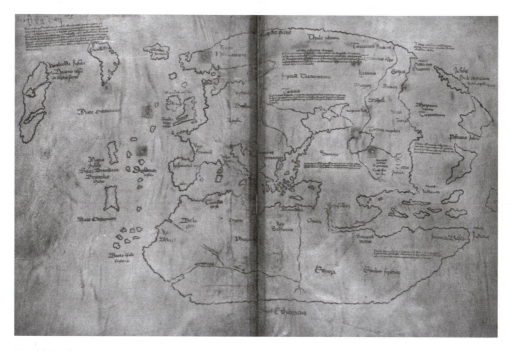

The Vinland map. If genuine, it is the earliest cartographic depiction of the New World. However, the chemical signature of the ink shows the presence of a chemical not known until the early twentieth century, indicating that it most likely is a fake. (AP Photo/ho)

experts in this way: "Not a single bona fide artifact of Old World origin has ever appeared in an Olmec archaeological site, or for that matter anywhere else in Mesoamerica" (2004, 14). In the most recent and complete synthesis of the Olmec (Pool 2007), van Sertima's claims do not warrant even a single mention.

Vinland Map

Archaeological evidence in Newfoundland (especially at the site called L'Anse aux Meadows), Ellesmere Island, Baffin Island, and even in the Canadian interior along the east shore of Hudson's Bay, shows unequivocally that the **Norse** journeyed to the New World, explored it, and even lightly colonized it beginning in the tenth century, more than 500 years before Columbus. With this in mind, the question of the authenticity of the famous—or perhaps infamous—Vinland Map loses much of its significance. Authentic or not, the map simply is not a crucial bit of evidence regarding a pre-Columbian Norse presence in the Americas.

The map ostensibly dates to 1440, just 52 years before Columbus's first voyage. On the right-hand side of the map, its cartographer very clearly depicts western Europe, including, with name labels, all of Spain, much of France, England, Ireland,

Scotland, Wales, Iceland, and Greenland. On the far left of the map, well across the Atlantic Ocean, the mapmaker placed a sizable island labeled "Vinlanda Insula," the Island of Vinland.

Vinland's location would seem to be in the correct geographic location for it to be North America, making the map of great interest to cartographers, as it would be the earliest world map showing the New World. Such a map would be worth quite a bit of money, and, in fact, it was purchased by Yale University's Beinecke Library for an estimated $1 million.

It has been difficult to come to a definitive determination concerning the authenticity of the Vinland Map. Much of its history is murky, and scholars have disagreed on the interpretation of various elements of the map. A few points are clear, though. A radiocarbon assay in 2002 of the parchment on which the map was made proves, at least, that the map was not made on modern paper. That is, while the map wasn't discovered until the middle of the twentieth century, the parchment on which it was made is far older, dating, in fact, to the early to mid-fifteenth century (about 1434, according to Donahue, Olin, and Harbottle 2002). That date does not prove that the map is authentic, since a clever twentieth-century forger might have obtained parchment of the appropriate age, guessing that it would be radiocarbon-dated to check its authenticity. However, it also does not rule out authenticity, as it would have had the parchment been significantly younger than the purported map date of 1440.

Famed forensic microscopist **Walter McCrone** was hired by Yale in 1974 to examine the map (though perhaps they should have done this before they purchased it). Using the tools of his trade, including a powerful scanning electron microscope and an electron and ion microprobe, to search for traces of the materials used to draw the image on the parchment, McCrone (1988) concluded that the map was a fake. He identified the presence of the yellow pigment anatase in the ink on the map. Anatase, whose chemical name is titanium dioxide, was unknown in the art and cartographic world in the fifteenth century and, in fact, was not developed until 1917. Thus, McCrone concluded, the map can be no older than 1917 and must be a twentieth-century forgery.

The details of the Vinland Map—its likely source and the motives behind its forgery—have been presented by Kirsten Seaver (2004) in her book *Maps, Myths, and Men: The Story of the Vinland Map*. She concludes that the map is a fake concocted by Josef Fischer, a Jesuit priest. Regardless of who might have forged the Vinland Map—and even regardless of whether or not it is a fake—the far more interesting issue is not in the least controversial. As stated at the outset of this entry, the Norse journeyed to the New World, interacted with the Native people they encountered here, and established a handful of short-lived colonies. The question of the Vinland Map's authenticity is interesting, but is significant largely for only cartographers and the trustees of Yale

University, who paid a hefty sum for what is either a very important historical map or a clever **fraud**.

Further Reading

If you are interested in the deep story behind the Vinland Map, read the book *Maps, Myths, and Men: The Story of the Vinland Map* by Kirsten Seaver (2004). For a marvelously illustrated and scholarly presentation supporting the map's authenticity, see *The Vinland Map and the Tartar Relation* by R. A. Skelton, Thomas E. Marston, and George O. Painter (1995).

Von Däniken, Erich

Erich von Däniken (1935–) is a Swiss fantasy and science fiction author masquerading as a writer of alternative prehistory and history. The primary themes of his **"ancient astronaut"** publications are:

1. The evolution of human beings was not solely the result of natural, evolutionary processes, but was instead the product of intentional and directed work by vastly technologically advanced extraterrestrial aliens. In other words, *Homo sapiens* is a species whose current appearance and behavior are the result of a process essentially similar to what we humans have accomplished through artificial selection of crops and domesticated animals. Von Däniken has stated clearly that this might have involved "an artificial genetic mutation" and, one might surmise, even interbreeding between extraterrestrials and prehuman females who, von Däniken explicitly states, would have been "fertilized" by the extraterrestrials.
2. The archaeological record is replete with artistic depictions and literary descriptions whose most reasonable interpretation is that they are of extraterrestrial aliens with whom primitive people had encounters. In other words, ancient people saw spaceships land and saw extraterrestrial aliens exit the ships, whereupon the aliens conducted a walkabout; collected soil, plant, or even animal specimens; and returned them to their ship for analysis and, perhaps, transportation to their home planet. Amazed and fascinated, our human ancestors then retired to the nearest cave or to their huts, where they attempted, as best they could, to preserve for posterity the remarkable sight they had just witnessed by drawing, painting, or recording it in a written language.
3. The archaeological record is replete with examples of intellectual great leaps—reflected in technology (like metallurgy), engineering (for example, pyramid construction), or subsistence (the development of agriculture)—that are far too great to have been the simple result of human development. Instead, these great leaps forward were the result of training by extraterrestrials, who represented a

sort of galactic Peace Corps, helping to raise our dimwitted ancestors to a higher level of civilization than they would otherwise have been capable through the application of their own native intelligence.

Erich von Däniken has no training in archaeology, history, geology, or, in fact, any scientific discipline. After a series of brushes with the law—in fairness, this was in his youth, but in the spirit of full disclosure, the court-appointed examiner labeled the young von Däniken a "liar and a criminal psychopath"—he produced a manuscript for a book originally titled (in its 1968 German publication) *Erinnerungen an die Zukunft* (Recollections of the Future). The book sold extraordinarily well, igniting a firestorm of interest in von Däniken's thesis concerning the role of ancient astronauts in human physical and cultural evolution. The English translation of the book was published in 1970 with the title **Chariots of the Gods** (the "chariots" being the vessels—spaceships—carrying the ones with godlike powers—that would be the extraterrestrial aliens—to Earth). Soon thereafter there was another book based on the same premise, but with a title a little less obscure for those not accustomed to metaphor: *Gods from Outer Space*. Next came *Gold of the Gods*, *Miracles of the Gods*, *Pathways of the Gods*, and a continuing list of books that, by von Däniken's own enumeration, includes 29 full-length works. Those books, again according to von Däniken, have been translated into 32 languages and together have sold more than 63 million copies. Not bad for a writer of fantasy and science fiction.

Von Däniken's books have spawned an entire ancient astronaut industry, which has included magazines, television shows, and, most recently, a late and not-so-lamented ancient astronaut theme park (**Mystery Park**). Now in his seventies, von Däniken remains active as a writer and lecturer, living in Beatenberg, Switzerland. He also likes to cook (I wonder when we can look forward to *The Joy of Cooking Like an Extraterrestrial*).

Vortex

I wish I could provide you with a concise definition of vortexes, but the literature is so scant and so laden with absolute gibberish that it is an impossibility to do so. Essentially, a vortex is a place that has so powerful an impact on the human psyche that, it is believed, in it resides some remarkable, little understood, perhaps supernatural power causing humans to get dizzy, to raise—or lower—their blood pressure, to get excited—or mellow—and simply to feel all warm and fuzzy, all one-with-the-universey, love peace and music, and all that. I am including the term in this encyclopedia devoted to fantastic claims made in archaeology because some ostensible vortexes are, in fact, archaeological sites.

Reading definitions of *vortex*, one finds reference to terms with actual scientific definitions, like *energy*, *force*, *amplify*, *magnetic*, and *electric*. Unfortunately, it is rather obvious that the purveyors of the vortex phenomena—though they do a great job of spelling these words—are not in the least bit acquainted with their actual scientific meaning. You will find no mathematical formulas in vortex guides, only vague statements about "forces," "power," and "energy."

Essentially, the vortex proponents claim that there are certain places on Earth—many of them, apparently, in the lovely community of Sedona, Arizona—where, by golly, our planet is just enormously "healthy," and, by visiting these healthy spots, that health sort of rubs off on you, resulting in the aforementioned feelings of well-being, happiness, at-oneness with the universe, and so forth.

Now, far be it for me to dispute the wonderfully therapeutic effect of hiking up a beautiful mountain trail to a scenic overlook of breathtaking beauty, perhaps especially in Sedona, a place I have been many times and for which I have enormous affection. I appreciate hiking and challenging myself as much as the next person. But, honestly, I am quite certain that the heart-pounding, short-of-breath feeling you obtain from hiking up mountain trails results from the challenge of the hike and the high altitude of the overlook. That sense of well-being is certainly the result of the endorphins released into your bloodstream by the time you reach the end of the trail, rather than some supernatural process of planetary energy—which, by the way, cannot be measured by any of the sophisticated technologies that have been developed to measure such things.

In his book *What Is a Vortex?* Dennis Andres (2000) poses the question, "Is Sedona a vortex simply because it is beautiful?" The answer is actually pretty simple: Yup.

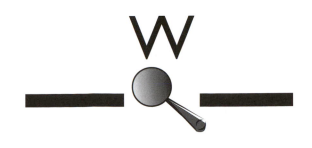

Walam Olum

One of the favored themes underlying the **moundbuilder myth** was that, whatever their ultimate geographical source, the people who built the ancient mounds in the American Midwest had created a splendid and peaceful civilization in the dim mists of antiquity. They had been overrun, decimated, and eliminated in a much more recent invasion by a wild, violent, and barbaric people. In this version of the myth, these barbarians were the ancestors of the American Indians.

One nineteenth-century hoaxer went so far as to concoct an entire epic story that followed this scenario. In 1836, **Constantine Samuel Rafinesque** claimed that 10 years earlier he had located and then deciphered an ancient historical text engraved on wooden tablets by the ancestors of the Lenape (Delaware) Indians of eastern North America (Oestreicher 1996). Rafinesque called the story he had discovered the Walam Olum. The tablets themselves had disappeared (of course), but Rafinesque claimed to have translated the saga they told of the migration of American Indians from Northeast Asia 3,600 years ago across a frozen waste that had once connected the Old and New Worlds. There is a certain irony in this; this part of Rafinesque's fake tale bolstered part of a scenario that we now know to be true—humans first entering the New World from Asia across a land bridge in the far north—though his timing is far too recent.

In Rafinesque's fantasy, the moundbuilders had migrated to the New World long before the arrival of the Indians. He went on to have his fictitious migrants overwhelm the moundbuilder people and then defeat them in battle. Where did the moundbuilders come from in this story? According to the Walam Olum, the moundbuilders originated on the Lost Continent of **Atlantis**.

Many Lenape people reject the authenticity of the Walam Olum, and researcher David Oestreicher (1996) has shown that the hieroglyphs in which the document was written were cobbled together using a jumble of Egyptian, Chinese, and **Maya** characters. The Walam Olum was an elaborate hoax in a series of hoaxes surrounding the mystery of the moundbuilders.

Further Reading
The article "Unraveling the Walam Olum" by David Oestreicher in *Natural History* (1996) is the best place to read more about this anthropological fake.

Westford Knight

An incised image of a sword in Westford, Massachusetts. Two boys were seen producing the image in the late 1800s. (K. Feder)

The so-called Westford Knight is a carved image that some—but by no means all—observers perceive on a fragment of bedrock located in Westford, Massachusetts. The carving is first mentioned in a local history published in 1883. Originally assumed to be a simple geometric carving by an American Indian, ever more speculative reconstructions have been suggested since. In its current iteration, the carving is viewed as a life-size image of a knight, including his sword and shield (with a coat of arms), and even the precise identity of the knight has been proposed: it is Sir James Gunn, a knight who ostensibly was a fellow traveler with Henry Sinclair, a Scotsman who, in another speculation unsupported by history or archaeology, traveled to the New World in 1398.

Actually, very little is known of Sinclair. We know that he was born near Edinburgh, Scotland, in 1345; became the Earl of the Orkney Islands in 1379; and died about 1400. There is very little else known definitively about him. There is, however, a body of unsubstantiated myth surrounding the Earl. The myth is based on the Zeno narrative, which tells the story of a voyage from the Orkneys to Greenland by an individual named Zichmni in 1398. Through a series of mental gymnastics, based on an absolute dearth of anything that might be claimed as historical or archaeological evidence, some have argued that Zichmni was, in actuality, a misspelling—or misreading—of the Sinclair name, and that he landed on Newfoundland in Canada rather than Greenland. This is utter nonsense.

Between 1883 when the image was first noted and 1954, nothing much was made of it. Then, in 1954, based on little more than his fevered imagination, **pseudoarchaeologist** Frank Glynn chalked in an entirely false elaboration of whatever image was actually there in the first place. Glynn's image included a knight in armor, a sword, and the coat of arms that have been identified as those of Sir James Gunn.

A detailed analysis of the image by David K. Schafer of the Peabody Museum of Archaeology and Ethnology at Harvard University has shown that the so-called knight exists only in Glynn's imagination (Weller 2006). The boulder itself is covered with glacial scratches and, according to Schafer (2003), the handle of the sword consists of nothing more than glacial striations, and the sword blade image that descends from the handle was produced with a metal punch by a pair of young boys in the late 1800s. Everything else on the boulder—the knight, his armor, his helmet, and his coat-of-arms-bearing shield—is nothing more than Glynn's fanciful painting. In fact, the evidence shows clearly that the Westford Knight doesn't exist. It is pure fantasy.

REFERENCES

Alexander, C. 2008. If the stones could speak: Searching for the meaning of Stonehenge. *National Geographic* 213 (6): 34–59.

Anderson, D., J. Halsey, and R. B. Stamps. 2004. Digging up controversy: The Michigan relics. Michigan Historical Center. http://www.hal.state.mi.us/mhc/michrelics/.

Andres, D. 2000. *What Is a Vortex? A Practical Guide to Sedona's Vortex Sites*. Sedona, AZ: Meta Adventures.

Aitken, M. J. 1959. Test for correlation between dowsing response and magnetic disturbance. *Archaeometry* 2:58–59.

Archaeological Institute of America. 2005. Insider: Fantastic footprints. *Archaeology* 58 (5). http://www.archaeology.org/0509/newsbriefs/insider.html.

Arguelles, J. 1987. *The Mayan Factor: The Path Beyond Technology*. Santa Fe, NM: Bear & Co.

Arnold, B. 1992. The past as propaganda. *Archaeology* 45 (4): 30–37.

Arnold, D. 1991. *Building in Egypt: Pharaonic Stone Masonry*. Oxford, UK: Oxford University Press.

Arthur, J. 1996. Creationism: Bad science or immoral pseudoscience? *Skeptic* 4 (4): 88–93.

Ashe, G., ed. 1971. *Quest for America*. New York: Praeger.

Bailey, R. 1983. Divining edge: Dowsing for medieval churches. *Archaeology* February: 5.

Bailey, R., E. Cambridge, and H. D. Briggs. 1988. *Dowsing and Church Archaeology*. Wimborne, UK: Intercept.

Balter, M. 2005. *The Goddess and the Bull: Çatalhoyuk: An Archaeological Journey to the Dawn of Civilization*. New York: The Free Press.

Barrett, T. H. 2002. *1421: The Year China Discovered the World* by Gavin Menzies: A Review. http://www.kenspy.com/Menzies/review2.html.

Brier, B., and J. P. Houdin. 2008. *The Secret of the Great Pyramid*. New York: Harper.

Bryce, I., B. E. Eng, J. Harris, and D. Wheeler. 1985. Physicists examine Karen Hunt's EPFT. http://www.skeptics.com.au/journal/beginning/book.pdf.

Buckley, T. 1976. The discovery of Tutankhamun's tomb. In *The Treasures of Tutankhamun*, ed. K. S. Gilbert, J. K. Holt, and S. Hudson, 9–18. New York: Metropolitan Museum of Art.

Burgess, D. 2009. Romans in Tucson? The story of an archaeological hoax. *Journal of the Southwest* 51:3–135.

Burl, A. 1995. *A Guide to the Stone Circles of Britain, Ireland, and Brittany*. New Haven, CT: Yale University Press.

Carroll, R. T. 2003. *The Skeptic's Dictionary*. New York: Wiley.

Castleden, R. 1993. *The Stonehenge People: An Exploration of Life in Neolithic Britain, 4700–2000 B.C.* London: Routledge.

Cayce, E. 1968. *Edgar Cayce on Atlantis*. New York: Hawthorn Books.

Chambers, H. 1969. *Dowsing, Divining Rods, and Water Witching for the Millions*. Los Angeles: Shelbourne Press.

Chippindale, C. 1983. *Stonehenge Complete*. Ithaca, NY: Cornell University Press.

Clayton, P. A. 1994. *Chronicle of the Pharaohs: The Reign-by-reign Record of the Rulers and Dynasties of Ancient Egypt*. London: Thames & Hudson.

Cohn, N. 1996. *Noah's Flood: The Genesis Story in Western Thought*. New Haven, CT: Yale University Press.

Colavito, J. 2005. Archaeological coverup? http://jcolavito.tripod.com/lostcivilizations/id8.html.

Cole, J. R. 1982. Western Massachusetts "Monk's Caves": 1979 University of Massachusetts field research. *Man in the Northeast* 17:27–53.

Conyers, L. 2004. *Ground-penetrating Radar for Archaeology*. Walnut Creek, CA: AltaMira Press.

Cremo, M. A., and R. L. Thompson. 1993. *Forbidden Archaeology: The Hidden History of the Human Race*. San Diego: Govardhan Hill.

Damon, P. E., et al. 1989. Radiocarbon dating of the Shroud of Turin. *Nature* 337:611–15.

Daniel, G. 1977. Review of *America B.C.* by Barry Fell. *New York Times*, March 13, 8ff.

de Camp, L. S. 1970. *Lost Continents: The Atlantis Theme in History, Science, and Literature*. New York: Dover.

Demarest, A. 2007. *Ancient Maya: The Rise and Fall of a Rainforest Civilization*. Cambridge, UK: Cambridge University Press.

Dexter, R. 1986. Historical aspects of the Calaveras Skull controversy. *American Antiquity* 51:365–69.

Diehl, R. A. 2004. *The Olmecs: America's First Civilization*. London: Thames & Hudson.

Dillehay, T. D. 2000. *The Settlement of the Americas: A New Prehistory*. New York: Basic Books.

DiPietro, V, and G. Molenaar. 1982. *Unusual Martian Surface Features*. Glen Dale, MD: Mars Research.

Donahue, D. J., J. S. Olin, and G. Harbottle. 2002. Determination of the radiocarbon age of parchment of the Vinland Map. *Radiocarbon* 44 (1): 45–52.

Donnelly, I. 1882. *Atlantis: The Antediluvian World*. Reprint, New York: Harper, 1971.

Faulkner, C. 1971. *The Old Stone Fort*. Knoxville: University of Tennessee Press.

Feder, K. L. 1984. Irrationality and archaeology. *American Antiquity* 49 (3): 525–41.

Feder, K. L. 1998/1999. Archaeology and Afrocentrism: An attempt to set the record straight. *A Current Bibliography on African Affairs* 29 (3): 199–210.

Feder, K. L. 2010. *Frauds, myths, and mysteries: Science and pseudoscience in archaeology*. New York: McGraw-Hill.

Fell, B. 1976. *America B.C.: Ancient Settlers in the New World*. New York: Demeter Press.

Fell, B. 1980. *Saga America*. New York: Times Books.

Fell, B. 1982. *Bronze Age America*. New York: Times Books.

Fitzhugh, W. W. 1993. Archaeology of Kodlunarn Island. In *The Archaeology of the Frobisher Voyages*, ed. W. W. Fitzhugh and J. S. Olin, 59–97. Washington, DC: Smithsonian Institution Press.

Fitzhugh, W. W., and J. S. Olin, (eds). 1993. *The Archaeology of the Frobisher Voyages*. Washington, DC: Smithsonian Institution Press.

Fitzhugh, W. W., and E. I. Ward, (eds). 2000. *Vikings: The North Atlantic Saga*. Washington, DC: Smithsonian Institution Press.

Flynn, S. 2006. Touro Park dig comes up empty. *Newport Daily News*. http://www.newportdailynews.com/ee/newportdailynews/default.php?pSetup=new portdailynews_archive.

Friedrich, W. L., B. Kromer, M. Friedrich, J. Heinemeier, T. Pfeiffer, and S. Talamo. 2006. Santorini eruption radiocarbon dated to 1627–1600 B.C. *Science* 312:548.

Frost, F. 1982. The Palos Verdes Chinese anchor mystery. *Archaeology* (Jan/Feb): 23–27.

Ghezzi, I., and C. Ruggles. 2007. Chankillo: A 2,300-year-old observatory in coastal Peru. *Science* 315:1239–43.

Goddard, I., and W. Fitzhugh. 1979. A statement concerning *America B.C. Man in the Northeast* 17:166–72.

Godfrey, W. 1951. The archaeology of the Old Stone Mill in Newport, Rhode Island. *American Antiquity* 17:120–29.

Goodman, J. 1977. *Psychic Archaeology: Time Machine to the Past*. New York: Berkeley Books.

Goodman, J. 1981. *American Genesis*. New York: Berkeley Books.

Gove, H. 1996. *Relic, Icon, or Hoax? Carbon Dating the Turin Shroud*. Philadelphia: Institute of Physics Publishing.

Griffin, J., D. Meltzer, and B. Smith. 1988. A mammoth fraud in science. *American Antiquity* 53 (3): 578–81.

Grove, D. 1995. The Olmec. *Arqueologia Mexicana* 12:26–33.

Gugliotta, G. 2007. The Maya glory and ruin. *National Geographic* 212 (2): 68–109.

Halsey, J. R. 2009. The "Michigan Relics": America's Longest Running Archaeological Fraud. Paper presented at the *Midwest Archaeological Conference*, Iowa City, IA.

Hancock, G. 1995. *Fingerprints of the Gods*. New York: Three Rivers Press.

Hawass, Z. 2005. *Tutankhamun and the Golden Age of Pharoahs*. Washington, DC: National Geographic Society.

Hawkins, G. 1965. *Stonehenge Decoded*. New York: Dell.

Haynes, C. V., and G. A. Agogino. 1986. *Geochronology of Sandia Cave*. Washington, DC: Smithsonian Institution Press.

Hertz, J. 1997. Round church or windmill? New light on the Newport Tower. *Newport History* 68 (2): 55–91.

Heyerdahl, T. 1968. *Kon-Tiki*. New York: Pocket Books.

Hoagland, R. C. 1987. *The Monuments of Mars: A City Of the Edge of Forever*. Berkeley, CA: North Atlantic Books.

Hoffman, C. 1987. The Long Bay Site, San Salvador. *American Antiquity* 62:96–101.

Hunt, K. A. 1984. *Point Creek Homestead Electro-magnetic Photo-field Survey*. Melbourne, Australia: Melbourne and Metropolitan Board of Works.

Ingstad, H., and A. S. Ingstad. 2000. *The Viking Discovery of America: The Excavation of a Norse Settlement in L'anse aux Meadows, Newfoundland*. St. John's, Newfoundland: Breakwater Books.

Irving, R. and J. Lundberg. 2006. *The Field Guide: The Art, History, and Philosophy of Crop Circle Making*. London: Strange Attractor Press.

Isaak, M. 1998. Problems with the global flood. http://www.talkorigins.org/faqs/faq-noahs-ark.html.

Jackson, K., and J. Stamp. 2003. *Building the Great Pyramid*. Toronto: Firefly Books.

James, G. G. M. 1954. *The Stolen Legacy*. New York: Philosophical Library.

Joltes, R. 2003. Burrows Cave: A modern hoax. http://www.criticalenquiry.org/burrowscave/burrows.shtml.

Jordan, P. 1998. *Riddles of the Sphinx*. New York: New York University Press.

Jordan, P. 2001. *The Atlantis Syndrome*. London: Sutton.

Kampschror, B. 2006. Pyramid scheme: Has a Houston contractor discovered the world's oldest pyramids in Bosnia? *Archaeology* 59 (4): 22–28.

Kehoe, A. B. 2005. *The Kensington Runestone: Approaching a Research Question Holistically*. Long Grove, IL: Waveland Press.

Krupp, E. C., ed. 1978. *In Search of Ancient Astronomies*. Garden City, NY: Doubleday.

Kuban, G. 2009. The Paluxy dinosaur/"man track" controversy. http://paleo.cc/paluxy.htm.

Lefkowitz, M. 1996. *Not Out of Africa*. New York: Basic Books.

Lehner, M. 1997. *The Complete Pyramids: Solving the Ancient Mysteries*. London: Thames & Hudson.

Lepper, B. 1998. Ancient astronomers of the Ohio Valley. *Timeline* 15 (1): 2–11.

Lepper, B. 2005. *Ohio Archaeology: An Illustrated Chronicle of Ohio's Ancient American Indian Cultures*. Wilmington, OH: Orange Frazer Press.

Lepper, B., and J. Gill. 2000. The Newark Holy Stones. *Timeline* 17 (3): 16–25.

Mainfort, R. C., and M. L. Kwas. 2004. The Bat Creek Stone revisited. *American Antiquity* 69:761–69.

Malin Space Science Systems. 1995. The "Face on Mars." Malin Space Science Systems. http://www.msss.com/education/facepage/face.html.

Manley, B., ed. 2003. *The Seventy Great Mysteries of Ancient Egypt*. London: Thames & Hudson.

Marinatos, S. 1972. Thera: Key to the riddle of Minos. *National Geographic* 141:702–26.

Martin, M. 1983–84. A new controlled dowsing experiment. *The Skeptical Inquirer* 8 (2): 138–42.

Martin, S., and N. Grube. 2008. *Chronicle of the Maya Kings and Queens*. London: Thames & Hudson.

Mazur, S. 2005. Dig of the century: Getting to the bottom of the Dorak Affair. http://www.scoop.co.nz/stories/HL0508/S00224.htm.

McCrone, W. 1976. Authenticity of Medieval document tested by small particle analysis. *Analytical Chemistry* 48 (8): 676A–679A.

McCrone, W. 1982. Shroud image is the work of an artist. *The Skeptical Inquirer* 6 (3): 35–36.

McCrone, W. 1988. The Vinland Map. *Analytical Chemistry* 60:1009–18.

McCrone, W. 1996. *Judgment Day for the Turin Shroud*. Chicago: Microscope.

McIntosh, G. 2000. *The Piri Reis Map of 1513*. Athens: University of Georgia Press.

McKusick, M. 1982. Psychic archaeology: From Atlantis to Oz. *Journal of Field Archaeology* 9 (1): 99–118.

McKusick, M. 1991. *The Davenport Conspiracy Revisited*. Ames: Iowa State University Press.

Mellaart, J. 1965. *Earliest Civilizations of the Near East*. London: Thames & Hudson.

Meltzer, D. J. 2009. *First Peoples in a New World: Colonizing Ice Age America.* Berkeley: University of California Press.

Menzies, G. 2002. *1421: The Year China Discovered America.* New York: Perennial.

Money, L. 1985. Down on the farm—In spirit at least. *The Herald* (Melbourne, Australia), July 26.

Moore, R. A. 1983. The impossible voyage of Noah's Ark. *Creation/Evolution* 11: 1–43.

Morgan, J. 2008. Dig pinpoints Stonehenge origins. http://news.bbc.co.uk/2/hi/science/nature/7625145.stm.

Murdock, D. M. 2010. What about the Anunnaki? *Truth Be Known.* http://www.truth beknown.com/anunnaki.htm.

Nelson, M. R. 2002. The mummy's curse: Historical cohort study. *British Medical Journal* 325:1482–84.

Neudorfer, G. 1980. *Vermont's Stone Chambers: An Inquiry Into Their Past.* Montpelier: Vermont Historical Society.

Nickell, J. 1983. *Inquest on the Shroud of Turin.* Buffalo, NY: Prometheus Books.

Noel Hume, I. 1974. *Historical Archaeology.* New York: Knopf.

Novella, S. 2006. The Starchild Project. http://www.theness.com/the-starchild-project/.

O Hehir, B. 1990. Barry Fell's West Virginia fraud. Unpublished manuscript.

Oestreicher, D. M. 1996. Unraveling the Walam Olum. *Natural History* 105:10.

Oestreicher, D. M. 2008. Grave Creek Stone. Unpublished manuscript.

Ortiz de Montellano, B. 1991. Multicultural pseudoscience: Spreading scientific illiteracy among minorities: Part 1. *Skeptical Inquirer* 16 (1): 46–50.

Ortiz de Montellano, B. 1992. Magic melanin: Spreading scientific illiteracy among minorities: Part 2. *Skeptical Inquirer* 16 (2): 162–66.

Page, C., and J. Cort. 1997. Secrets of Lost Empires: Stonehenge. *NOVA:* WGBH, Boston.

Peterson, N. 1988. *Sacred Sites: A Traveler's Guide to North America's Most Powerful and Mysterious Landmarks.* New York: Contemporary Books.

Phoenix Gazette. 1909. Explorations in Grand Canyon. April 5. http://grandcanyontreks.org/fiction.htm.

Picknett, L., and C. Prince. 2007. *The Turin Shroud: How da Vinci Fooled the World.* New York: Touchstone.

Pool, C. 2007. *Olmec Archaeology and Early Mesoamerica.* Cambridge, UK: Cambridge University Press.

Powell, E. 2004. Theme park of the gods. *Archaeology* 57 (1): 62–67.

Quinion, M. B. 2008. *Cidermaking.* Oxford, UK: Shire Publications.

Raloff, J. 1995. Dowsing expectations: New reports awaken scientific controversy over water witching. *Science News* 148:90–91.

Randi, J. 1979. A controlled test of dowsing abilities. *Skeptical Inquirer* 4 (1): 16–20.

Randi, J. 1984. The great $110,000 dowsing challenge. *Skeptical Inquirer* 8 (4): 329–33.

Ross, A., and P. Reynolds. 1978. Ancient Vermont. *Antiquity* 52:100–107.

Rowland, I. D. 2004. *The Scarith of Scornello: A Tale of Renaissance Forgery.* Chicago: University of Chicago Press.

Russell, M. 2003. *Piltdown Man: The Secret Life of Charles Dawson and the World's Greatest Archaeological Hoax.* Gloucestershire, UK: Tempus.

Sagan, C. 1996. *The Demon-haunted World: Science as a Candle in the Dark.* New York: Random House.

Schaafsma, P. 1980. *Indian Rock Art of the Southwest*. Albuquerque: University of New Mexico Press.

Schafer, D. K. 2003. Westford Knight. *Bulletin of the Massachusetts Archaeological Society*.

Schele, L., and D. Freidel. 1990. *A Forest of Kings*. New York: Quill/William Morrow.

Schmid, R. E. 2008. Study: Stonehenge Was a Burial Site for Centuries. http://news.yahoo.com/s/ap/20080529/ap_on_sc/sci_stonehenge_8.

Schnabel, J. 1994. *Round in Circles: Poltergeists, Pranksters, and the Secret History of Cropwatchers*. Armherst, NY: Prometheus Books.

Schwartz, S. 1978. *The Secret Vaults of Time*. New York: Grosset & Dunlap.

Schwartz, S. 1983. *The Alexandria Project*. Bloomington, IN: iUniverse.

Seaver, K. A. 2004. *Maps, Myths, and Men: The Story of the Vinland Map*. Palo Alto, CA: Stanford University Press.

Silverberg, R. 1989. *The Moundbuilders*. Athens: Ohio University Press.

Sitchin, Z. 1976. *The 12th Planet*. New York: Avon Books.

Skelton, R. A., T. E. Marston, and G. O. Painter. 1995. *The Vinland Map and the Tartar Relation*. New Haven, CT: Yale University Press.

Slifer, D. 2000. *Guide to Rock Art of the Utah Region*. Santa Fe, NM: Ancient City Press.

Smith, C. B. 2004. *How the Great Pyramid Was Built*. Washington, DC: Smithsonian Books.

Spence, L. 1924. *The Problem of Atlantis*. London: William Rider & Son.

Spence, L. 1925. *Atlantis in America*. London: Ernest Benn.

Spence, L. 1926. *The History of Atlantis*. New York: Bell.

Spencer, F. 1990. *Piltdown: A Scientific Forgery*. Oxford, UK: Oxford University Press.

Stiebing, W. 1984. *Ancient Astronauts, Cosmic Collisions, and Other Popular Theories About Man's Past*. Buffalo, NY: Prometheus Books.

Suggs, R. C. 1970. The *Kon-Tiki* myth. In *Cultures of the Pacific*, ed. T. G. Harding and B. J. Wallace, 29–38. New York: Free Press.

Sutherland, P. 2000. Scattered signs: The evidence for native/Norse contact in North America. Paper presented at the Vikings: The North Atlantic Saga conference, Washington, DC.

Terrell, J. 1986. *Prehistory in the Pacific Islands*. Cambridge, UK: Cambridge University Press.

Thomas, C. 1894. *Report on the Mound Explorations of the Bureau of Ethnology*. Washington, DC: Bureau of American Ethnology.

Thompsen, L. 2008. The Oklahoma Runestones: Possibilities, probabilities, and realities. MA thesis, University of Leicester.

Trace Genetics. 2003. Report on the DNA analysis from skeletal remains from two skulls conduced [*sic*] by Trace Genetics. http://www.starchildproject.com/reports_dna.htm.

Tribble, S. 2009. *A Colossal Hoax*. New York: Rowman & Littlefield.

Van Leusen, M. 1999. Dowsing and archaeology: Is there something underneath? *Skeptical Inquirer* 23 (2): 33–41.

Van Sertima, I. 1976. *They Came before Columbus*. New York: Random House.

Van Tilburg, J. 1994. *Easter Island: Archaeology, Ecology, and Culture.* Washington, DC: Smithsonian Institution Press.

Von Däniken, E. 1970. *Chariots of the Gods.* New York: Bantam Books.

Von Däniken, E. 1973. *Gold of the Gods.* New York: Bantam Books.

Von Däniken, E. 1980. *Pathways to the Gods: The Stones of Kiribati.* New York: G.P. Putnam's Sons.

Walsh, J. E. 1996. *Unraveling Piltdown: The Science Fraud of the Century and Its Solution.* New York: Random House.

Walsh, J. M. 2008. Legend of the crystal skulls. *Archaeology* 61 (3).

Wauchope, R. 1974. *Lost Tribes and Sunken Continents: Myth and Method in the Study of American Indians.* Chicago: University of Chicago Press.

Webster, D. 2002. *The Fall of the Ancient Maya: Solving the Mystery of the Maya Collapse.* London: Thames & Hudson.

Weller, D. 2006. A preliminary report on a survey of the "Westford Knight." http://www.ramtops.co.uk/westford.html.

Williams, S. 1991. *Fantastic Archaeology: The Wild Side of American Prehistory.* Philadelphia: University of Pennsylvania Press.

INDEX

Page numbers in italics refer to images.

About the Author

Kenneth L. Feder is a professor of anthropology at Central Connecticut State University. He is the director of the Farmington River Archaeological Project and the author of several books, including *The Past in Perspective: An Introduction to Human Prehistory*; *A Village of Outcasts: Historical Archaeology and Documentary Research at the Lighthouse Site*; *Linking to the Past: A Brief Introduction to Archaeology;* and *Frauds, Myths, and Mysteries: Science and Pseudoscience in Archaeology*.

ML   1/11